DATE DUE

MEDICINE AND THE REFORMATION

THE WELLCOME INSTITUTE SERIES IN THE HISTORY OF MEDICINE

Edited by W.F. Bynum and Roy Porter
The Wellcome Institute

Florence Nightingale and the Nursing Legacy
Monica Baly

Vivisection in Historical Perspective
Nicholaas A. Rupke

Abortion in England, 1900–1967
Barbara Brookes

The Hospital in History
Lindsay Granshaw and Roy Porter

Women as Mothers in Pre-industrial England
Valerie Fildes

The Charitable Imperative
Colin Jones

Medicine at the Courts of Europe, 1500–1837
Vivian Nutton

Mad Tales from the Raj
Waltraud Ernst

British Medicine in an Age of Reform
Roger French and Andrew Wear

Doctor of Society
Roy Porter

Medical Journals and Medical Knowledge
W.F. Bynum, Stephen Lock and Roy Porter

Medical Theory, Surgical Practice
Christopher Lawrence

The Popularization of Medicine, 1650–1850
Roy Porter

Women and Children First
Valerie Fildes, Lara Marks and Hilary Marland

Psychiatry for the Rich
Charlotte MacKenzie

Literature and Medicine during the Eighteenth Century
Marie Mulvey Roberts and Roy Porter

The Art of Midwifery
Hilary Marland

MEDICINE AND THE REFORMATION

Edited by

Ole Peter Grell

and

Andrew Cunningham

London and New York

First published in 1993
by Routledge
11 New Fetter Lane, London EC4P 4EE

Simultaneously published in the USA and Canada
by Routledge
29 West 35th Street, New York, NY 10001

Typeset in 10/12pt Baskerville by Witwell Ltd, Southport

Printed in Great Britain

British Library Cataloguing in Publication Data

A catalogue record for this book is available from the British Library.

Library of Congress Cataloging in Publication Data
Medicine and the Reformation / edited by Ole Peter Grell and Andrew
Cunningham.
p. cm. - (The Wellcome Institute series in the history of
medicine)
Includes bibliographical references and index.
1. Medicine-History-16th century. 2. Medicine-History-17th
century. 3. Reformation. I. Grell, Ole Peter. II. Cunningham,
Andrew, Dr. III. Series.
[DNLM: 1. History of Medicine, 16th Cent. 2. Religion and
Medicine. WZ 56 M4891]
R146.M43   1993
261.5′61′09409031—dc20
DNLM/DLC
for Library of Congress   92-49047
CIP

ISBN 0-415-08974-3

Contents

List of illustrations and tables vi
List of editors and contributors vii

Introduction 1
Ole Peter Grell and Andrew Cunningham

1. Wittenberg anatomy 11
 Vivian Nutton

2. *Aspectio divinorum operum*: Melanchthon and astrology for
 Lutheran medics 33
 Sachiko Kusukawa

3. Paracelsus: medicine as popular protest 57
 Charles Webster

4. Caspar Bartholin and the education of the pious physician 78
 Ole Peter Grell

5. Spiritual physic, Providence and English medicine, 1560–1640 101
 David Harley

6. Physicians and the Inquisition in sixteenth-century Venice 118
 Richard Palmer

7. The Church, the Devil and the healing activities of living
 saints in the Kingdom of Naples after the Council of Trent 134
 David Gentilcore

8. The Inquisition and minority medical practitioners in
 Counter-Reformation Spain: Judaizing and Morisco
 practitioners, 1560–1610 156
 Luis García-Ballester

Index 192

Illustrations and tables

Illustrations

1 Anatomia M Lutheri (Coburg *c*.1567) 1
2 'Tabula exhibens insignoria maris viscera' (Anatomical sheet: Wittenberg 1573) 18
3 'Tabula foeminae membra demonstrans' (Anatomical sheet: Wittenberg 1573) 19
4 Title page of Paracelsus: 'Practica gemacht auf Europen 1530–1534' 60
5 Title page of Paracelsus: 'Vom Holtz Guaiaco, gründlicher heylung' 63
6 Caspar Bartholin: print by Simon de Pas, 1625 80
7 Seal of the Medical Faculty of the University of Copenhagen, 1537 84
8 Map of Spain, Portugal and North Africa 157
9 Warrant signed by the Inquisitor of Toledo, Don Francisco de Múxica 170
10 Signature of the Converso physician, Felipe de Nájera 183
11 Confession of the Morisco healer, Juan de Toledo 184

Tables

1 Offences recorded by the Court of the Inquisition of Toledo (1575–1610) 162
2 Medical training of Judaizing practitioners prosecuted by the Inquisition (1560–1610) 164

Editors and contributors

Editors

Andrew Cunningham is Wellcome Lecturer at the Wellcome Unit for the History of Medicine, University of Cambridge.

Ole Peter Grell is Carlsberg Fellow at the Wellcome Unit for the History of Medicine, University of Cambridge.

Contributors

Luis García-Ballester is Professor at Consell Superior d'Investigacions Cientifiques, Barcelona, Spain.

David Gentilcore is Wellcome Trust Fellow at the Wellcome Unit for the History of Medicine, University of Cambridge.

David Harley is an associate of the Wellcome Unit for the History of Medicine, University of Oxford.

Sachiko Kusukawa is a Research Fellow at Christ's College, University of Cambridge.

Vivian Nutton is Senior Lecturer in the History of Medicine at the Wellcome Institute, London.

Richard Palmer is Librarian and Archivist at the Lambeth Palace Library, London.

Charles Webster is a Fellow at All Souls College, University of Oxford.

Introduction

Ole Peter Grell and Andrew Cunningham

ANATOMIA M. LVTHERI.

Illustration 1 The anatomy of Martin Luther, issued by Vitus Jacobaeus in Coburg, *c*.1567. Original in the Kupferstichkabinett of the Kunstsammlungen der Veste Coburg. Reproduced here from Walter L. Strauss, *The German Singleleaf Woodcut, 1550–1600: a pictorial catalogue*, New York, 1975, vol. 3, p. 1184, by permission of the Syndics of Cambridge University Library and of the Kunstsammlungen der Veste Coburg.

Martin Luther (1483-1546) is the man whose act of protest against the papacy in 1517 has always been seen as the first public act of the Reformation: he posted for debate, on the door of the university church at Wittenberg, the famous 95 theses challenging the Roman Church's view of indulgences.

Fifty years later the propaganda battle between defenders of the Catholic faith and the new 'Protestants' still continued. Here, in this broadsheet issued by the Ingoldstadt Jesuit Vitus Jacobaeus in Coburg in 1567, Luther is portrayed as being anatomized, tortured, and even eaten, by those who followed him and went yet further down the path of 'protestant' religious reform.[1] 'Does a new astonishment seize your doubting mind, and do you silently wonder about the meaning of this picture?', the propagandist asks in the accompanying Latin poem. 'Hear about the practices of this false sect.' All the followers of Luther rage as they tear his body apart. John Calvin, the director of the Genevan Reformation, is first singled out for attack. Calvin became the intellectual leader of the 'second' Reformation, and he is accordingly portrayed as seizing the head of Luther, piercing his chest and dragging him into league with himself. Ulrich Zwingli, Luther's contemporary and the instigator of the Swiss Reformation, is fittingly equipped with a battle-axe and shown chopping off Luther's arms: reminding the viewer of Zwingli's dual role as preacher and soldier, and of his violent death in battle. Peter Viret, a colleague of Calvin in Geneva and then the reformer of Lausanne, appropriately assists Calvin by strangling Luther; he is here called 'Virus', 'poison', because of his 'poisonous tongue' in writing satirical pamphlets in defence of Calvin. Johannes Brenz (Brettiades), the Lutheran controversialist and reformer of Württemberg, who in matters of church order inclined towards the Calvinist position, 'stands near and smiles on the efforts of Calvin'.[2] Phillip Melanchthon, Luther's own close friend and adviser at Wittenberg, the Achates to Luther's Aeneas, is present, dolefully witnessing the sad destruction of his friend. Other Reformers – amongst them Paul Eber, Cyriacus Spangenberg and Mattaeus Flacius Illyricus – roughly dissect Luther, they rub his gore into their beards, they eat his flesh and drink his blood, as if he were some second Christ. The anti-Protestant message is that the punishment for heresy is to be betrayed, chopped up and devoured by your own followers.

In a number of ways this broadsheet serves as a natural introduction for our theme of 'Medicine and the Reformation'.

In the first place it quite unexpectedly brings together into one visual field the Protestant Reformers and the act of public anatomizing, thus unifying medicine and the Reformation in one picture. For public anatomizing was something that was performed in universities by medical teachers for the benefit of future physicians and for a public audience. It was in the course of the lifetime of Luther that public

2

anatomizing of the human body, having been only an occasional practice in the medical faculties of medieval universities, was promoted to a role of great importance, especially through the advocacy of Andreas Vesalius when he was teaching at Padua in the 1530s. Vesalius' great illustrated volume which presented such public anatomizing sumptuously in print, the *De humani corporis fabrica libri septem* ('Seven books on the fabric of the human body'), published in 1542, has been widely celebrated by historians of medicine as the beginning of the modern tradition of anatomizing and medicine. Obviously, scenes of anatomizing had become familiar enough as an image to educated audiences by the 1560s for them to be used as metaphors for other messages, such as this anti-Protestant one.

For Vesalius and those who followed him, such anatomizing had two functions: to show to medical students the inside of the human body, with which their later practice as physicians would deal; and to display the design, plan and workmanship of the Creator in the highpoint of His creation, the body of man, in order to invoke admiration for Him and gratitude for His care and providence for mankind. In the public anatomies performed in universities the corpses used were those of criminals, and anatomies were therefore timed to coincide with the sessions of the local law courts. So public anatomies were acquiring new importance for medicine in this period, and they centrally displayed the divine handiwork of the Christian God.

Second, this combination of anatomy and Protestantism in a single broadsheet is more than a convenient occasion for topical satire on the part of its artist and author. For the picture conveys other, symbolic, messages as well, as such pictures always do. The image of the anatomized body represents at least three persons, in different ways. First it represents a common criminal, for this was the conventional subject of anatomizing. Second, it represents Luther, and the fate of the Lutheran heritage, as we have just seen. But third, and most significantly, the body being anatomized also represents Christ. For portrayed in the background to the left of the dissection scene is an image of the crucifixion of Christ: after Christ was put to death (like a common criminal) His body was taken to its tomb (to await resurrection on the third day), and the Roman soldiers played dice for His clothing. In the background to the right is the kitchen scene in which Peter denied Christ. At the dissection table one of the Reformers (Calvin) is shown piercing the side of the corpse with a spear, just as is reported happened to Christ in St John's Gospel (19, xxxiv): 'one of the soldiers with a spear pierced his side, and forthwith came there out blood and water'. And around the table where this body is being anatomized, two other Reformers are portrayed as (sacrilegiously) eating its flesh and drinking its blood, following Christ's injunction to His disciples at the Last Supper:

And he took bread, and gave thanks, and brake it, and gave unto them, saying, This is the body which is given for you. Do this in remembrance of Me. Likewise also the cup after supper, saying This is the cup of the new testament in my blood, which is shed for you.

(Luke 22, xix–xx)

What the events of the Mass meant and symbolized, and how literally Christ's injunction to 'Do this in remembrance of Me' should be taken by true Christians, were matters of the most vigorous debate amongst Protestants and were the cause of division between Lutherans and Reformed. Moreover, the dissection table may also be seen as a symbolic 'Last Supper' table: and this is how some of the Reformers were themselves portrayed, as Christ's disciples at the Last Supper.[3]

And to add to the complexities, Luther himself came to be seen as a Christ figure among Protestants. From as early as 1520 he was presented to the public as a 'living saint'. One of the most common images of Luther showed him as a friar with a halo, holding the open Bible in his hands, while the Holy Spirit floated above him. He was often compared with the greatest saints of the Church, such as St Augustine or Gregory the Great, and even with Christ himself. Eventually it became a veritable 'Luther cult' associated with miracles, which continued well into the eighteenth century.[4] The interesting thing about this woodcut is that it indirectly accepts these Protestant claims, and turns them on their head. It uses the association of Luther with Christ to create an image of Luther as a false Christ: an image further developed in the association of Luther with the person anatomized – normally a criminal.

Thus we have seen how the worlds of medicine and religion could be organically linked in a popular broadsheet. And this underlines how the Reformation was not merely a religious phenomenon, but affected all aspects of sixteenth and early seventeenth century life. This wider context has been the theme of much recent work on the Reformation.[5] Not only has considerable attention been given to the national contexts of the Reformation, and to the effects of the Reformation on education in general, and university education in particular, but in the social sphere historians have begun to investigate the impact of the Reformation on social conditions such as poor relief, hospital provision, charity, and social welfare within local communities, and this has led to questioning about the success of the Reformation in improving social welfare. Likewise the issue of social discipline in the Reformation, meaning the relationship between the state and church and the relationship between 'official' religion and 'popular' religion, has come to prominence. Recent studies indicate a common interconfessional pattern of conflict between popular religion and official confession.[6] Questions such as the extent of church attendance and of knowledge of the tenets of faith among the laity

are being investigated, while functionalist and anthropological approaches have been applied to the role of 'superstition' and magic in the
daily life of people, following the lead of Keith Thomas.[7]

Within the history of medicine too this categorization of 'official' and
'popular' has gained currency in recent years, thereby incorporating
witchcraft, healing and superstition into the realm of medical history.
Thus there have been a number of studies on healers other than
university-trained physicians, including women, midwives and 'cunning
women'. This concentration on 'popular medicine' has also helped to
bring to attention the importance of religion and popular belief in
medicine. It is implicit in this approach that the Reformation must to
some extent have brought about major changes in the practice of
medicine. But so far there has been little if any systematic investigation of
the relation of the Reformation to such changes.[8]

Accordingly, we intend this volume to explore some of the effects of the
Protestant Reformation and of its Catholic counterpart or response, the
'Counter-Reformation', on medicine: on the teaching of medicine, on
medical thinking and on medical practice, with special attention to
'popular' attitudes to medicine and healing.

In some ways, of course, the Reformation had little effect on medicine.[9]
The texts used for teaching and learning medicine were much the same in
both Protestant and Catholic universities, the therapies applied to ill
people were for the most part similar for both Protestants and Catholics
and the diseases seem to have shown no particular distinction in their
incidence, affecting Protestants and Catholics alike. The Reformation in
fact coincided with the renaissance of classical learning and practice in
the universities, known as 'humanism'. Medical scholars were therefore
seeking out ancient Greek medical manuscripts, especially the writings of
Galen, the second century AD Greek physcian, and Hippocrates from the
fifth century BC. These texts were edited and printed and, what is more
important, translated into Latin for use in the medical faculties of the
universities. Thus, for the first time, Western medical scholars had
available the full authentic texts of the medical ancients and set about
reforming their medical knowledge, practice and teaching on the basis of
them. Galen had propounded a medical system which demanded detailed
knowledge of the anatomy and functioning of the human body, and of a
highly elaborate method of assessing the cause of illness in individual
patients and of reasoning toward the treatment necessary. This ration-
alistic and very learned medicine was being introduced into the medical
faculties of universities across Europe and was becoming the basis of all
formal medical education.

However, there were many important ways in which the Reformation
did indeed affect medicine and beliefs about the body and about healing
and some of these are dealt with by our contributors.

5

With the chapters by Vivian Nutton and Sachiko Kusukawa our story starts in the heartland of the Reformation, at Wittenberg. Wittenberg was of course the university where Luther was professor of theology, and into which he introduced the young scholar of Greek, Phillip Melanchthon, to assist in teaching people to read the Bible in the original languages. But after Luther's 'blinding flash' of insight about justification by faith alone (rather than by works or learning), he and Melanchton adopted a negative attitude toward traditional learning, and Luther wanted to throw out the works of the heathen Aristotle completely. However, the emergence of Protestant radicalism in the 1520s forced the Wittenberg reformers to rethink their attitude toward academic learning. Consequently they began to look at the writings of the Ancients with new eyes, gradually accepting them, and shaping them to the service of their new theology. In his chapter Nutton draws attention to the way in which the Wittenberg Lutherans, especially Melanchthon, took a new, very positive and detailed interest in anatomy in the arts course. This was determined (Nutton claims) by the particular importance for Protestants of the relationship between body and soul in revealing the workings of God and promoting Christian morality. It led Melanchthon to master the new anatomical work of Vesalius and to have anatomical figures printed for the use of Wittenberg students. Kusukawa, writing about the study of astrology in Wittenberg, similarly demonstrates how Melanchthon managed to extend the indispensability of this subject from medicine (where it had long been a basic part of the physician's education) to the education of Lutheran arts students in general. Melanchthon managed to make astrology acceptable in spite of its heathen and supersititious antecedents. Melanchon felt obliged to introduce astrology in order to assert the Protestant doctrine of providence and the sovereignty of God, against the radical enthusiasts who, listening mainly to the Spirit speaking within them, in Melanchthon's view threatened the whole Lutheran reformation by making themselves the authorities, rather than God. Melanchthon thought that the book of Nature should be understood and interpreted as God's intentions and plan for the world.

Among the radical enthusiasts against whom Melanchthon was writing was the famous physician Paracelsus and, as Charles Webster shows in Chapter 3, an important feature of the medicine promoted by Paracelsus was that it arose from popular protest, and that its practice was simultaneously an act of popular protest. The religious radicals claimed that none of the learning, priesthood or hierarchy of the Church was necessary for the true Christian: all the true Christian needs to do is to follow the teachings of the Spirit, who reveals everything to him. Paracelsian medicine itself was like this: the true physician is someone inspired by the Spirit to recognize (by some intuitive act) the nature of diseases and to identify the correct cures amongst the products of nature, and to use them by the light of nature. Webster draws attention to how Paracelsus advocated his 'religion' of medicine, and shows how, like the radical reformers' attack on the authority of the Church, it was an attack on the established and learned medicine of the universities; likewise, the radical reformers' emphasis on the priesthood of all believers is paralleled by the way that Paracelsus' medicine gave primacy to the medical knowledge of the laity. Webster stresses that the religious and populist inspiration of Paracelsian medicine needs to be recognized if we are properly to understand its nature.

It is in such ways that Paracelsianism radically differs, both as an approach to conceptualizing what is happening in disease and as a theory and practice of therapeutics, from the medicine of the universities. It could not be adopted outside radical circles until its revolutionary sting had been drawn. It was never adopted by Catholic institutions because of its links with heterodoxy. Even in Catholic countries like France, Paracelsianism was the prerogative of Protestants such as the Huguenots Theodore de Mayerne and Joseph du Chesne (Quercetanus).[10] It was adopted and adapted in a sanitized and modified form by some Protestant individuals like Petrus Severinus from the 1570s, as Ole Peter Grell points out in Chapter 4, and versions of it were introduced into the medical faculties of some Protestant universities, such as the University of Copenhagen.

The development of orthodox Lutheranism in the second half of the sixteenth century, with its obsession with doctrine, came to dominate a number of Lutheran universities, including Wittenberg. Denmark, though Lutheran, remained relatively unaffected by this development. Consequently, the University of Copenhagen remained a relatively liberal place throughout the sixteenth century, both in theology and in medicine. This open-minded and practical approach to medicine was maintained by revivalist Lutheranism with its emphasis on a full reformation of life to follow Luther's reformation of doctrine. A consequence of this was Caspar Bartholin's concept of the 'pious physician' as the only true and properly qualified doctor.

In England, too, physicians needed to be 'divines in some measure' by the late sixteenth century. As David Harley shows in Chapter 5, this attitude was a practical consequence of the rigorous Calvinist doctrine of Providence, which pointed directly to the necessity of a pious and Godly life. For Calvinists, the sovereign God governed the world through secondary causes, and disease was a product of such causes. Illness had to be considered as much a blessing or a trial as a punishment. Doctors looked on their role as a calling sanctified by God, and saw this vocation as a religious duty.

The 'Counter-Reformation', the delayed Catholic response in southern and central Europe to the Protestant Reformation, led to a revival of the

7

Inquisition, a growing intolerance of dissent and a hunt for heretics. New orders were created, such as the Jesuits, with the specific tasks of promoting Catholic piety and learning, and of helping to root out heterodoxy. In the wake of the Council of Trent (1545–63), Catholic doctrine and discipline were established more firmly, and propagated out to the laity.

Medicine was affected by this in a number of ways. Even in relatively tolerant Venice, the Inquisition insisted on stamping out heresy. Doctors were particularly high on their list of suspects as can be seen in Richard Palmer's chapter, not least on account of their university education, especially at Padua, where Catholic students mingled with foreign Protestant students. In its attempt to make the index of Prohibited Books as comprehensive as possible, the Inquisition included all books by Protestant authors, even medical books. Furthermore, the Inquisition was deeply worried about the social role of heterodox physicians, not least through their contacts with patients and their families. Faced with persecution, Italian Protestant physicians were left with three options: flight, abjuration or pretending to be Catholics (Nicodemism).

Furthermore, the Counter-Reformation also affected the practice of popular medicine in Italy. As David Gentilcore demonstrates in Chapter 7, the Catholic Church tried to control and regulate local attempts to 'tap the power of the sacred', and in particular with respect to disease and healing. The Church authorities were particularly worried about 'cunning' men and women who came to be considered 'living saints'. The Church simultaneously tried to regulate such phenomena while not discouraging them, since they related directly to the sacred and to sainthood, which constituted domains which were essential to the attempts of the post-Trent Catholic Church to restore and maintain orthodoxy. This in effect meant that there was a fine and often unpredictable line in healing practices between what was orthodox and acceptable and what was heterodox and unacceptable – and by implication diabolical and dangerous.

By the time of the accession of Philip II in 1556, Spain had become financially, militarily and intellectually the leader of the Counter-Reformation. Gone were Illuminism and Erasmianism, the great intellectual forces of spirituality which had been behind Charles V's visions for Church reform and reconciliation with the Protestants. The Jesuits and the Inquisition were in the forefront of the campaign to extirpate all forms of heterodoxy.[11] This development did not only affect Christians, but also a significant proportion of the Jewish and Moslem population, often recently converted to Christianity. In Chapter 8 Luis García-Ballester demonstrates how physicians from both these groups were policed and persecuted by the Inquisition. In the case of the Converted Moslem healers, the rationale behind the Inquisition's attention was as much based on the unorthodox and 'popular' medicine they practised, as on suspicion of possible backsliding into their former Islamic faith. The converted Jewish physicians, by contrast, practised orthodox medicine, but were persecuted primarily for suspicion about insincerity in their professed Christianity.

The Reformation not only seriously affected the practice of medicine and the medical profession in both Protestant and Catholic countries, but also the way medicine was taught in a number of Protestant universities, while Catholic universities, subject to the control of the Inquisition, remained more restrictive in what was allowed to be taught. Popular medicine, on the other hand, was particularly affected by the increased social control which was one of the effects of the Reformation. Indeed, the major changes in religious belief and practice that constituted the Reformation and Counter-Reformation meant that taking up even a profession as seemingly innocuous as medicine could lead to one being put to death, not only for heterodox beliefs but also for the type of healing that one engaged in.

Notes

1. On this broadsheet see Wolfgang Harms (ed.), *Deutsche illustrierte Flugblätter des 16 und 17 Jahrhunderts*, 4 vols., Munich, 1980-9, and Frederick Stopp, 'Der religiöspolemische Einblattdruck "Ecclesia Militans" (1569) des Johannes Nas und seine Vorgänger', *Deutsche Vierteljahrsschrift für Literaturwissenschaft und Geistesgeschichte* 39 (1965), 588-638. We are grateful to Dr R.W. Scribner for supplying us with these references.
2. Here we are using the original Latin version of this broadsheet; in the significantly different German versions of 1568 and 1582, the figure of Johannes Brenz (Brettiades) is considered to be Johann Aurifaber (1519-75); see Harms, vol. 2., numbers 16 to 17. For both a picture and biography of Johannes Brenz, see M. Greschat (ed.), *Gestalten der Kirchengeschichte*, vol. 6, 'Die Reformationszeit II' (Stuttgart, 1981), 103-17.
3. See Carl C. Christensen, *Art and the Reformation in Germany* (Ohio, 1979).
4. See R.W. Scribner, 'The Reformation movements in Germany' in G.R. Elton (ed.), *The New Cambridge Modern History*, vol. 2, 2nd edn, 'The Reformation 1520-1559', pp. 69-93, especially p. 75; for development of the Luther cult, see Scribner, 'Incombustible Luther: the image of the reformer in early modern Germany', *Past and Present* 110 (1986), 38-68.
5. See for instance the recent survey by E. Cameron, *The European Reformation* (Oxford, 1991).
6. G. Oestreich, *Strukturprobleme der frühen Neuzeit*, Berlin, 1980; H. Schilling (ed.), *Die reformierte Konfessionalisierung in Deutschland: das Problem der 'Zweiten Reformation'* (Gütersloh, 1986); R. Po-Chia Hsia, *Social Discipline and the Reformation: Central Europe 1550-1750* (London, 1989).
7. Keith Thomas, *Religion and the Decline of Magic: Structures and Popular Belief in Sixteenth and Seventeenth Century England* (London, 1971); L. Rothkrug, *Religious Practices and Collective Perceptions: Hidden Homologies in the Renaissance and Reformation* (Waterloo, Ontario, 1980); R.W. Scribner,

'Religion, society and culture: reorientating the Reformation', *History Workshop* (1982), 14, 2–22; R.W. Scribner, *Popular Culture and Popular Movements in Reformation Germany* (London, 1987); B. Moeller, 'Religious life in Germany on the eve of the Reformation', in G. Strauss (ed.), *Pre-Reformation Germany*, London, 1972.

8. The relationship of *science* and religion in this period has of course been the subject of a number of important studies, from the Weberian investigations of R.K. Merton, through the writings of R. Hooykaas and others, and to the more recent work such as Charles Webster, *The Great Instauration: Science, Medicine and Reform 1626–1660* (London, 1975), and D.C. Lindberg and R.L. Numbers (eds), *God and Nature* (Berkeley, California, 1986); see also Olivier Fatio (ed.), *Les Eglises Face aux Sciences du Moyen Age au XX^esiecle* (Geneva, 1991) and the 500th anniversary of Luther's birth issue of *Wissenschaftliche Zeitschrift der Martin-Luther-Universität* (Halle-Wittenberg, vol. 34, 1985). However, the relationship between *medicine* and religion has been less well explored. It has only recently been recognized as an important topic, as shown by the collections of R.L. Numbers and D. Amundsen, *Caring and Curing: Health and Medicine in the Western Religious Traditions* (New York, 1986), W.J. Sheils, *The Church and Healing* (Oxford, 1982), and R.K. French and A. Wear, *The Medical Revolution of the Seventeenth Century* (Cambridge, 1989). Both Numbers/Amundsen and Sheils are chronologically and thematically very broad, while French/Wear addresses itself to the relationship between religion and medicine rather than the influence of the Reformation on medicine. While there are studies on individual Reformation figures involved in medicine, such as Walter Pagel's important work on Paracelsus (*Paracelsus*, 2nd edn, (Basle, 1982); *From Paracelsus to Van Helmont*, ed. M. Winder (London, 1986), and C.D. O'Malley's *Michael Servetus* (Philadelphia, 1953), there has been no attempt to assess the impact of the Reformation more generally on sixteenth and seventeenth century medicine.

9. For a strong defence of this position, see Richard Toellner, 'Die medizinischen Facultäten unter dem Einfluß der Reformation', *Renaissance Reformation: Gegensätze und Gemeinsamkeiten* (Wolfenbüttel, 1984), pp. 287–97.

10. See A.G. Debus, *The French Paracelsians* (Cambridge, 1992).

11. H.G. Koenigsberger, 'The Empire of Charles V and Europe', pp. 339–76, see 376; in *New Cambridge Modern History*, vol. 2, 2nd edn, 'The Reformation 1520–1559', ed. G.R. Elton (Cambridge, 1990).

1

Wittenberg anatomy

Vivian Nutton

The history of anatomy in the sixteenth century is frequently described in terms of the triumph of observation over book-learning, and of the penetration into Northern Europe of techniques, ideas and discoveries first formulated in Bologna and, above all, Padua.[1] It is a trail that leads inexorably from Berengario, through Vesalius, Falloppio and Fabricius, to William Harvey, with, occasionally, a special mention for Leonardo da Vinci and his drawings. Statutes and university records are combed for the first references to chairs of anatomy or actual anatomical demonstrations on a corpse in order to confirm the participation of a particular institution in the march of medical progress. There is, in short, widespread agreement that by the end of the century Vesalian anatomy had replaced Galenic, that human dissection was both commonplace and central to any medical study, and that the message from Padua had been received swiftly and enthusiastically. Areas such as Spain, where the new anatomy does not seem to have conquered so easily, are usually forgotten or held up as dire examples of the follies of conservative academics, short-sighted administrators and religious obscurantists.[2] From such a perspective, the history of anatomy at the Saxon University of Wittenberg becomes almost inexplicable, for here, as the first part of this chapter will show, Vesalian anatomy was established early, held a central place in the curriculum, yet disappeared quietly in the first years of the seventeenth century, some time before the social, economic, and academic disasters of the Thirty Years' War, without, apparently, contributing much to the annals of medical discovery.

This paradox can be resolved only if we set the study of anatomy in a wider setting, as part of a broader movement for the understanding of man's place in God's creation. As the academic home of Martin Luther, the University of Wittenberg swiftly gained fame (or notoriety) for its theology, and the educational ideals formulated and put into practice there by Phillip Melanchthon (1497–1560) were adopted by many schools and universities within the Lutheran world. They aimed to produce

11

Christian intellectuals, both learned and Lutheran. The methods of teaching employed there, whether in theology, arts, or medicine, were as modern as any in Europe, and, as we shall see, they could be adapted to changing needs and to new discoveries. But, far more than in most other universities, they were employed at Wittenberg within a specifically religious context. True, the notion that man inhabited a divinely ordered universe was commonplace, and the claim that anatomy could reveal something of the wondrous handiwork of the Creator can be found across the religious spectrum, but at Wittenberg the links were much tighter.[3] Melanchthon, and his Lutheran followers, posited a strong interaction between body and soul, and hence a knowledge of medicine, the art of the healthy body, was essential if one was to preserve the health of the soul. Anatomy revealed not only the structures, arrangement, and purpose of the body, but also the ways in which the activities of the Christian soul were mediated in thought, imagination, or will. Such a theme was far too important to be left to the physicians or medical students alone; theologians, pastors, teachers, arts students, even pupils in the gymnasia required this information, and the Wittenberg faculty provided it for them. In lectures, books and prints, the coherent message of the Lutheran anatomists was transmitted from Wittenberg to other areas of Germany for a century or more. In this perspective, the tradition of anatomy teaching at Wittenberg was no less important, and on its own terms scarcely less successful, than that of Padua and, as this chapter will show, it deserves more than the neglect of medical and religious historians.

Origins

The University of Wittenberg owed its creation, in large part, to a medical man, Martin Pollich von Mellerstadt (*c.*1450–1513), Professor of Medicine at Leipzig and personal physician to Elector Frederick of Saxony. Although his published writings hardly suggest a typical humanist, his support for new Italian ideas brought him into bitter conflict with his fellow professors at Leipzig over both theology and medicine. In 1498 he held the first of a series of public disputations with his colleague Simon Pistoris in which he upheld the views of the Ferrarese professor, Niccolò Leoniceno, on the origin and treatment of the newly arrived syphilis. The debate was not only about a disease; it called into question the whole basis of contemporary medical learning, for Leoniceno (and Mellerstadt after him) derided the authority of Avicenna and his medieval interpreters for propagating doctrines based on misunderstandings and mistranslations of classical sources. A return to these purer, and older, springs would, so Leoniceno and Mellerstadt argued, be of practical advantage even in the treatment of an apparently new disease. Two years later, Mellerstadt took up his cudgel to defend the value of poetry in Christian education against the 'Spartan barbarism' of Konrad Wimpina and other Leipzig theologians.[4]

The bitterness of these controversies, which increasingly degenerated into mere personal abuse, hardly made for comfortable cooperation. Hence, when the Elector Frederick mooted the creation of a new university in his own territory of Ernestine Saxony, Mellerstadt was more than eager to assist. Indeed, he was its leading spirit, 'duxque parensque scole'. Vice-chancellor for the first eleven years of Wittenberg's existence, he was largely responsible for the choice of the new body of teachers and was himself at first the sole professor of medicine. The statutes of the medical faculty, as codified in 1508, are thus likely to reflect his wishes and interests. They can hardly be called novel. In the four-year course of *practica* and *theoretica*, the emphasis was on the standard authors of the medieval curriculum, the *Articella*, Avicenna, and Rhazes, with appropriate medieval commentators. The only concessions to the new medical humanism may be found in the specified translation of Hippocrates' *Aphorisms* (by Laurentianus) and, perhaps, in the setting of passages on fever from Galen's *Method of healing, for Glaucon*.[5] Of anatomy there is no word, despite the fact that Mellerstadt himself had, some years previously, in 1493, produced at Leipzig an edition of the most famous of medieval anatomy textbooks, the *Anatomia* of Mondino dei Liuzzi.[6]

The success of the new university in quickly attracting students in large numbers had immediate repercussions on the older university of Leipzig. Its overlord, Duke George of Augustine Saxony, carried out a 'Reformation' in November 1502, and a further reorganization followed in 1511, which involved the medical faculty more deeply.[7] On both occasions it was proposed that dissection be introduced into the medical curriculum. In 1502 Dr Benedict Staetz pleaded for a dissection every three years so that the students might learn 'the inner organisation of the body; for whoever has not seen this is not a proper doctor'. In 1511 an anonymous proposer suggested that the dissection of an animal or executed criminal in front of students in their final year would show them the inner layout of the human body. Both proposals were turned down, but in the next set of reforms, Duke George acceded to the 'unanimous and universal' wish of the medical faculty for an annual dissection. This was introduced for the first time in 1519, when the list of medical lectures announced that 'an anatomy or dissection of a dead body will take place once a year. For without this a knowledge of diseases and the human constitution is defective'.[8]

Wittenberg in this now lagged behind. This was hardly unexpected, for after Mellerstadt's move to the faculty of theology, the two chairs of medicine were filled only by young doctors staying for brief periods and were occasionally left vacant. It was not until 1518, with the arrival of Peter Burchard (1487–1539) as professor, that the numbers of students began to rise, and the first signs of a new approach to medicine in Wittenberg can be seen. The preface to Burchard's *Parva Hippocratis tabula* (1519) contains a plea for the superiority of Greek medicine over that of the Arabs.[9] It was contributed by Phillip Melanchthon, whose influence over the whole development of the university, including its medicine, was to remain paramount until his death. On Burchard's return in 1521 to the university of Ingolstadt, his post was divided between Stephan Wild (who stayed for only a year) and Augustin Schurff, who continued to teach until his death in 1548. It was Schurff who, in 1526, carried out the first recorded dissection at Wittenberg, of a human head, in the presence of the medical faculty and students. He repeated the dissection on other occasions, and his example was followed by other colleagues, Caspar Lindemann (professor 1532–36) and Jacob Milich (1501–59), who in 1536 was the first occupant of a new third chair in medicine specifically devoted to anatomy. From now on, lectures on anatomical authors were a central part of the medical curriculum.[10]

The rise and fall of Wittenberg anatomy?

The history of Wittenberg anatomy over the next eighty years could well take the form of a moral fable. True, there are no reports of spectacular disasters like that of Antonio Pigafetta, an Italian exile, whose failure to demonstrate at Heidelberg in 1574 the passage of blood from one side of the heart to the other via tiny capillaries in the heart wall was swiftly bruited around Europe and could still serve, years later, as a pointed contrast to the sounder methods of Fabricius of Aquapendente at Padua.[11] Instead, Wittenberg anatomy is the province of men of solid worth, like Milich, Caspar Peucer (1525–1602), and Salomon Alberti (1540–1600), whose writings on anatomy show how well they fulfilled their academic duties.[12] One can point also to a student interest in public anatomies, like that carried out in 1554 in the presence of Professors Milich and Fend.[13] The highpoint in such a story would be reached with the new statutes of 1572, when the duties of the third professor of medicine were extended. As well as being responsible for the teaching of medical botany, he had to lecture on the anatomical writings of Galen, Vesalius and Falloppio (or on a suitable modern introductory textbook), pointing out what had been 'accurately written', and correcting 'the mistakes of earlier centuries'. At the same time, the university also received the statutory right to ask the relevant civil authorities, at an appropriate moment, for the bodies of executed criminals for use in an anatomy.[14] But from then on, there is an apparently swift decline. Anatomies rarely took place, and, in 1601, the most capable of Wittenberg anatomy professors, Johann Jessen (1566–1621), left in high dudgeon for Prague after a brush with the civil powers. The medical professors complained of a lack of support for anatomy by the authorities and bewailed the interference of what Jessen called 'importunate busybodies'.[15] When Tobias Tandler, professor from 1607–17, managed to conduct a public anatomy of a male corpse in 1609, this was the result of pure chance: more often, as he complained officially in 1614, there was a distinct lack of bodies.[16] If this was the case, it is hardly surprising that Wittenberg anatomy rose and fell unnoticed by all save its local historians.

An explanation for this decline in anatomy in terms of outside interference is not entirely without foundation. In 1585, the court apothecary had created difficulties over the dispatch of a skeleton to be used in university teaching, and the protest by Aegidius Hunnius to the authorities against Jessen's anatomical activities, allegedly 'for his own private advantage', undoubtedly contributed to Jessen's move soon afterwards to Prague.[17] But in all these disputes, the rulers of Saxony backed their professors. Even though Jessen's desire to get hold of corpses, of both men and women, from all over Saxony might appear to some 'scandalous', he was not prevented from dissecting. Provided that the corpse was treated with dignity and the skeleton returned for burial when no longer needed, neither civil nor religious authorities withheld their permission. Indeed, they continually upbraided the local officials who put difficulties in the way. Elector Christian I accepted the excuse of the medical professors in 1587 that their inability to carry out anatomies was the direct result of the reluctance of local sheriffs and magistrates to hand over corpses of executed criminals, and in his new statutes of 1588 he expressly repeated the regulations of 1572 which allowed the medical faculty to seek such bodies. The University Visitors in 1609 were specifically enjoined to find out if the anatomies had been performed diligently, and there is no reason to believe that the complaints of Tandler and his colleagues in 1614 would have fallen on deaf ears. Indeed, so much were the Visitors of 1623 in favour of anatomy that in the new statutes of 1624 the number of anatomies was increased to two a year. Their comments on the 'lack of diligence' in the performance of the public anatomies, and on the chaos over the supply of medical simples, suggest that, in their eyes, the fault lay with the university, and no one else.[18]

But there is a much stronger objection to this account of Wittenberg anatomy: to think of the teaching and study of anatomy solely in terms of dissection, whether public or private, is to misunderstand what was actually taking place. In common with all other universities, the study of anatomy at Wittenberg was throughout this period largely a book anatomy. It was imparted in lectures that took as their starting point anatomical writings, not the evidence of a corpse in front of the class. Its teachers employed in their investigations the same types of intellectual enquiry and argument as were used to explicate Galen's doctrine of fevers, Hippocrates' *Aphorisms* or Aristotle's *Physics*. This is not to say that the choice of author remained constant, far from it; one of the features of early Wittenberg anatomy is its readiness to change its set texts in order to gain the best of modern learning. Instead of setting up an opposition between book and body – which, to the Wittenberg anatomists, would have revolved around mere trivial points of detail – it is better to consider the study of anatomy as an education process in which a variety of messages was transmitted from master to pupil, and beyond. On this definition, Wittenberg anatomy has more than a passing claim on the historian's attention, for there the bonds of collegiality, reinforced by those of religion and marriage, ensured that a general consistency of aims, methods and priorities persisted through the century that separates Peter Burchard from Tobias Tandler. The same message can be found in prefaces and in theses, in lecture notes and in formal orations, in letters and in illustrations and, perhaps even more significantly, outside the bounds of the university and of Saxony. In its own way, it is arguably as influential as the more familiar north Italian anatomy of the years after Vesalius.

The Wittenberg message

The formulation of the Wittenberg approach to anatomy derives from Melanchthon, theologian, educator and universal scholar, although it would be wrong to attribute it entirely to him or to see it as a totally new creation of Lutheranism. There are parallels with developments elsewhere, although Wittenberg anatomy does not fit easily into the traditional categories of medical historians. For example, Melanchthon continually stressed the importance of the Greek heritage within medicine: 'medicine is entirely Greek, and it cannot be perfectly understood without Greek'.[19] It was a message that he had first delivered in his preface to Burchard's *Parva Hippocratis tabula* in 1519 and one that he continued to repeat from then on.[20] But it was not a case of the Greeks or nothing. Arabic authors continued to form the mainstay of the medical curriculum until the end of the century, and Melanchthon himself was perfectly willing to adopt Vesalian anatomy as an improvement on that of Galen. He obtained a copy of Vesalius' *De humani corporis fabrica* soon after it appeared, reading and annotating it throughout and expressing his admiration of it in an elegant poem.[21] The second edition of his *De anima* carefully adapted as much as possible of the new anatomy and may have been more responsible than any other book for spreading a knowledge of Vesalian anatomy throughout north Germany.[22] Melanchthon's criterion was truth, not Hellenism. He had sought informed advice on the best sources of anatomical information for inclusion in the first edition of the *De anima* (Wittenberg, 1540), and his choice of Galen to supplement the 'thin and babyish little book' on anatomy by Benedetti was, at the time, entirely justified. There was no book then on the market that incorporated fully the extensive anatomical discoveries of the ancient Greek physician, which had become accessible in their original Greek only after 1525.[23] Hence, too, the need to provide detailed lexicographical equivalents for terms that would be found in the new 'Hellenic' anatomy and in the older, medieval and arabised texts. The later statutes of 1572 recommended the study of Vesalius, Falloppio or, if necessary, a suitable modern textbook of anatomy.[24] This willingness to incorporate criticisms of Galen and new textbooks contrasts with the violent denunciations of Vesalius by such Hellenists as Cornarius, Sylvius and Caius, or with the conservative lists of set texts put out by the University of Ingolstadt and the London College of Physicians.

Nor does the anatomical tradition of Wittenberg fit easily into a schema that contrasts the written with the visual. As we have already seen, the authorities encouraged public anatomies, and dissections were performed well before they became a statutory obligation. Even if, as Friedensburg suggested, the professors themselves became less keen on public dissection, that does not mean they abandoned visual information. Melanchthon himself had praised the *Fabrica* for its remarkably beautiful illustrations (and, interestingly, for its elucidations of Galen), while a series of illustrated anatomical sheets were published by the university printer well into the next century for the benefit of those studying the *De anima*.[25] Such visual aids might well be necessary, if, as Jessen once implied, the seats in the hall were arranged in such a way that not everyone could see properly even when a public anatomy was held.[26] Besides, this visual information supplemented that of the lecture and demonstration and served a valuable function as an aide-mémoire.

Melanchthon and his successors at Wittenberg chose their set texts and visual materials pragmatically; they incorporated the best information available into their lecture courses on anatomy without apparent concern for the controversies taking place elsewhere between Galenists and Vesalians. The reason is not far to seek: at Wittenberg anatomy was taught within a broad context that emphasized the theological and moral dimensions of the subject as much as the merely technical or therapeutic.[27] The points that divided John Caius from Andreas Vesalius were thus relatively minor when compared with the importance of correct religious belief or of understanding the workings of the body and its relationship with the soul. It is this theological and moral emphasis that explains why, in the various prefaces, orations and books presented by Wittenberg scholars, relatively little attention is given to justifying anatomy in terms of its contribution to the understanding and cure of disease or its necessity as the basis for surgery – though these points are made – and much to its wider role.

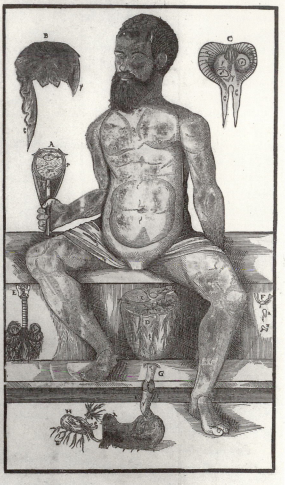

Illustration 2 Anatomical fugitive sheet: 'Tabula exhibens insignoria maris viscera', Wittenberg, 1573. Male figure, with head of Andreas Vesalius. Wellcome Institute Library, London, reproduced by permission.

The arguments advanced go far beyond the standard rhetoric of an exordium. To claim that anatomy revealed the majesty of God, the divine Creator, was commonplace.[28] The idea of a purposeful designer went back to Galen, Aristotle and Plato, who all acknowledged the 'architectural Mind' that had formed man. The wonderful fabric of the human body, all were aware, provided clear and unmistakable revelations

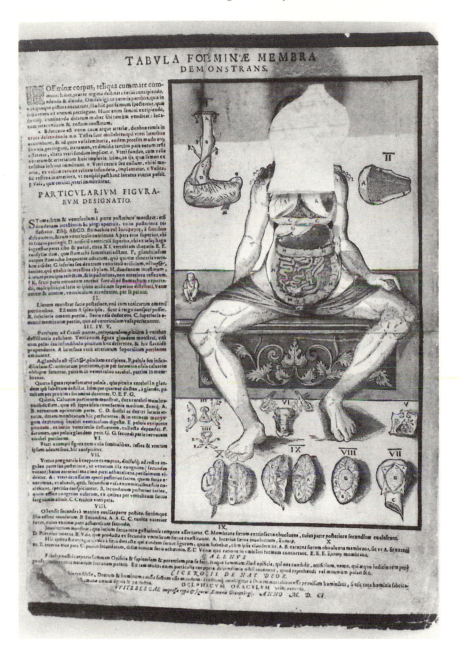

Illustration 3 Anatomical fugitive sheet: 'Tabula foeminae membra demonstrans. Edita Witebergae in gratiam studiosae iuventutis, discentis elementa doctrinae Anatomicae in libello de Anima, M.D. LXXIII', Wittenberg, 1573. Female figure, with hinged flap raised to show the internal organs. Wellcome Institute Library, London, reproduced by permission.

of the wisdom and foresight of its Creator.[29] In the human body, just as in the whole theatre of nature, God had left his footprints, testimonies and evidence for man to contemplate.[30] The handiwork of God was indeed wonderful; the way in which the foetus, which had before birth derived breath through the umbilical cord, suddenly at birth began to breathe and, simultaneously, the link that had formerly joined the foetal artery and vena cava began to disappear was nothing short of miraculous.[31] But this whole argument was in Wittenberg given a further theological twist by being directly associated with an attack on atheism and Epicurean atomism; anatomy demonstrates that man cannot be a chance concatenation of atoms but is a purposeful work of a divine Creator.[32]

Such an argument from purpose and organization was scarcely new or unusual.[33] But not every anatomist would assert publicly that anatomy would improve individual morality as well as health. Nor was it immediately obvious that a knowledge of the workings of the body would lead to a reduction in one's capacity for anger and to a life lived in love and charity with one's neighbours. Yet such claims were made by Melanchthon and his pupils and formed the basis for anatomical teaching within the Wittenberg tradition.[34]

The connection between anatomy and morality was made in a variety of ways. Anatomy might serve as a meditation on death: it showed how fragile was man, how delicate his brain, how easily damaged his veins and nerves. It was thus a perpetual reminder of the transitory nature of this life and of the judgement of God to come.[35] Alternatively, a knowledge of anatomy would reveal in man the 'dwelling-place of God', the home of the soul, and hence impart in the observer a desire to maintain this divine temple in as neat a condition as one would a local church.[36] Such messages were, however, far from unique to Wittenberg; they could be found, in words and pictures, in a variety of renaissance anatomy books.[37] But few of their authors would have stressed as much as the Wittenbergers the role of anatomy in revealing the workings of the soul. In this, so Melanchthon argued, anatomy was almost as important as religion for imparting morality, a sentiment he associated with Luther, who had encouraged his son Paul to study medicine.[38]

It was not just that contemplation of the order of the body, with its own senate and ministers, would provide a model for the ordered moral life in society or even that the body's evacuation of sooty residues through the lungs was a nice counterpart to the way in which the Christian might get rid of sin.[39] Rather, what one gained from anatomy was a direct insight in to the way in which the faculties of the soul worked and acted together, for good or ill. To reveal this was the task of the Christian anatomist.[40] Only by means of anatomy could one properly learn how the heart and the nerves functioned and how the various spirits (including the Holy Spirit) operated throughout the body. Anatomy would also prove that the human mind was not just a machine, but had within it free will.[41] Indeed, only by anatomy could one really know how the mind or soul could go wrong.

This malfunctioning was expressed in two ways: in directly physical manifestations, as with madness and hallucinations, or in immorality. Melanchthon and his pupils, following a strongly Galenic line that linked soul and body closely together, made little distinction between the two types of disorder; both were disorders of the *anima*. So, just as corporal wounds could weaken, and ultimately destroy, the machine of the human body, so the soul could be also destroyed by wounds.[42] These wounds could be physical – excessive drinking or damage to the chambers, nerves or faculties of the brain – or moral. Lust, greed, pride, 'human wounds', could not only obscure the ways of God and impede one's understanding of the mind of the creator but also block and damage in some way the 'cells' of the brain. In other words, sin had a physical effect, corrupting both soul and brain and preventing them from functioning as well as they ought. In some cases this corruption might be reversed by medicine; in others only by the aid of prayer and the gospel.[43] Hence not only had the authorities the right and duty to lay down the appropriate religious regulations for the Christian community, they also should perform a similar function with regard to medicine, educating, upbraiding and, if necessary, removing those whose medical knowledge and practice fell short of what was needed.[44]

Melanchthon, who was the originator of this Wittenberg programme of anatomy, did not confine himself to theoretical exhortations. He had long contemplated introducing medicine, as represented by Hippocrates and Galen, into other faculties than that of medicine, as a replacement for (or supplement to) Aristotle, since he was convinced that what they had to say about the human body gave a more accessible insight into *physice*, the world of nature.[45] Unfortunately, it was not until 1525–6 that Greek texts of these authors were published and perhaps not for a decade or so that Latin versions of their works became widely available. For all his claims for Greek, Melanchthon's wishes could not be fulfilled for many years. Nonetheless, his influence can be detected, for example, in the anatomical information imparted at Wittenberg in the lectures on Aristotle's *Physics* by Johannes Velcurio in the early 1530s.[46] By this date Melanchthon was already contemplating, and may even have embarked on, his exposition of the soul, ostensibly commenting upon Aristotle's *De anima* but going far beyond any commentator before or since in his introduction of anatomical material. Although he himself modestly referred to his book as a student guide, he took great pains over it. The first edition, of 1540, took him five or six years to write; the second, of 1552, perhaps a decade or more, and was substantially revised. He sought to be as up-to-date as possible. The first edition is a monument to the new

Greek medicine; the second incorporates the latest Vesaliana. He took advice from scholars at home and elsewhere – Milich and Fuchs for the first edition, and, additionally, Peucer for the second – and incorporated their criticisms in his revised edition.

By far the most unusual feature of his exposition is Melanchthon's attention to anatomy. His original plan had not included any extensive discussion of anatomy, but he had soon come to realize that the workings of the soul could not be understood properly without a knowledge of the body. Hence his decision to devote almost half his book to a description of the body, the domicile of the soul. Besides, the newly discovered Galen included important anatomical writings of direct relevance to philosophy. The Middle Ages had known relatively little of his treatise *On the use of parts*, a treatment of anatomy in Aristotelian terms, and nothing of his *Anatomical procedures* and *On the opinions of Hippocrates and Plato*, a Platonic interpretation of the same anatomical material. All this Melanchthon read and incorporated in his own synthesis. He also devoted a considerable amount of space to lexicographical problems, recording and identifying the various terms for parts of the body found in Greek, Arabic and medieval Latin sources. This was no philological frivolity, but an essential activity at a time when nomenclature was far from settled and when considerable confusion had already arisen over the meaning of technical anatomical terms. In short, in his *De anima*, in both the first edition of 1540 and the second edition of 1552, Melanchthon provided for the studious youth of Wittenberg a work that was as modern as possible in its presentation of anatomical knowledge.[47]

In his *De anima* Melanchthon offered to Wittenberg a pattern for the integration of anatomical instruction with philosophy and with theology. His successors in the university followed his example in a variety of ways. The publications of the medical faculty that are concerned with anatomy repeat the message of the *De anima*, and it is no coincidence that their subjects are closely related to the major theme of the book. Peucer on the brain, Johann Mathesius the younger (1544–1607) on the organ of hearing, Alberti on tears are all concerned with problems discussed at length in *De anima*.[48] A later product of the Wittenberg school, the *Disputationes anatomicae* edited by Tobias Knobloch, reveals the long survival of the tradition.[49] Its subtitle, 'explicantes mirificam corporis humani fabricam et usum', hints at God and Vesalius simultaneously, and its twenty-four chapters, each one representing a thesis by one of Knobloch's pupils, culminate in four sections on the soul in general, its faculties, the sensitive soul and the rational soul. The earlier chapters, nicely illustrated, describe the individual bones and organs and incorporate recent Italian anatomy; those in the second half, on physiology, pile up authorities in scholastic fashion as they repeat at length the doctrines of Melanchthon. They differ from contemporary theses in philosophy only in the extent to which they emphasize their shared anatomical material.[50]

In all this there is no sense among the Wittenbergers that they are not being progressive. Mostelius, Mathesius, Alberti and Jessen all claim to be bringing into their teaching the very latest of discoveries, some made by themselves, most deriving from elsewhere. Nor should one deride as foolish their commitment to using anatomy to define and investigate the workings of the soul and its interrelationship with the body. The fact that more accurate conclusions on the anatomy and physiology of the brain were reached in the late nineteenth century is no reason to despise these attempts, which, in their own terms, are often superior to those of other contemporary anatomists. After all, when Vesalius in the later books of the *Fabrica* came to describe the workings of the body, as opposed to its structure, he was equally fallible.

Spreading the word

Looked at from another angle, however, the Wittenberg tradition of anatomy is far from negligible. Melanchthon was convinced that both moral philosophy and natural philosophy were essential for the education of the Christian; hence anatomy was too important to be left solely to the physicians. At Wittenberg, perhaps from the early 1530s, the philosophical lectures on Aristotle's *De anima* incorporated anatomical material, a tendency that became still more pronounced after the publication of Melanchthon's own textbook, *De anima*. In 1545 Melanchthon could expect all the arts students to be acquainted with the '*doctrina* on the nature of the human body, the rudiments of medicine, and the description of the faculties (*virtutes*)', and his book was again a set text in the revised statues of the mid-1550s.[51] In the elucidation of this book philosophers and medical men collaborated to an unusual extent. In the first place, the lectures were given to students in the arts and theological faculties. They were thus central to the whole system of education at Wittenberg; they were not confined to the handful of students aiming at a higher degree in medicine. Second, by being included in the arts course, these lectures gave a preliminary orientation to the anatomy course that would be followed later on in medicine. They determined the perspective in which the good Lutheran would learn his medicine. And, third, although in the arts faculty, they were frequently given by lecturers with a more than passing interest in actual anatomy and dissection. Paul Luther, Peucer, Mathesius, Alberti and Valentin Espich (1544–99), who succeeded Alberti in the anatomy chair, all lectured on *De anima*, and Hieronymus Schaller, Peucer's son-in-law, was already a doctor of medicine at the time of his appointment to the chair of *Physica* in the fateful year of 1574. Nor should one underestimate the anatomical interests of Paul Eber (1511–69), one of Melanchthon's closest friends, or of Esrom Rüdinger, a learned and pious scholar who held the chair of *Physica* from 1557–70.[52]

To find a work on the soul set in the arts course was not unusual. Park and Kessler have drawn attention to the presence of Aristotle's *De anima* in the Bologna arts curriculum of 1405, which was intended as an essential preliminary to the study of medicine, and they have also noted that medicine and philosophy were often taught in Italy within the same faculty and by the same persons.[53] At the end of the sixteenth century, Jacopo Zabarella (1533–89) was emphasizing in his arts course at Padua on Aristotle's *De anima* just how much his theme related to medicine, and how much philosophers' discussions of life, growth and the soul could benefit the would-be physician.[54] In these Italian discussions, however, the flow was one way – the philosopher instructed the medical man. The new anatomy of Vesalius and Colombo provided a few new facts, but their interpretation was still the province of the philosopher.[55] The career patterns of the Italian lecturers also differ significantly from those of Wittenberg. A glance at Lohr's lists of commentators on Aristotle reveals just how very few were the lecturers on his *De anima* who passed on to the more lucrative career of a medical professor.[56] Those arts teachers who did make the move had more usually taught logic or the *Physics*. They did not go to chairs of anatomy, but to chairs of medical theory, where their philosophical and logical expertise suited well the knotty theoretical problems raised by Galen and Avicenna. Professors of anatomy and surgery were among the humbler members of the medical faculty and paid appropriately, even if they were a Vesalius. The Wittenberg synthesis of anatomy and philosophy thus stands apart from the way in which similar discussions were conducted in the best Italian medical universities.[57]

The diffusion of this synthesis did not stop at the gates of Wittenberg or at the door of the lecture-room. In 1583, Zacharias Brendel, professor of philosophy and later of medicine, was lecturing on Melanchthon's *De anima* at the Lutheran University of Jena.[58] Thirteen years later, when the statutes of the University of Greifswald were revised, the *De anima* was among the texts set for comment in the medical faculty.[59] It also served as a textbook in schools. At Jüterbog, on the borders of Brandenburg and Saxony, Johann Grün, the first rector of the grammar school, prepared for his young charges in 1580 a summary of the *De anima* in the form of Ramist tables, 'methodical diagrams'. According to one of the townsfolk, the new rector had succeeded admirably in encompassing so briefly the 'fabric of the human body and the vigour of the mind' (*corporis humani fabricam mentique vigorem*).[60] At almost the same time, at the other end of Saxony, Matthaeus Dresser, rector of the gymnasium at Pirna, was preparing his own abridgement for the instruction of his pupils. He did not use Grün's trendy tables (which are by no means as easy to follow as their author had hoped), but concentrated on providing basic information, long lists of names and synonyms in Latin, Greek and German.[61] However different their methods, both schoolmasters put forward the same justification for their books. The Christian needs to know about the ills of the body as well as of the soul; the intending physician can learn from them how evil tendencies within the soul may be corrected, while the theologian can see just how the physical body is controlled by the soul. Above all, everyone, however old, however intelligent, however industrious, can be brought by a contemplation of man to wonder at a great work of God and to find therein proofs of God's wisdom and understanding.[62]

This theological message was not confined to books or the words of a teacher. From at least the early 1560s, the Wittenberg printers were producing cheap pairs of anatomical sheets to accompany the study of the *De anima*.[63] By cutting out the internal organs of the male and female body and then sticking them down in order on the so-called 'Adam and Eve Figures', a student could gain a basic idea of the structure and organization of the body, which he could supplement from the brief verbal description printed around the edges of the sheets. The anatomy is crudely Vesalian; the inspiration is made plain by the close likeness of the head of the Adam figure to that of Vesalius at the front of his *Fabrica*. It is thus at one and the same time both learned and popular (for these anatomical sheets cost far less than a printed book), and it was aimed at an audience that was not confined to medicine. The 1573 set put out by Gronenburg at Wittenberg was intended 'for those who study anatomy from *De anima*', a comment repeated by him on a set of *c*.1589 and also on the two sets published there by Schönborn *c*.1590. The same female figure was reprinted by Gronenburg at Wittenberg in 1601, and as late as 1625 by Johann Germanus there.[64] The message of Wittenberg anatomy was not restricted to the specialist or to the physician.

Seen in this perspective, Wittenberg anatomy was no trivial pursuit. Its tradition was long-lasting, widespread and accessible to a broad section of the community, from schoolboys to professors, and from book-pedlars to pastors. If to modern eyes the number of 'discoveries' made by the Wittenberg anatomists is minimal, the same could be said about teachers in other areas of Europe at the same time.[65] But, as this chapter has tried to show, making discoveries was not what Wittenberg anatomy was all about. What one learned through it was not only to preserve health, but also to control one's behaviour, to recognize God and to understand the doctrine of the Church.[66] It was but one part of a plan to produce within Lutheran Saxony a learned, Christian community, free from Epicurean and atheist heresies, and firm in its knowledge of Christian principles.[67] It was an ambition that was followed even after the theological crisis of

1574 that sent Peucer to gaol and forced his medical son-in-law to leave the university and his lecturing on *Physica*. If anything, the later productions of Wittenberg anatomists stuck even closer to the line first formulated for them by Melanchthon and repeated the same aspirations. To talk of the soul might well be the duty of the theologian or the philosopher but, as Johann Grün somewhat grudgingly admitted, the physician and anatomist also had much to contribute. True, the anatomists were often forced by 'philosophical considerations' (logic) and the necessity imposed by the very order of dissection to follow a method of exposition that concentrated on the body's structures and members, not on humours or spirits. But when the moment came, and their 'history of the parts of the body' allowed them, then they too could talk about the Christian soul.[68]

Wittenberg anatomy, then, was a joint enterprise of specialists for a common and universal purpose, the advancement of true religion through an understanding of man. It was a high aim, pursued, and in part achieved, by men of talent and learning. In their own eyes, its adherents were no conservatives, clinging to every word that Galen had ever uttered, but realists, willing to use whatever new discoveries had been made in Italy or beyond. But, if their anatomy derived from Vesalius, their outlook was focussed on a different series of questions and priorities.[69] By dissecting, and by learning from others' dissections, they were not only saving the body from disease and defeating illness in this life. More importantly, they were gaining and imparting knowledge that would save the soul and preserve it in the eternal life of heaven that they so earnestly sought. To describe or criticize the Wittenberg tradition of anatomy teaching solely in terms of this world is thus to miss the point. For Melanchthon, Peucer, Grün and Alberti, the Christian life encompassed both heaven and earth, body and soul. To misunderstand the workings of the one would be to risk losing both. In this sense, anatomy, as Luther was alleged to have said, was almost as effective as religion in saving man's soul.[70]

Notes

I gratefully acknowledge the help of Frau Leistner and the staff of the Ratsschulbibliothek, Zwickau, where much rare Wittenberg material is still to be found; and of Professor Thom and the staff of the Sudhoff Institut, Leipzig. Early versions of this chapter were given to audiences in Pennsylvania and Newcastle, and I am grateful for their comments.

1. There is little change in perspective between e.g. Charles Singer, *A short history of anatomy*, first published in 1925, and Allen G. Debus, *Man and nature in the Renaissance* (Cambridge, 1978).

2. A useful survey is by Luis S. Granjel, *La medicina española renacentista* (Salamanca, 1980), who points out that, despite the publicity gained for the new anatomy by Valverde, anatomy teaching in Spain was far from universally Vesalian, and dissections were not taking place in every Spanish university even at the end of the century.

3. Some of these linkages are hinted at by Roger French, 'Natural philosophy and anatomy', in J. Céard, M.M. Fontaine, J.C. Margolin (eds), *Le corps à la Renaissance* (Paris, 1990), 447-60, but his attempt to differentiate a Catholic from a Protestant anatomy is too schematic to be convincing.

4. For Mellerstadt, see W. Friedensburg, *Geschichte der Universität Wittenberg* (Halle, 1917), chaps. 1-2, is fundamental. The two debates are discussed at length by G. Bauch, *Geschichte des Leipziger Frühhumanismus, Zentralblatt für Bibliothekswesen, Beiblatt* 22, 1899, to which add the further document published by Otto Clemen, *Kleine Schriften zur Reformationsgeschichte, I-VIII* (Leipzig, 1982-6), III, 253-5. An overview is provided by P.A. Russell, 'Syphilis, God's scourge or nature's vengeance? The German printed response to a public problem in the early sixteenth century', *Archiv für Reformationsgeschichte* 80 (1989), 286-307. The conflict with Wimpina is studied at length by J.H. Overfield, *Humanism and scholasticism in late medieval Germany* (Princeton, 1984), 173-85. All authors rightly note the difficulty of categorizing Mellerstadt as a humanist, although by comparison with his Leipzig colleagues he shows himself more open to Italian ideas, and the new Wittenberg University in general was more humanist in tone than Leipzig, even if far more medieval than the Wittenberg of the 1530s.

5. W. Friedensburg, *Urkundenbuch der Universität Wittenberg*, (Magdeburg, 1926), 48-50.

6. The frontispiece of the *Anathomia Mundini emendata per doctorem Melerstat* (Leipzig, n.d.), has been often reproduced, e.g. N.G. Siraisi, *Medieval and early renaissance medicine* (Chicago University Press, 1990), 87. It shows a professorial figure seated in a chair while a second figure draws back the skin over the viscera of a corpse on a table in the foreground. The rural setting cautions against a too literal interpretation of the scene. See also J.J. Bylebyl, 'Interpreting the *Fasciculo* Anatomy Scene', *Journal of the History of Medicine* 45 (1990), 304 and pl. 10.

7. H. Helbig, *Die Reformation der Universität Leipzig im 16. Jahrhundert* (Gütersloh, 1953), 18-31.

8. O. Clemen, *Kleine Schriften, III*, 34-7; *VIII*, 30, 100. One should note the purely practical aims of the proposals.

9. Originally, Wittenberg, 1519; reprinted in O. Clemen, *Melanchthons Briefwechsel* (Leipzig, 1926), no. 48; and in H. Scheible, *Melanchthons Briefwechsel* (Stuttgart, 1977), no. 37.

10. For all this, see Friedensburg, *Geschichte der Universität Wittenberg*, 62-4, 136-9, 181 (the new statutes), 210-12. The Statutes of 1536 provided that the third professor 'soll . . . anatomicos libros lesen'.

11. L. Scholz (ed.), *Johannis Cratonis et aliorum medicorum consilia et epistulae*, V (Hanover, 1619), 431-2; VI (Hanover, 1611), 95.

12. J. Milich, *De cordis partibus et motibus* (Wittenberg, 1551); C. Peucer, *Oratio de cerebro* (Wittenberg, 1560); S. Alberti, *Historia plerarunque partium humani corporis* (Wittenberg, 1583; edn 2, Wittenberg, 1585).

13. Friedensburg, *Geschichte der Universität Wittenberg*, 273-4. On Fend (1486-1564), who held the third chair from 1543 until his death, see Clemen, *Kleine Schriften*, VI, 110-16.

14. Friedensburg, *Geschichte der Universität Wittenberg*, 278; *Urkundenbuch*, 381–2.

15. Friedensburg, *Geschichte der Universität Wittenberg*, 456–7; *Urkundenbuch*, 616–17.

16. Friedensburg, *Geschichte der Universität Wittenberg*, 460.

17. Friedensburg, *Geschichte der Universität Wittenberg*, 328, 456; *Urkundenbuch*, 510, 616–18.

18. Friedensburg, *Urkundenbuch der Universität Wittenberg*, 525, 537, 563, 723; II: 23, 50, 58. Ibid., 515, shows that no formal anatomy had taken place in the two years before 1587, with the exception of a brief dissection of a young child.

19. Melanchthon, *Ep.* 497 = Scheible, *Melanchthons Briefwechsel*, n. 583 (of 1527). Cf. his enthusiasm for the new Greek edition of Galen, *Ep.* 496 = *Melanchthons Briefwechsel*, n. 590.

20. See note 9 above.

21. The poem is written in his copy of the *Fabrica*, now Bethesda, MD., National Library of Medicine, classmark, WZ 240fV 1543; it was printed in the *Corpus Reformatorum* edition of Melanchthon's works (Halle, 1834–60), X.102.

22. Melanchthon, *De anima*, edn 2, (Wittenberg, 1552), reprinted in *Corpus Reformatorum* XIII.1–178. I have discussed this in detail in 'The anatomy of the soul in early Renaissance medicine', in G.R. Dunstan (ed.), *The human embryo: Aristotle and the Arabic and European Traditions* (Exeter, 1990), 136–57. For the role of this book in the spread of Vesalian ideas, see Moritz Roth, *Andreas Vesalius Bruxellensis* (Berlin, 1892), 244–5.

23. He sought the aid of Milich (*Ep.* 1145 = Scheible, *Melanchthons Briefwechsel* 1384) and Leonhard Fuchs (*Ep.* 1182 = Scheible, *Melanchthons Briefwechsel* 1430) in securing the most up-to-date anatomical information. Benedetti's textbook, *Anatomice, sive De historia corporis humani*, was several times printed in the first half of the century, at Venice, Paris, Cologne, and Strasbourg.

24. For the statutes, see above, p. 13–15; what they had in mind may be divined from the small textbook of Professor Salomon Alberti, *Historia plerarunque partium humani corporis, in usum tyronum edita*, which appeared a few years later (Wittenberg, 1583); and in a revised second edition (Wittenberg, 1585).

25. Melanchthon, *De anima*, edn 2, sig. A.5r. Thobias Mostelius, *Exortus et distributionis omnium venarum . . . quemadmodum delineantur in amplissimo opere Andreae Vesalii brevissima descriptio, ita, ut velut in tabula cujuslibet venae ramus ad quas partes feratur facile occurrat* (Wittenberg, 1557).

26. Friedensburg, *Urkundenbuch der Universität Wittenberg*, 608.

27. Cf. the letter of Milich to Symon Grynaeus, January, 1531, emphasizing that for a committed Christian Wittenberg was the best place to study medicine – and that Grynaeus' proficiency in Greek could be put to good use, G.T. Steuber (ed.), *Grynaei Epistulae* (Basle, 1847), 183 = Herbert Rädle, 'Simon Grynaeus (1493–1541): Briefe', *Basler Zeitschrift für Geschichte und Altertumswissenschaft* 90 (1990), no. 9, 48–9.

28. Melanchthon, 'Laus artis medicae' (1529?), *Corpus Reformatorum* XI.194; Mostelius, *Exortus*, sig. iii verso; Alberti, *Historia partium*, edn 2, pf.; J. Wilkofer, *De hominis praestantia*, (*c.*1604), in T. Knobloch, *Disputationes anatomicae* (Wittenberg, 1661), 3–6.

29. Melanchthon, 'De studio doctrinae anatomicae' (1550), *Corpus Reformatorum* XI.946; 'De pulmone' (1558), *Corpus Reformatorum* XII.209; on the 'mens architectrix', Melanchthon, *Encomium medicinae* (1529?), *Corpus*

Reformatorum XI.201; 'De anatomia' (1553?), *Corpus Reformatorum* XI.32; 'An virtutes sint habitus' (1559), *Corpus Reformatorum* XII.325; C. Peucer, *De cerebro* (Wittenberg, 1560), sig. b iv recto.

30. Melanchthon, 'De dignitate artis medicae' (1548), *Corpus Reformatorum* XI.808; 'De studio doctrinae anatomicae', *Corpus Reformatorum* XII.272-3.

31. Melanchthon, 'Quaestio' 45 (1550), *Corpus Reformatorum* X.803-6, deriving from Galen, *On the use of parts*, VI.21, with an interesting comparison between the church and the foetus; Mostelius, *Exortus*, sig. a ii verso; J. Mathesius, *De **admirabili** auditus instrumenti fabrica et structura*, Wittenberg, 1577 (my emphasis).

32. Melanchthon, 'De pulmone' (1557), *Corpus Reformatorum* XII.209; 'De consideratione corporis humani' (1559), *Corpus Reformatorum* XII.323; 'An virtutes', *Corpus Reformatorum* XII.326; Mostelius, *Exortus*, sig. a ii recto; J. Wilkofer, *De hominis praestantia*, (c.1604), in T. Knobloch, *Disputationes anatomicae*, (Wittenberg, 1661), 9. Cf. C.B. Schmitt, 'The rise of the philosophical textbook', in C.B. Schmitt, Q. Skinner (eds), *The Cambridge history of renaissance philosophy* (Cambridge, 1988), 797. One may well doubt, however, how far Epicurean atomism had at this stage penetrated into Germany, and believe that this use of the argument derives directly from Galen or is aimed at Lucretius.

33. Cf. Roger French, 'Natural philosophy and anatomy', in Céard, Fontaine, Margolin (eds), *Le corps à la Renaissance*, although overschematized and theologically shaky.

34. Melanchthon, 'De studio doctrinae anatomicae', *Corpus Reformatorum* XI.939; 'De anatomia', *Corpus Reformatorum* XII.28-31 (referring to the teaching of Paul Eber); *De arte medica*, XII.116; Peucer, *De cerebro*, sig. b iv verso; J. Grün, *Liber De anima Philippi Melanthonis in diagrammata methodica digestus* (Wittenberg, 1580), sig. a iii verso.

35. Melanchthon, 'De studio doctrinae anatomicae', *Corpus Reformatorum* XI.946; De consideratione corporis humani, XII.320-1, with thoughts on the death of Martin Luther; the frontispiece to Alberti's *Historia*, displays a skull, with a crucifix and an hourglass, on which see W.M. Schupbach, 'The paradox of Rembrandt's "Anatomy of Dr. Tulp" ', Medical History, Suppl. 2 (1982), 95 and plate 31.

36. Melanchthon, 'De anatomia', *Corpus Reformatorum* XI.33; 'De arte medica', *Corpus Reformatorum* XI.116; 'De studio doctrinae anatomicae', *Corpus Reformatorum* XI.942, 944; Mostelius, *Exortus*, sig. a ii verso.

37. Schupbach, *Anatomy*, 66, 90, lists examples linking the practice of anatomy to a knowledge of God, and, second, to an acceptance of the fragility of man. Add to his list, Wilkofer, *De hominis praestantia*, 2-3, for 'know thyself' as a justification of anatomy and a revelation of God and his angels.

38. Melanchthon, 'De aphorismo', *Corpus Reformatorum* XII.273: this was young Luther's doctoral oration, and is traditionally ascribed to Melanchthon. Cf. M. Dresser, *De vita et morte D. Pauli Lutheri medici* (Leipzig, 1593), sig. b ii verso.

39. Melanchthon, 'De consideratione corporis', *Corpus Reformatorum* XII.324; 'De pulmone', *Corpus Reformatorum* XII.213 (an oration delivered by Milich on the occasion of Paul Luther's doctorate). Cf. T. Knobloch, *Disputationes anatomicae* (edn 2, Leipzig, 1612), preface (dated Nov. 1609); the body is a state (*politeuma*) in which the mind functions as counsellor, the heart as prince, and the external senses as the ministers.

40. Melanchthon, 'De aphorismo', *Corpus Reformatorum* XII.275-6; 'De consideratione corporis', *Corpus Reformatorum* XII.322 (the 'discrimen

potentiarum animae'). Cf. Knobloch, *Disputationes anatomicae*, edn 2, pf.; theologians and lawyers will thereby understand more of the 'jus naturae' and of what governs our moral actions. This approach to 'psychology' by considering the faculties and organs of the soul, and by linking moral and physical disorders, was already well established by Melanchthon's own day, cf. K. Park, 'The organic soul', in Schmitt, Skinner, *Cambridge history of renaissance philosophy*, 464–86, with, p. 466, a table of the parts of the soul taken from Gregor Reisch. Schmitt, ibid., 798, draws attention to Melanchthon's lack of interest (shared with other north Europeans) in the intellectual functions of the soul, and in discussions of the soul's immortality.

41. Melanchthon, 'De anatomia', *Corpus Reformatorum* XII.29–32. Park, 'The organic soul', 481–3, notes a growing tendency in the (late) sixteenth century to incorporate anatomical and physiological information into philosophical discussions of the organic soul, citing Francesco Piccolomini (1575) and, still later, Francisco Suárez. But by apparently dating the *De anima* to the 1550s, p. 483, she misrepresents the novelty of Melanchthon's position, as well as underestimating the extent of his general use of anatomical knowledge.

42. Melanchthon, 'De anatomia', *Corpus Reformatorum* XII.33; 'De consideratione corporis', *Corpus Reformatorum* XII.322. So S. Stangius, *De partibus continentibus capitis, Disputatio 13*, in Knobloch's *Disputationes anatomicae*, talks in the same paragraph of the cures of melancholy, misanthropy and lykanthropy.

43. Peucer, *De cerebro*, sigg. a v-vi recto; b ii-v recto.

44. Peucer, *De cerebro*, sigg. d i-ii verso. The attack on quacks and lesser practitioners made here by Melanchthon's son-in-law and the major influence of the university until the 1580s was only a continuation of what Melanchthon himself had urged in his 'Encomium medicinae', *Corpus Reformatorum* XI.197; 'Laus artis medicae' (1529?), *Corpus Reformatorum* XI.194; and 'Contra empiricos medicos' (1531), *Corpus Reformatorum* XI.202–10 (recommending a touch more Galen).

45. See V. Fossel, 'Philip Melanchthon's Beziehungen zur Medizin', *Festschrift Hermann Baas*, (Leipzig, 1908), 33–40; Wilhelm Maurer, *Melanchthon-Studien* (Gütersloh, 1964), 51–5; idem, *Der junge Melanchthon* (Göttingen, 1967), I, 163–6.

46. Johannes Velcurio, *Commentarii in Aristotelis Physicam* (Tübingen, 1540), an edition seen through the press by Melanchthon after Velcurio's death in 1534. Velcurio used the anatomical textbooks of Benedetti and Berengario da Carpi, certainly the best available in his day, but in no edition of his lectures are his anatomical comments printed.

47. On all this, see my 'The anatomy of the soul', and, for the new Galen, my '*De placitis Hippocratis et Platonis* in the Renaissance', in M. Vegetti, P. Manuli (eds), *Le opere psicologiche di Galeno* (Naples, 1988), 281–310.

48. Peucer, *De cerebro*; Mathesius, *De auditu*; Jessen, *De lachrymis*; (Wittenberg, 1581) (not seen, but cited by Friedensburg, *Geschichte der Universität Wittenberg*, 305). Mathesius, who had studied at Wittenberg, had gained much anatomical knowledge and expertise during a stay in Bologna, and was appointed to the third (anatomy) chair in the reorganization that followed Peucer's imprisonment in 1574 for theological error. He held it briefly before being moved to the first chair.

49. T. Knobloch, *Disputationes anatomicae explicantes mirificam corporis humani fabricam et usum, in gratiam studiosae juventutis elaboratae* (Wittenberg, 1608). (I have used the copy in the Ratsschulbibliothek, Zwickau,

classmark 22.7.37.) The copy in the National Library of Medicine, Bethesda, MD, classmark 6460, to judge from the catalogue, would seem to contain only the first twenty disputations, and omits those on the soul. The second edition has an extended title, *Disputationes anatomicae et physiologicae recens editae . . . additis humani corporis affectibus praecipuis* (Leipzig, 1612); I have used it in the reprint (Wittenberg, 1661) (Wellcome Library, M.S.L. collection). In the latter, the running heads for *Disp.* 1–20 have 'anatomicae', those for the last four 'psychologicae'.

50. G. Schvegler, *De sede animae* (Wittenberg, 1596), defends Melanchthon's position (and rejects Galenic tripartition) with the aid of Zabarella's interpretation of Aristotle and N. Italian anatomy. J. Wessel, *De motus cordis causa* (Wittenberg, 1596), is a philosophical investigation of the 'Harveian' problem, but incorporating Fracastoro's views on sympathy, Vesalian anatomy, and Melanchthon's ethics in an attempt to establish why mental states and emotions produce physical changes in the movement of the heart. Note also another thesis by a pupil of Knobloch, N. Becker, *Disputationum libelli de anima secunda, de cute, pinguedine, musculis et peritonaeo* (Wittenberg, 1602).

51. Friedensburg, *Urkundenbuch der Universität Wittenberg*, 257 (only the *De anima* incorporated all these topics, and I am tempted to translate 'doctrina' as textbook), 303.

52. For Espich, Friedensburg, *Geschichte der Universität Wittenberg*, 308, 317; for Schaller, ibid., 283 (rightly seeing a planned career for him in the medical faculty); for Rüdinger, 282; for Eber, 259, and Melanchthon, 'De anatomia', *Corpus Reformatorum* XII.28.

53. Park, and Kessler, 'The concept of psychology', in *Cambridge history of renaissance philosophy*, 457.

54. C.B. Schmitt, 'Aristotle among the physicians', in A. Wear, R.K. French, I.M. Lonie (eds), *The medical renaissance of the sixteenth century* (Cambridge 1985), 1–15 (citation on p. 7).

55. See Nutton, 'The anatomy of the soul', 143–5.

56. C.H. Lohr, *Latin Aristotle commentaries: II, Renaissance authors* (Florence, 1988).

57. Dr Kusukawa reminds me that medical (and anatomical) topics were disputed on in the arts faculty, e.g. Erasmus Flock, *De balneis caena, somno* (May, 1541); J.B. Aepelius, *De victu, exercitiis corporis, balneo* (1542); Caspar Peucer, *De differentiis coctionum generibus* (June, 1554); H. Paxmann, *De partibus humani corporis et methodo* (December, 1556), see J. Köstlin, *Baccalaurei und Magistri der wittenberger philosophischen Facultät, 1538–1546*, (Osterprogramm der Universität Halle-Wittenberg, Halle, 1890), 23–4; J. Köstlin *Baccalaurei und Magistri der Wittenberger philosophischen Facultät, 1548–1560*, (Osterprogramm der Universität Halle-Wittenberg, Halle, 1891), 30. Melanchthon's ideas on the centrality of medicine were thus reflected also in the practice of the arts faculty.

58. E. Giese, B. von Hagen, *Geschichte der medizinischen Fakultät der Friedrich-Schiller-Universität Jena* (Jena, 1958), 97.

59. K. Pielmeyer, *Statuten der deutschen medizinischen Fakultäten* (Diss., University of Bonn, 1981), 83.

60. Grün, *Liber De anima*. According to his preface, sig. a iv verso, he had been teaching on this theme privately at Wittenberg and then at Jena for almost sixteen years, correcting and improving on Melanchthon with the aid of Aristotle and Vesalius.

61. M. Dresser, *De partibus corporis humani et de anima* (Wittenberg, 1581).

Dresser was a friend of Paul Luther and wrote his biography, *De vita et morte D. Pauli Lutheri medici* (Leipzig, 1593).

62. Grün, *Liber De anima*, sigg. a ii–iii verso; Dresser, *De partibus corporis*, sigg., a ii verso–a iv verso.

63. For these sheets, see my 'The anatomy of the soul', 151, 157. According to the *Allgemeine deutsche Biographie*, vol. 19 (Leipzig, 1884), Paul Luther was responsible for publishing at Wittenberg a set of 2 (coloured) anatomical plates and 3 anatomical tables. This is possibly to be identified with the set described to me by Dr. H.G. Koch (Merseburg) and dated to *c.*1562 (cf. also Dresser, *Vita Lutheri*, sig. b ii verso).

64. See L. Crummer, 'Early anatomical fugitive sheets', *Annals of Medical History* 5 (1923), 189–209; 'Further information on early anatomical fugitive sheets', ibid., 7 (1925), 1–5; J.G. de Lint, 'Fugitive anatomical sheets', *Janus* 24 (1924), 78–91; and L.H. Wells, 'A remarkable pair of anatomical fugitive sheets', *Bulletin of the History of Medicine* 38 (1964), 470–6. Neither of Schönborn's two versions of the male (Vesalius) figure can be accurately dated. A copy of the 1601 printing (female only) is in the Sudhoff Institute, Leipzig.

65. Friedensburg, *Geschichte der Universität Wittenberg*, 305, credits Alberti with the discovery of the so-called Wormian little bones in the sutures of the skull.

66. Melanchthon, 'De anatomia', *Corpus Reformatorum* XII.28.

67. Cf. Friedensburg, *Urkundenbuch der Universität Wittensburg*, 255–68. Combating the Epicurean heresy still figured in the dissertations published by Knobloch, e.g. J. Wilkofer, *De hominis praestantia*, chap. 1.

68. Grün, sig. a v verso. Alberti's textbook of 1583 bore the title *History of parts of the body*, but there is no necessary reason to connect the two men, save for the fact that Grün moved in 1581 to become professor of dialectic at Wittenberg; the title is not uncommon.

69. One might, for instance, compare with the views of Vesalius, Fabricius, and Harvey on the heart the oration *De partibus et motibus cordis* by Melanchthon, *Corpus Reformatorum* XI.947–54, and the thesis by Wessel, *De motus cordis causa*, above, note 48.

70. Melanchthon, *De Aphorismo* (spoken by Paul Luther), *Corpus Reformatorum* XII.273.

2

Aspectio divinorum operum

Melanchthon and astrology for Lutheran medics

Sachiko Kusukawa

Introduction

Astrology was important for medics as an essential part of prognosis, that is, the identification of the cause and prediction of the course and termination of an illness.[1] Usually a horoscope of the patient at the time of decumbiture was constructed. In order to arrive at a prognosis from this horoscope, basic interpretive knowledge such as the following was necessary: each 'house' (named after the zodiac sign) ruled part of the body, e.g. Cancer ruled the lungs, Pisces the feet; each planet has two qualities, e.g. the moon is cold and moist, the sun is hot and dry: planets such as Jupiter are beneficent while Saturn and Mars are maleficent; the relative position of planets could be 'favourable' (trigonal or sextile) or 'bad' (quartile or in opposition); the moon (because it was nearest to earth) had greatest influence on the body and it governed the 'critical' times of acute diseases; the sex and age of the patient were also related to planets. Thus an astrological prognosis could take the following form:

A patient falls ill with with inflammation of the lungs when the moon is waning in Cancer, Saturn being in opposition, and Jupiter approaching trine. The moon is cold, moist, and situated in the house governing the lungs. Saturn, cold and dry, is placed in a bad aspect and greatly aggravates the condition by contributing a dry, hacking cough. The chief hope lies with Jupiter which, in addition to being a generally beneficent planet, has special powers over the lungs, and is moving to the favourable trine aspect. Much will also depend upon the moon. If the patient can hold his ground until the new moon, when everything begins to 'grow' again, his chances will be much strengthened, and Luna's moistness will help to mitigate the hard cough. A powerful, hot planet like the Sun could also be beneficial if well placed, for Sol's heat would drive out the cold humours. Medication should take the form of warming applications, and possibly, bleeding on the right days, to release the heavy Saturnine humours.[2]

The practical skill to construct horoscopes and the interpretive knowledge were thus crucial for medical prognosis. When medics studied astrology, it was therefore often for this practical purpose of medical prognosis.

Italian universities where the arts curriculum was strongly orientated towards medical learning attest to this medical and practical orientation of the study of astrology. For instance, at the 'faculty of astrology' at Bologna, an impressive number of texts were prescribed: Euclid's *Elements*, the *Theorica Planetarum*, *Algorismus*, Sacrobosco's *De Sphaera*, Alcabitus' *Introduction to Astrology*, Ptolemy's *Centiloquium*, *Tetrabiblos*, the *Almagest*, the *Alfonsine Tables* with Canons, Massahala on the astrolabe, a treatise on the quadrant and William of England's *Urine Unseen*.[3] As often noted, it is impossible to strictly classify such texts into astrology, astronomy or mathematics in our modern sense since these quadrivial subjects were not necessarily independent of each other.[4] The content and format of such quadrivial teaching point to a strong orientation towards astrology, as was the case at Padua.[5] The education provided by such texts and commentaries was not primarily intended to provide proficiency in the prediction of stellar positions, but rather, they served as introductions to the canons, tables and instruments such as astrolabes, with which one could work out planetary positions.[6]

At northern European universities where the arts curriculum was mainly orientated towards theology, the study of astrology or of other quadrivial subjects seems to have been less prominent. Yet there is ample evidence that medics educated at Paris or Montpellier actively used medical astrology.[7] Although statutory prescriptions may not have offered sufficient training in astrology, the study of quadrivial arts again seems to have been orientated towards astrology.[8]

As can be seen in the *De caelo* commentaries, that celestial bodies had influence on terrestrial bodies had also become part of scholastic Aristotelian philosophy. The astrological works of Arabic authors such as Abumashar had preceded the introduction of Aristotle's nature books to the West,[9] and by the mid-thirteenth century astrology was integrated into the standard philosophical outlook of the universities. Aristotelian philosophy touching on celestial influences could thus be drawn upon by those medics such as Peter of Abano who felt the need to justify the study of astrology.[10]

By the mid-fifteenth century, medical astrology thus seems to have been the primary reason for astrology and its ancillary quadrivial arts to have been studied in the universities. Aristotelian philosophy could also provide a strong defence of the study of astrology for medics. It should be noted, however, that we can discern no explicit or general consensus among university-educated medics as to the kind of astrology to be studied at universities, the level of mathematical competence necessary for the medical profession, or indeed why astrology should be studied at all. In other words, we can identify no group of medics educated at the same university, for instance, promoting the same type of study of astrology. Instead, it seems, people who did voice their position on the status and value of the study of astrology, such as Martin Polich von Mellerstadt at pre-Reformation Wittenberg (as we shall see), had their individual reasons for doing so.

The Reformation, as I hope to show in this chapter, at least in one important instance directly affected the status of the study of astrology in the university. As a result of the educational reforms carried out by Phillip Melanchthon (1497–1560), the humanist ally and colleague of Martin Luther, a particular type of astrology came to be promoted and taught by medics at Wittenberg, not primarily because of its medical use but because of its specific significance to Lutherans. Although it is certainly the case that astrological beliefs permeated all walks of life in this period,[11] here I shall be concentrating on the status of astrology as a study, in particular at the University of Wittenberg, since it has so far not received the scholarly attention it deserves in this respect.[12]

Wittenberg during the Reformation is the time and place we might expect to see the overthrow of astrological beliefs, especially in the light of earlier humanist critiques of astrology and of the later Protestants' (Puritans', to be precise) attempt to eliminate magical practice by replacing it with the doctrine of Providence.[13] Yet, at Wittenberg, we find astrology actively taught and promoted, mainly by medics who claim that it teaches the manifest 'testimony of the Providence of God'. As I shall argue, the study of astrology thus promoted was an important part of Melanchthon's natural philosophy, which was based on a Lutheran understanding of God's governance of the physical world. Furthermore, Melanchthon made the study of astrology part of a body of learning designed to consolidate Luther's message. A tradition of the study of astrology which (I claim) was distinctive to Lutherans was thus initiated by Melanchthon and his medical colleagues.

Martin Polich von Mellerstadt and astrology

I begin with a brief summary of the status of astrology at the University of Wittenberg before the Reformation. The University of Wittenberg was founded in 1502 by Frederick the Wise, Elector of Saxony.[14] It was comprised of the faculties of arts, theology, law and medicine. As was mostly the case with other German universities, the Wittenberg medical faculty seems to have been the least active of those four faculties.[15] The statutes of the medical faculty dating from 1508 do not prescribe any texts specifically pertaining to medical astrology.[16] We have very little information on the extent to which these statutes were implemented during the early years of the university.[17] Nor is there any indication that studies useful for medical astrology were taught in the arts curriculum. The arts curriculum exhibits a typically theology-orientated programme with heavy emphasis on scholastic logic and Aristotelian philosophy, to the virtual exclusion of quadrivial subjects: in the statutes of the arts faculty of 1508, mathematics appears as an appendage to lectures on Aristotle's *Ethica* and *Metaphysica*.[18] I have been unable to find any positive confirmation that any quadrivial subject was actually taught before 1514.

This absence at Wittenberg of the teaching of quadrivial arts, particularly for the sake of medical astrology, may be due to the presence there of Martin Polich von Mellerstadt (1450–1514), the Elector's personal physician and one of the influential founding members of the University.[19] Polich had taken his medical doctorate at Leipzig in 1486, but despite his medical background, he seems to have been more interested in theology by the time the University of Wittenberg was founded. He became the first doctor of theology there, was teaching theology in 1507[20] and his interest in the medical faculty seems to have been minimal.

Just prior to moving to Wittenberg, Polich had been embroiled in a bitter dispute with his medical colleague at Leipzig, Simon Pistoris, over the nature of the 'French disease'.[21] This dispute also extended to the use of astrology for medicine. Pistoris originally claimed that the French disease was caused not by the mutation of the air in its manifest qualities, but by an occult quality in the air.[22] Though the issue was irrelevant to the main question about the cause of the French disease, Pistoris also claimed that while astrology was not part of medicine, it was nevertheless necessary and useful for medicine.[23] Polich, who had earlier maintained that the French disease was pestilential and caused by corruption of the air, took Pistoris' tract as a personal attack on himself and his main authority in this matter, Nicolao Leoniceno.[24] A war of pamphlets ensued. Polich pointed out the logical absurdity of Pistoris' claim that astrology is not part of, but is necessary for medicine.[25] Although alluding frequently to the arguments of Giovanni Pico della Mirandola to reinforce his rejection of judicial astrology as irreligious, Polich first seems to approve of astrologers publishing lunar almanacs without the sensational or diabolical forecasts.[26] It is difficult to see what use Polich saw in these lunar almanacs were it not for medical purposes. Polich is indeed known to have published several almanacs himself.[27] Yet as the controversy with Pistoris dragged on, the arguments escalated. Polich eventually rejected the necessity of astrology for medicine altogether.[28] His attacks quickly degenerated into *ad hominem* remarks such as that Pistoris lacked literary sophistication, that he was ignorant of astrology and that he did not know his medical authorities well enough. Quite patronizingly, Polich explained in great detail the definitions and subtle distinctions between different kinds of diseases and, at great length, he listed authorities who concurred with his view.

Though Polich here projects himself as a literary, sophisticated and learned medic, he also wrote commentaries on Aristotle following Thomas Aquinas, using the 'quaestio' method and leaning heavily on Scholastic authors.[29] It would thus be rash to characterize Polich as a straightforward 'humanist' or his objection to astrology as his 'humanist rationalism'.[30] His attack on astrology occurs as part of his comprehensive attack (which became increasingly acrimonious) on a colleague who he believed had attacked his own views. The personal nature of the dispute should not be forgotten.[31] Although Polich did draw up the horoscope for the foundation of the University of Wittenberg,[32] he may well have been less than enthusiastic to promote medical astrology as a study in the new university, still with fresh memories of this debate. Polich died in December 1513.

In 1514 a lectureship specifically for mathematics was created because mathematics was 'the most certain scientia, without which Aristotle can hardly be understood'.[33] It became a subject required to be heard for both degrees in the arts: those studying for the BA degree were required to hear lectures on the *Computus ecclesiasticus* and the text of the *De sphaera* of Sacrobosco; for the MA degree, students were required to hear lectures on some books of Euclid's *Elements* or Muris on arithmetic or on music, or the *Theorica Planetarum*.[34] It is unclear to what extent this stipulation was followed by the first lecturer, Bonifazius Erasmi, if at all.[35] Erasmi's successor, Johannes Volmar (d.1536), seems to have been more active. By 1521, his task was to teach the 'major' (= for MAs) and the 'minor' (= for BAs) mathematics on alternate days and the choice of texts and authors was left to his discretion.[36] Judging from his unpublished manuscripts and later testimonies, it seems that Volmar, who had studied at Cracow before coming to Wittenberg, had an active interest in medical astrology.[37] Yet, as we shall see, it is only after 1531, at the instigation of Melanchthon, that we see an active and explicit promotion of the study of astrology and other related quadrivial arts at Wittenberg.

Melanchthon, astrology and Lutheran natural philosophy

In 1531 Melanchthon wrote his first defence of the study of astrology. It was a preface to Sacrobosco's *De sphaera*[38] addressed to Symon Grynaeus, Melanchthon's school friend and a mathematician. Melanchthon starts off by defending the study of astronomy as valuable because it confirms men's view of God, that is, by looking at this 'manifest vestige of God in nature', we may acknowledge that the whole universe has been created and is guided by a Mind.[39] Then follows a lengthy defence of the study of astrology, which Melanchthon sees as having been revitalised by

37

Peurbach and Regiomontanus in Germany. He brushes aside Pico della Mirandola's rejection of astrology as contrary to experience by pointing out that the conjuncton of burning planets gives rise to dryness and that of moist planets increases the humours.[40] Passages from Aristotle (*Meterologica* 339a 19) and Hippocrates (*Airs, Waters and Places* ii) are cited to endorse the validity of astrology. Melanchthon then goes on to claim that astrology does not contradict Christian teaching. Rather, it is worthy of a Christian because it distinguishes between actions common to God and nature, and what pertains only to God and is beyond nature.[41] There are three kinds of human actions. One is 'inclinations' which follow the temperaments of qualities. It is due to celestial influences that people exhibit diverse inclinations. Another kind is supernatural and is caused by God, namely miracles such as Moses' passage through the Red Sea and Peter's liberation from prison. These did not happen because of planetary influences and we should correctly assign their cause to God. As taught in the Bible, celestial signs which indicate terrible incidents should not be feared, but ought to be seen as a consolation to the pious for divine justice. The third is caused by the Devil, such as Nero's tyranny and other such monstrous acts or murders.[42]

We can see in this preface to Grynaeus that Melanchthon is more concerned with defending the validity of astrology than that of astronomy, though both were undoubtedly necessary for a proper understanding of the heavens. Besides drawing on the validity of medical astrology for his defence, Melanchthon argues that the study of astrology is not inimical but useful to Christian teaching.

In an oration 'De dignitate astrologiae' delivered by Jacob Milich (1501–59),[43] medical student, friend and collaborator, Melanchthon clarifies how this study of astrology is useful for Christians. God has placed as signs eclipses, conjunctions, comets and other celestial portents, so that republics may anticipate major incidents and political commotion.[44] It is not irreligious to observe these signs because God has placed them there in order that we may be more vigilant. At an individual level, this astrology is useful to understand our own inclination so that we may cultivate discipline in cherishing virtue and avoiding vice.[45] Melanchthon's astrology is thus useful as an aid to political stability and self-discipline.

In a disputation on whether astrological prediction is prohibited by law, Melanchthon concedes that there are some predictions which are. These are predictions of augurs who predict murders or names of thieves. These predictions do not have their causes in nature.[46] Then Melanchthon nevertheless goes on to make a strong case for a legitimate kind of astrology:

To observe the governance of God (*ordinationes Dei*) is pious and

useful and not superstitious . . . astrological observations are observations of physical causes which are the governance of God. Just as
predictions by medics are physical observations of causes and effects:
[for instance] the speed of the pulse in the arteries signifies the
excessive heat and motion of the heart because the motion of the
heart drives the spirit into the arteries; so too the astrologer learns
that the sun has the power of heating and the moon of dampening.
Thus he predicts that the moon gives rise to more humid temperaments in the air and in animated bodies and secondary qualities arise
[thus] from primary ones. Therefore, such an observation, since it
arises from physical causes, which are divine governance, is pious
and useful for life.[47]

Melanchthon again stresses the positive value of the study of astrology in
Christian terms – its subject-matter, that is, physical causes, has become
godly because physical causes are the means by which God governs the
world.

Whilst Melanchthon felt the need to defend vigorously this study of
astrology, the validity of medical astrology was in fact very much taken
for granted by him. Thus in a disputation held on the occasion of
Milich's promotion to a medical doctorate, Melanchthon provides an
emphatically positive answer to the question of whether astrological
observations are useful for medics in judging and curing illnesses.
Against those medics who do not turn to astrology in order to judge or
cure illnesses, Melanchthon lists the testimonies of Hippocrates, Diocles
and Galen that celestial power effects change in the body. He then
recounts an anecdote noted by Johannes Volmar, the mathematics
lecturer, about a mathematician to the King of Hungary. The King was
suddenly taken ill, but his doctors could not find the cause of his illness.
The mathematician judged from the horoscope that the eclipse in the
moon was affecting the heart of the King. Thus the mathematician
recommended medication that would strengthen the heart. When the
doctors followed his advice the King recovered swiftly.[48] This example
shows that astrological prediction is useful for medics.

While the validity of medical astrology lay in curing illnesses
effectively, the validity of Melanchthon's astrology lay in its Christian
content and moral utility. This difference is due to the fact that, although
based on medical astrology, Melanchthon made astrology (as well as
astronomy) a part of his natural philosophy.

In 1549 Melanchthon published a textbook on natural philosophy, the
Initia doctrinae physicae, which was based on his lectures on Ptolemy's
Tetrabiblos.[49] Indeed the first book of the *Initia* deals with the subject-
matter of the *Tetrabiblos* as well as that of the *Almagest*, namely
descriptions of the planetary motions and their effects. The second book

deals with general causes of changes in the inferior bodies and much of the argument is taken from Aristotle's *Physica*. In the third and last book Melanchthon deals with the elements, their qualities and causes of change in matter such as generation, nutrition, alteration and corruption – topics discussed in Aristotle's *De generatione et corruptione*.

It is in the second book that Melanchthon incorporates his earlier defence of astrology. And from here we may appreciate what part astrology plays in Melanchthon's natural philosophy. After reciting various distinctions among the kinds of causes, Melanchthon proceeds to deal with accidental causes. Following Aristotle, accidental causes are defined as causes by which an effect does not necessarily follow but may or may not follow. They are divided into two kinds, fortune and chance. Fortune is an accidental cause in agents with deliberation, whose actions are concomitant with other events and thus unforeseen and unintended, and can be good or bad for the agent. Chance on the other hand is an accidental cause in agents without deliberation.[50] Melanchthon firmly points out, as Aristotle had done, that it is not that there are no causes for these events but that they are indeterminable or unknown to us. Then diverging from the arguments in Aristotle's *Physica*, Melanchthon gives a biblical example of David's sufferings and delivery as being God's doing, whereby he argues that accidental causes can be further reduced to causes *per se*. There are six kinds of causes *per se*: God; angels; evil spirits; temperaments and planetary effects; man's own behaviour; and instability of matter.[51] At the end of his illustration (with biblical and classical examples) of what each of these causes *per se* means, Melanchthon explains why this reduction of accidental events to causes *per se* is necessary:

> It befits men to consider causes *per se* of such [accidental] events, as much as can be enquired, so that we may perceive (*aspiciamus*) the series of those things which governs nature and life, and by heeding this order we may recognise more firmly that this world did not come into being without a Maker-mind, and that a guiding Mind is presiding over it.[52]

Melanchthon is thus concerned with causal investigation, even of seemingly accidental events, which attests to the existence of a Creator.

Melanchthon then proceeds to the topic of fate. One kind of fate signifies divine Providence such as miracles. They are immutable not because of Stoic necessity, but because of necessity of consequence following the fact that God has decreed them.[53] There is another kind of fate which signifies the series of natural causes, namely the linkage of planets with temperaments and inclinations.[54] Here Melanchthon is careful to point out that not all happenings should be attributed to stars, since evil spirits can incite actions and sinful man's wicked deeds may invoke God's wrath. Furthermore, Melanchthon rejects the idea of Stoic fate which binds God to secondary causes. God's miracles indicate that God is not subject to natural causes. Thus leaving aside God's extra-ordinary power and the devil's working, Melanchthon calls the order of natural causes 'physical fate'.[55] It is in this section on physical fate that Melanchthon's defence of astrology reappears.

Melanchthon characteristically starts with his defence of both astrology and astronomy. Knowledge about celestial motions, based on mathematics, is necessary because God has decreed that light be a sign to distinguish time, day and year. Because it is knowledge of things created and ordained by God, it is good. Similarly, divinations which are physical predictions, namely those which take signs from nature, are knowledge of God's works and order.[56] Medical astrology is a good example. Predictions which do not have their causes in nature, however, should be banned. Melanchthon added a long list of the illegitimate kind of predictions (mainly taken from the Old Testament), including crystal-ball gazing, augury, sortes and magic.[57] Although Melanchthon concedes that proper and legitimate physical astrology contains few demonstrations, he nevertheless stresses that, since all demonstration in nature is a truth and was placed by God for human consideration on account of some utility, to consider those few demonstrations is noble and useful.[58] Thus this astrology is useful for preserving health and curing illnesses; for regulating manners and behaviours by inspecting temperaments; for distinguishing between good and evil events; for knowing something about the political conditions and dangers.[59] As always, Melanchthon stresses the positive utility of the study of astrology.

In Book Two of the *Initia doctrinae physicae*, although he allowed space for miracles, the working of the devil and man's sin, and hence was not attributing everything to the influence of the stars, Melanchthon was concerned with establishing an unbroken chain of physical causation by linking the heavenly motion and effects (discussed in Book One) with the changes in matter in the sublunary world (discussed in Book Three). Astrology was essential to this programme.

What this demonstration of a series of physical causes achieves for Melanchthon is the point of departure of natural philosophy from medicine: unlike medics who stop their investigation at the visible level of matter, natural philosophers should investigate more remote and invisible causes of change.[60] Melanchthon does not simply mean more general causes. A natural philosophical consideration of causes should lead to knowledge of the 'primary composition of things'.[61] This 'deduction to the primary origin', Melanchthon says, is a 'pointer to God' (*monstratrix Dei*).[62] The essence of Melanchthon's natural philosophy is precisely this, to point to God: that the whole natural world is governed by orderly physical causation attests to the existence of an architect-like

Mind who has created and sustains everything. In other words, Melanchthon's ultimate purpose in natural philosophy is to demonstrate the manner of God's government in this world, namely Providence.[63]

The emphasis on Providence – enhanced by an effort to ascribe to God's doing all matters previously regarded as achieved by the meritorious man – is a notable feature in the Protestant tradition. When we look at what John Calvin, the leader of the other main Reformed tradition, had to say about astrology and Providence, however, we find an emphasis markedly different from that of Melanchthon. In his *Traité ou Advertissement contre l'astrologie qu'on appelle iudiciaire* (1549), Calvin warns 'the simple and unlearned multitude' of the superstitions of 'bastardly astrology'.[64] Since the planets can at best only incline people to certain qualities, Calvin sees predictions from horoscopes of the exact duration of life and manner of death as absurd. Calvin also rejects divination which predicts the rise and fall of kingdoms as bogus since it would mean that an enormous number of people will have the same horoscope. Calvin's main objection to this judicial astrology of soothsayers and sorcerers is that:

> in attributing the causes of our prosperous success and afflictions to the stars and to their influence, we put as it were clouds before our eyes to drive us away from the Providence of God . . . moreover this followeth that those men which wander amongst the stars, do descend no more into their consciences to examine their life . . .[65]

Furthermore, by attributing to stars the cause of evils men may forget about their sins.[66] Judicial astrology for Calvin is thus detrimental to the proper godly life of the common people and to appreciating divine Providence.

On the other hand, Calvin admits that there is a legitimate and 'true' astrology which he defines as:

> the knowledge of the natural order and disposition that God hath set in the stars and planets to judge of their office[,] property and virtue and to bring all to their end and use.[67]

Such a knowledge is praiseworthy because it glorifies God and is useful.[68] Although Calvin concedes that planets have influence on complexions and the human body (and he therefore allows medical astrology), he nevertheless stresses that planets are not the primary cause of such changes.[69] Famine, pestilence and wars are due to God's wrath to make us repent, and proliferation of good health and peace means God's blessing and encouragement to love God and obey His will.[70] Calvin's emphasis is thus always on the fact that we should not stray from the will of God.[71] He thus exhorts the reader to fear God, study in order to know His will, follow the teaching of the Bible and pursue one's vocation.[72] Even with 'true astrology', Calvin is thus concerned to preserve God's Providence over and against the working of nature and human knowledge.

Calvin sought to glorify God's infinite wisdom, rather than His intelligible wisdom and thus he also spoke out against natural philosophy which preoccupied itself with secondary causes.[73] To my knowledge, Calvin never showed any active interest in promoting a study of astrology or of natural philosophy which demonstrated God's Providence over the world. In fact, it seems as if there was a stronger concern for Calvinists to strictly reorientate traditional subjects such as natural philosophy towards Scripture, as we can see in the attempt at a natural philosophy based on Scripture and the Church Fathers, which was made by Lambert Danaeu, Calvinist theologian and polemicist.[74]

In stark contrast to Calvin, Melanchthon insisted on demonstrating the Providence of God in his natural philosophy. As I argue elsewhere,[75] that the Providence of God is knowable through *this world* is a specifically Lutheran interpretation. Furthermore, that such Providence of God over the physical world *ought* to be seen in natural philosophy is ultimately derived from the need to address a problem that Lutheranism had been facing. In short, in the late 1520s Melanchthon feared that civil unrest caused by radical evangelicals would jeopardize Luther's cause. This led to his re-evaluation of Aristotelian philosophy and the reintroduction in the universities of Aristotelian moral philosophy which emphasized obedience to civil authorities. Melanchthon developed a natural philosophy precisely in order to prove the starting point of this moral philosophy: the whole world, including man, was created for a purpose and that purpose for man was the pursuit of moral virtue (as dealt with in moral philosophy). Melanchthon's astrology was indeed part of this natural philosophy in that it demonstrated the Providence of God and was useful for moral purposes.

When we understand the reason why Melanchthon created a Lutheran natural philosophy and how he made astrology an important part of it, we may realize why, despite his humanist tendencies, his writings on astrology seem virtually oblivious to the contemporary humanist and other (quite sophisticated) debates on the validity of astrology. It was not that such astrological literature was not available to him. Circumstantial evidence indicates quite the reverse: the works of Marsilio Ficino and Giovanni Pico della Mirandola were available in the Wittenberg University Library (where Melanchthon was known to be an avid borrower) by 1513;[76] Melanchthon is known to have read Gianfrancesco Pico della Mirandola's *De providentia Dei* and numerous texts on Aratus, Proclus and Julius Firmicus by 1536;[77] he was also familiar with Bellantius' *Astrologiae defensio contra Ioannem Picum Mirandulanum*;[78] and his teacher at Tübingen, Johannes Stöffler, was involved in a famous dispute about the meaning of the conjunction of 1524.[79] Yet, neither

Pico's concern to preserve human freedom from the determinism of astrology nor Ficino's 'spiritual medicine' which was based on astrological magic, nor Bellantius or Stöffler can be identified as the singular inspiration behind Melanchthon's defence of astrology.[80] Nor does the reading of Melanchthon's astrology as 'neo-Platonism' or 'humanist superstition'[81] explain why Melanchthon's astrology should have been about the Providence of God and should serve moral purposes. This is because Melanchthon was addressing an issue which was quite different from the concerns of his predecessors. His natural philosophy was designed to address an issue which was specific to the Lutherans and thus Melanchthon created a natural philosophical astrology of his own. His main sources were Pliny and Ptolemy. Hence, by 1545, the second book of Pliny's *Historia naturalis*, which deals with planetary motions and effects in a geocentric universe, was taught at Wittenberg as introductory natural philosophy;[82] Melanchthon himself taught the *Tetrabiblos* until the publication of the *Initia doctrinae physicae*, which became a text in natural philosophy lectures; and basic skills for drawing horoscopes were taught in mathematics lectures.[83] Melanchthon himself promoted this study of astrology through numerous prefaces to quadrivial textbooks and was actively engaged in preparing texts of classical authors on the subject, such as Ptolemy, Pliny and Aratus.[84]

When we look at Melanchthon's natural philosophy as a whole, we get the impression that most of his natural philosophy is based upon medical knowledge:[85] Galenic anatomy (mainly understood through the works of his friends Camerarius and Fuchs who were involved in the production of the 1538 Basle edition of Galen's writings) in the *Commentarius de anima*; Vesalian anatomy in the *Liber de anima*; and lectures on Nicander's *Alexipharmaca* and the inclusion of Dioscorides in natural philosophy lectures by his students.[86] These all count as natural philosophy because by providing an explanation of how human organs are made for certain functions and herbs for certain medicinal uses, the Providential design of God in creating this world can be confirmed. The medical content of Melanchthon's natural philosophy in fact constitutes an integral part of his definition of philosophy:

> The Gospel is the teaching of the spiritual life and of justification in the eyes of God; but Philosophy is the doctrine of the corporeal life (*doctrina vitae corporalis*), just as you see that medicine serves health, judgements about storms serve navigators, civil manners serve the common peace of men. The use of philosophy in this way is very necessary and approved of by God; as Paul says in many places, that creatures of God may be used with thanksgiving.
>
> (I. Timothy 4. 41).[87]

Philosophy is teaching about the physical (as opposed to the spiritual) welfare of man and it is for this reason that medical knowledge becomes a legitimate and important part of philosophy.[88]

Thus it was almost always medics or those studying for a medical degree that taught natural philosophy and/or astrology at Wittenberg:[89] Jacob Milich, whom we have already encountered defending the study of astrology, also lectured and wrote a commentary on the second book of Pliny's *Historia naturalis*;[90] Erasmus Flock who taught natural philosophy also disputed on astrology in 1540;[91] Bartholomaeus Schönborn lectured and wrote a commentary on the second book of the *Historia naturalis*;[92] Sebastianus Theodoricus taught both mathematics and natural philosophy for a long period;[93] Caspar Peucer, son-in-law of Melanchthon, actively disputed, lectured and wrote on astrology and natural philosophy.[94] These men are known to have taught astrology and all obtained medical degrees,[95] with the exception of Paulus Eberus who taught Pliny's *Historia naturalis* and wrote the *Oratio de doctrina physica* (1550) and became a theologian.[96] Numerous writings by these men survive which promote the study of astrology (and of natural philosophy) and in the way that Melanchthon did. For instance, Bartholomaeus Schönborn promoted the study of astronomy (which he identified with that of astrology) in his *Oratio de studiis astronomicis* (1564) and Sebastianus Theodoricus advertised in 1549 that he would teach the second book of the *Historia naturalis* because 'the view of nature and order is itself testimony of divine Providence'.[97]

Medics at Wittenberg thus taught and promoted a new kind of astrology which had a Lutheran content and purpose. This did not mean, however, that medical astrology lost its importance. After all, as knowledge about God's creation, it also pertained to the study of the divine:

> Just as in the medical art, the art both of judging and of predicting the many changes in bodies is based on the knowledge of causes, signs and effects, and just as this kind of prediction was taken as a matter of physics and quite distinct from superstition because it is a view of the divine works (*aspectio divinorum operum*), of their causes, signs and effects, so too in this divinatory art [astrology], by judging from the position of the stars, the causes, signs and effects may be known. Consideration of such things is in itself very much a view of the divine works (*aspectio divinorum operum*).[98]

We therefore find Lutheran medics such as Janus Cornarius (as a Christian) promoting medical astrology.[99] Even into the next century, we can find medics belonging to the orthodox Protestant tradition using astrology for their profession.[100]

Conclusion

The Reformation at Wittenberg changed the nature of the study of astrology in the arts faculty. From a study with primarily a medical purpose, it became part of a natural philosophy which was designed to address an issue that Melanchthon saw as jeopardizing Lutheranism, and it was based on a Lutheran idea of God's Providence. This new study of astrology was therefore about the Providence of God and served political and moral purposes. It was also inseparable from astronomy and required knowledge of geometry and arithmetic. Such a study became a crucial part of the educational programme of the *Praeceptor germaniae*, who regarded education as essential for Lutherans in order to maintain orthodox doctrine. It was mainly the medics who taught and promoted this new kind of astrology which had a specifically Lutheran content and purpose. To my knowledge, it is the first time in this period that we can identify medics, all from the same university, professing and promoting the same type of study of astrology for reasons of Christian faith. I call this a tradition of Lutheran astrology.[101] It is a tradition that is important not least because Johannes Kepler was heir to it,[102] but also because it is a channel through which part of Copernicus' achievements was disseminated.[103] In this regard the reaction of medics to Copernican ideas deserves further investigation.[104] Most significantly, however, the case of Lutheran astrology indicates that we cannot simply equate the Protestant tradition with anti-astrological tendencies. Quite the reverse.

Whether insisting on its persistence throughout the ages until its natural death in the face of 'Newtonian science'[105] or concentrating on the erosion of such 'superstitious beliefs' through Puritan struggle against magic, historians have traditionally regarded astrology as the other 'dark side' of the coin of 'science'. For them astrology *per se* represents an 'occult tradition' which is independent of and should be separated from the 'scientific tradition'.[106] In this chapter I have tried to show that at least in one important instance, astrology was a key part of a particular natural philosophy. It is only after resisting the temptation to draw (modern) disciplinary boundaries onto natural philosophy and instead acknowledging that astrology and astronomy were both part of Melanchthon's natural philosophy – which in turn was deeply related to the issue of faith – that we can appreciate what effect the Lutheran Reformation had on the study of astrology.

Notes

1. The following section is based on S.J. Tester, *A History of Western Astrology* (Bury St Edmunds, 1987); N.G. Siraisi, *Medieval and Early Renaissance Medicine: An Introduction to Knowledge and Practice* (Chicago, 1990); Ptolemy,

Tetrabiblos, ed. and transl. F.E. Robbins (Loeb Classical Library 435; London, 1980).

2. As constructed by A. Chapman, 'Astrological Medicine', *Health, Medicine and Mortality in the Sixteenth Century*, ed. C. Webster (Cambridge, 1979), 290.

3. L. Thorndike, *University Records and Life in the Middle Ages* (New York, 1975), 281f.

4. That the medieval study of astronomy, for instance, was never an independent discipline in the modern sense is amply demonstrated in C.A. McMenomy, 'The Discipline of Astronomy in the Middle Ages', Ph.D. thesis (Los Angeles, California, 1984).

5. N.G. Siraisi, *Arts and Sciences at Padua: The Studium of Padua before 1350* (Toronto, 1973), 67–94.

6. For the limited nature of the *De sphaera* and the *Theorica planetarum* for achieving calculatory competence, see McMenomy, 'The Discipline of Astronomy in the Middle Ages', 104–79. For the technological contribution of medieval medical astrologers to the development and refinement of astronomical instruments and machines, see L. White, Jr, 'Medical Astrologers and Late Medieval Technology', *Viator* 6 (1975), 295–308.

7. See for instance E. Poulle, 'Astrologie et tables astronomiques au XIIIe siècle: Robert le Febvre et les Tables de malines', *Bulletin philologique et historique* (1964), 793–831 and M. Préaud, *Les Astrologues à la fin du Moyen Age* (Paris, 1984).

8. For the practical orientation of the quadrivial arts at Montpellier, see L. Demaitre, 'Theory and Practice in Medieval Education at the University of Montpellier in the Thirteenth and Fourteenth Centuries', *Journal of the History of Medicine and Allied Sciences* 30 (1975), 108f.; for Paris, see R. Lemay, 'The teaching of Astronomy in Medieval Universities, principally at Paris in the fourteenth century', *Manuscripta* 20 (1976), 197–217.

9. R. Lemay, *Abu Ma'Shar and Latin Aristotelianism in the Twelfth Century: The Rediscovery of Aristotle's Natural Philosophy through Arabic Astrology* (Beirut, 1962), 1–40.

10. For Peter of Abano, see G.F. Vescovini, 'Peter of Abano and Astrology', *Astrology, Science and Society: Historical Essays*, ed. P. Curry (Bury St Edmunds, 1987), 19–39. For the use of Aristotelian philosophy by medics in general, see C.B. Schmitt, 'Aristotle among the physicians' in *The Medical Renaissance of the Sixteenth Century*, ed. A. Wear, R.K. French and I.M. Lonie (Cambridge, 1985, reprinted 1987), 1–15. Medical astrology was taken for granted most of the time, as seen in medieval commentaries on Avicenna's Canon 1.1, N.G. Siraisi, *Avicenna in Renaissance Italy: The Canon and Medical Teaching in Italian Universities after 1500* (Princeton, 1987), 139–46, 179.

11. For instance, for astrological symbolism in art, see J. Seznec, *The Survival of the Pagan Gods: The Mythological Tradition and Its Place in Renaissance Humanism and Art*, trans. B.F. Sessions (Bollingen Series 38; Princeton, 1972), 63–83 and E.H. Gombrich, *Symbolic Images: Studies in the Art of the Renaissance II* (3rd edn, London, 1985), esp. 109–18. For medieval popular astrological beliefs, see R. Kieckhefer, *Magic in the Middle Ages* (Cambridge, 1989, reprinted 1990), 116–33.

12. The standard works on Lutheran astrology are: A. Warburg, 'Heidnischantike Weissagung in Wort und Bild zu Luthers Zeiten', *Sitzungberichte der Heidelberger Akademie der Wissenschaften* 26 (1919); J.W. Montgomery, 'L'astrologie et l'alchimie Luthériennes à l'époque de la Réforme', *Revue d'histoire et de philosophie religieuses* 46 (1966), 323–45; S. Caroti, 'Comete, portenti,

causalità naturale e escatologia in Filippo Melanthone' in *Scienze, Credenze Occulte, Livelli di Cultura* (Florence, 1982), 393–426 and 'Melanchthon's Astrology' in *Astrologi Hallucinati: Stars and the End of the World in Luther's Time*, ed. P. Zambelli (Berlin, New York; 1986), 109–21; D. Belluci, 'Mélanchthon et la défense de l'astrologie', *Bibliothèque d'Humanisme et Renaissance* 50 (1988), 587–622. None of these deal specifically with astrology as a study in the universities. The Lutheran interest in astrological pamphlets for propaganda purposes is well known, see for instance the popularization of the sole authority of the Bible by Lutheran authors of practica pamphlets (in contrast with Catholic practicas in which the Biblical texts held 'additional authority'), in H.R. Hammerstein, 'The Battle of the Booklets: Prognostic Tradition and Proclamation of the Word in early sixteenth-century Germany', *Astrologi Hallucinati*, 129–51.

13. E. Cassirer, *The Individual and the Cosmos in Renaissance Philosophy*, transl. M. Domandi (Oxford, 1963), 98–122; K. Thomas, *Religion and the Decline of Magic* (London, 1988), 87–132, 425–40. Cf. now the case for the seventeenth and eighteenth centuries in P. Curry, *Prophecy and Power: Astrology in Early Modern England* (Cambridge, 1989).

14. The standard history of Wittenberg is W. Friedensburg, *Geschichte der Universität Wittenberg* (Halle, 1917).

15. *Geschichte der Universität Wittenberg*, 62; Siraisi, *Medieval and Early Renaissance Medicine*, 57.

16. According to the statutes of the medical faculty dating from 1508, the following texts were prescribed to be heard in the medical faculty: *Practica medica seu expositio vel commentarii in nonum Rhazis Arabis* by Giovanni Arcolani; Gentile de Foligno's *Expositiones in Canonem Avicennae* (on the Canon 1.4); the *Practica* of Avicenna; Hippocrates' *Aphorisms* translated by Laurentius Laurentianus with commentaries by Jacobus Forliviensis or by Hugo Senensis; Galen's *Ars medica* with commentaries by Foroliviensis and Turisanus; the *Chyrugia* following the exposition of Dino di Garbo; and Galen on fever. *Urkundenbuch der Universität Wittenberg*, I, 1502–1611, ed. W. Friedensburg (Magdeburg, 1926), 49f.

17. Out of the eighteen men who took a medical degree in one way or another between 1502 and September 1518, some details of twelve of them are known, see H.-T. Koch, 'Medizinischen Promotionen an der Universität Wittenberg in der Vorreformationszeit' in *Medizin und Naturwissenschaften in der Wittenberger Reformationsära*, ed. W. Kaiser and A. Völker (Wissenschaftliche Beiträge der Martin-Luther-Universität Halle-Wittenberg 82/7; Halle, 1982), 75–9.

18. '[Legantur hora] secunda libri ethicorum et post illos metaphisica [sic], item in mathematica, . . . ' 'Statuta collegii artistarum' (1508), *Urkundenbuch der Universität Wittenberg*, I, 1502–1611, 56.

19. For Polich, see C.H. Lohr, *Latin Aristotle Commentaries: II, Renaissance Authors* (Florence, 1988), 346f.

20. *Urkundenbuch der Universität Wittenberg*, I, 1502–1611, 14.

21. The pamphlets pertaining to this dispute are reprinted in *Die ältesten Schriftsteller über die Lustseuche in Deutschland von 1495 bis 1510*, ed. C.H. Fuchs (Göttingen, 1843), 127–288. A brief summary of the dispute is given in G. Bauch, *Geschichte des Leipziger Frühhumanismus: mit besonderer Rücksicht auf die Streitigkeiten zwischen Konrad Wimpina und Martin Mellerstadt* (Leipzig, 1899), 96–101.

22. 'Morbus iam currens, malum francum appellatus, non proprie male morigeratum dictus, non ex mutatione aëris in qualitatibus manifestis, puta

calido et humido, sed ex occulta in aëre proprietate est causatus.' Simon Pistoris, 'Positio de morbo franco' (1498), *Die ältesten Schriftsteller*, 130.

23. 'Licet astrologia pars medicinae non dicatur, multum tamen medico utilis, imo necessaria, ut conciliator refert, comprobatur. . . . Medici possunt ex aegritudinibus ventura prognosticare; similiter astrologus ex astris futura praedicare.' *Die ältesten Schriftsteller*, 130.

24. R. French, 'The Arrival of the French Disease in Leipzig', in *Maladie et Société (XIIe–XVIIIe siècles): Actes du Colloque de Bielefeld* (Editions du CNRS, Paris, 1989), 139f.

25. Martin Polich, 'Defensio Leoniceniana' (1499), *Die ältesten Schriftsteller*, 149f.

26. 'Laudaremque itaque, si nostri temporis astrologi quotannis supputarent almanach conjunctionum et oppositionum lunarium atque eorum eclipses, omittendo sceleratas divinatoris atque diabolicas practicas . . .', *Die ältesten Schriftsteller*, 152.

27. L. Thorndike, *A History of Magic and Experimental Science*, (8 vols.; London, 1923–58) iv, 456f.

28. 'Esse necessarium medico, scire causas morborum inter sidera, error . . . Astrologiam esse partem medicinae, error.' Polich, 'Castigationes' (1500), *Die ältesten Schriftsteller*, 176, 178.

29. See Polich, *Cursus physici collectanea* (Leipzig, 1514) and G. Bauch, 'Wittenberg und die Scholastik', *Neues Archiv für Sächsische Geschichte und Altertumskunde* 18 (1897), 326–8.

30. As do M. Grossmann, *Humanism in Wittenberg 1485–1517* (Bibliotheca Humanistica et Reformatorica, 11; Nieuwkoop, 1975), 43 and Fuchs, *Die ältesten Schriftsteller*, 152f.

31. For the individualistic nature of humanist controversies in Germany, see J.H. Overfield, *Humanism and Scholasticism in Late Medival Germany* (Princeton, 1984).

32. Thorndike, *A History of Magic and Experimental Science*, iv, 456.

33. ' . . . mathematica teste Apolonio prima et certissima scientia est, sine qua Aristoteles, illud omnium artium robor et fundamentum, minime intelligi potest . . . ' *Urkundenbuch der Universität Wittenberg*, I, 1502–1611, 73.

34. ' . . . statuimus pro utilitate . . . scholasticorum . . . computum aliquem ecclesiasticum et textum spherae materialis Joannis de Sacrobusto [sic] . . . publice legi . . . idem lector aliquot libros Euclidis vel arithmeticam [sic] communem Joannis Muris aut musicam ejusdem, sive theoricas planetarum pro complentibus ad magisterium [legat], . . . ' *Urkundenbuch der Universität Wittenberg*, I, 1502–1611, 73.

35. For Erasmi, see *Geschichte der Universität Wittenberg*, 134.

36. *Geschichte der Universität Wittenberg*, 134.

37. It was reported in the eighteenth century that the Jena University Library possessed a collection of manuscripts by Volmar on topics such as the 'Summa astrologiae' and the 'de electionibus ad flebothomiam', see J.C. Mylius, *Memorabilia Bibliothecae Academicae Ienensis* (Jena, 1746), 405. For Melanchthon's testimony on Volmar, see below p.39. For the prominence of astrology instruction at Cracow during the late fifteenth century, see R. Lemay, 'The late medieval astrological school at Cracow and the Copernican system', *Studia Copernicana* 19 (1978), 337–54.

38. For the fortuna of this preface, see I. Pantin, 'La lettre de Melanchthon à S. Grynaeus: les avatars d'une apologie de l'astrologie' in *Divination et Con-*

troverse Réligieuse en France au XVIe siècle (Collection de l'Ecole Normale Supérieure de Jeunes Filles, 35: Paris, 1987), 85–101.

39. 'Quare si astronomia confirmat hanc de Deo opinionem in animis hominum, Plato non solum erudite, sed etiam religiose dixisse iudicandus est, astronomiae causa nobis oculos datos esse. Sunt enim certe ob hanc causam praecipue dati, ut ad quaerendam aliquam Dei notitiam duces essent. Proinde ex philosophis soli isti, qui Astronomiam aspernati sunt, ex professo fuerunt, atheoi, et sublata providentia etiam immortalitatem animorum nostrorum sustulerunt: qui, si attigissent hanc doctrinam, manifesta Dei vestigia in natura deprehendissent, quibus animadversis coacti fuissent fateri, mente aliqua hanc rerum universitatem et conditam esse et gubernari.' 'Sim. Gryneo' (August 1531), *Corpus Reformatorum Philippi Melanthonis Opera quae supersunt omnia*, ed. C.B. Bretschneider and H.E. Bindseil (28 vols.; Halle and Brunswick, 1834–60), iii, 531.

40. '[Q]uamquam mihi neque Picus, neque quisquam alius persuaserit, sidera nullos habere effectus in elementis et in animantium corporibus, praeterea nullas significationes in hac inferiore natura. Nam experientia ostendit, ardentium stellarum congressus vere haec corpora et siccitates affere, rursus etiam congressus humentium siderum augere humores. Deinde varie mixta lumina, variaeque temperatae qualitates, ut in pharmacis res dissimillimae, aliter temperatae, alios habent effectus.' *Corpus Reformatorum Philippi Melanthonis Opera quae supersunt omnia*, iii, 533.

41. *Corpus Reformatorum Philippi Melanthonis Opera quae supersunt omnia*, iii, 533.

42. *Corpus Reformatorum Philippi Melanthonis Opera quae supersunt omnia*, iii, 532–6.

43. For Milich, see Eusebius Menius, *Oratio de vita Iacobi Milichi Medicae artis doctoris* (Wittenberg, 1562).

44. 'Quanto est autem illa maior utilitas, non solum in aegrotis corporibus, sed multo magis in Rebuspub. considerare mutationum maximarum seu causas seu significatiationes, ut accommodare ad eas nostra consilia possimus, et arte mitigare incommoda. . . . Etenim si significationes illae non sunt considerandae, cur divinitus in coelo scriptae et pictae sunt? Cum autem Deus has notas impresserit coelo, ut Rebuspub. denunciaret ingentes casus, impietas est, animos ab hac observatione prorsus avertere. Eclipses, coniunctiones, prodigia, traiectiones, cometae, quid sunt nisi Dei oracula, qui minitatur vitae hominum ingentes calamitates ac mutationes? Haec si quis contemnit, Dei monitus aspernatur.' 'Dignitas astrologiae' (1535), *Corpus Reformatorum Philippi Melanthonis Opera quae supersunt omnia*, xi, 265.

45. 'Sed videamus privatos mores. Si quis naturae suae inclinationem intelligit, alere bona et confirmare, et vitare vitia diligentia ac ratione potest. . . . Ita prodest videre, quo quenquam ducat natura, ut disciplina idonea ad virtutem flectatur, et a vitiis abducatur.' *Corpus Reformatorum Philippi Melanthonis Opera quae supersunt omnia*, xi, 266.

46. 'Quaestio: an leges damnent praedictiones astrologicas' (17 April 1536), *Corpus Reformatorum Philippi Melanthonis Opera quae supersunt omnia*, x, 713.

47. 'Ordinationes Dei in natura observare, pium et utile est, non est superstitiosum. . . . Sed observationes Astrologicae sunt observationes causarum Physicarum, quae sunt ordinationes Dei. Sicut medicorum praedictiones sunt observationes Physice causarum et effectuum, celeritas pulsuum in arteriis, significat vehementem calorem et motum cordis, Nam motus cordis pellit spiritus

in arterias. Ita comperit Astrologus Solem habere vim calefaciendi, Lunam humectandi. Quare praedicit Lunam in aëre et corporibus animantium humidiora temperamenta efficere, et a primis qualitatibus secundae oriuntur. Talis igitur observatio, cum oriatur a causis Physicis, quae sunt divina ordinatio, pia est et utilis vitae.' *Corpus Reformatorum Philippi Melanthonis Opera quae supersunt omnia*, x, 714. (My interpolation in translation.)

48. 'Doctissimus vir, Ioannes Volmarus, annotavit historiam de Mathematico Regis Hungariae, Matthiae. Cum enim Rex subito et gravi morbo laboraret, nec Medici causam morbi invenire possent, Mathematicus eos admonuit, causam morbi esse Eclipsin, quae fuisset in signo Horoscopo Regis, nec alium morbum esse, nisi cordis debilitatem, ortam propter Eclipsin. Ideo hortatus est, ne aliis medicinis vexarent corpus, sed tantum darent iuvantia cor. Huic consilio cum Medici obtemperassent, experti sunt, curationem recte et foeliciter procedere, et Rex brevi convaluit. Existimo itaque saepe posse Medico prodesse obscrvationes Astrologicas.' 'Quaestio: Utrum Astrologia sit adiungenda Medicinae?' (16 November 1536), *Corpus Reformatorum Philippi Melanthonis Opera quae supersunt omnia*, x, 716.

49. Melanchthon lectured on the *Tetrabiblos* in 1535, 1536, 1537, 1543, 1544 and 1545. K. Hartfelder, *Philipp Melanchthon als Praeceptor Germaniae* (Monumenta Germanicae Paedagogica, 7; Berlin, 1889).

50. *Initia doctrinae physicae, Corpus Reformatorum* xiii, 316–21.

51. *Corpus Reformatorum Philippi Melanthonis Opera quae supersunt omnia*, xiii, 322–30.

52. ' . . . consideratio digna est homine, causarum per se talium eventuum, quantum fieri potest inquirere, ut seriem earum rerum, quae naturam et vitam gubernat, aspiciamus, et ordine animadverso firmius statuamus, non sine mente opifice hunc mundum exortum esse, et mentem ei gubernatricem praeesse.' *Corpus Reformatorum Philippi Melanthonis Opera quae supersunt omnia*, xiii, 328.

53. *Corpus Reformatorum Philippi Melanthonis Opera quae supersunt omnia*, xiii, 329.

54. 'Fatum significat seriem causarum naturalium, id est, copulationem stellarum cum temperamentis et inclinationibus.' *Corpus Reformatorum Philippi Melanthonis Opera quae supersunt omnia*, xiii, 329.

55. *Corpus Reformatorum Philippi Melanthonis Opera quae supersunt omnia*, xiii, 331.

56. *Corpus Reformatorum Philippi Melanthonis Opera quae supersunt omnia*, xiii, 335f.

57. *Corpus Reformatorum Philippi Melanthonis Opera quae supersunt omnia*, xiii, 337–9.

58. 'Cum omnis demonstratio in natura sit veritas, a Deo proposita considerationi humanae propter aliquam utilitatem, has ipsas demonstrationes, etiamsi paucae sunt, considerare honestum et utile est.' *Corpus Reformatorum Philippi Melanthonis Opera quae supersunt omnia*, xiii, 342f.

59. *Corpus Reformatorum Philippi Melanthonis Opera quae supersunt omnia*, xiii, 343–45.

60. 'Ex his [= Ignis, Aër, Aqua, Terra] Medici componunt mixta, et in haec resolvunt. Nec alia extrema oculis cerni possunt. Quaerat igitur aliquis, cum haec sint prima corpora oculis subiecta, cur non in his resistit Physicus? quid opus est quaerere ultra haec materiam, quae non cernitur oculis, nisi quatenus ipsa elementa cernuntur? Hac quaestione explicata, facilius intelligi poterit, quid sit apud Physicos materia. Sic igitur respondeo: Physici non solum gignunt mixta

51

corpora ex elementis, sed quaerunt etiam causas, cur elementa inter sese misceri, ac transmutari possint, quia causas generationum et corruptionum in natura scrutantur.' *Corpus Reformatorum Philippi Melanthonis Opera quae supersunt omnia*, xiii, 294f.

61. 'Haec consideratio primum movit aliquos ingeniis praestantes, ut ordinem huius doctrinae instituerent, discernerent corpora et qualitates, et causas mutationum et mixtionum quaererent, ac deinde progrederentur ad quaerendas causas remotiores, et ut ita dicam, *primam corporum compositionem.*' *Corpus Reformatorum Philippi Melanthonis Opera quae supersunt omnia*, xiii, 292. (My emphasis.)

62. 'Et haec ipsa deductio ad primam originem *monstratrix est Dei*, et doctrina de ordine causarum convincit mentes, ut fateri cogantur, esse Deum mentem architectatricem, cum reliquae totius naturae, tum vero humanae, cui impressit noticias, quae ostendunt aliquo modo, et quid sit Deus, et qualis sit eius voluntas, scilicet regulam tenens discernentem honesta et turpia. Haec deductio ad primam causam ex vestigiis naturae, valde grata est bonae menti, et honestas de Deo opiniones confirmat.' *Corpus Reformatorum Philippi Melanthonis Opera quae supersunt omnia*, xiii, 292f. (My emphasis.)

63. Melanchthon's definition of Providence is as follows: 'Usitatum est vocare providentiam, et cognitionem, qua Deus omnia cernit et prospicit, et gubernationem, qua naturam universam servat, id est, ordinem motuum, vices temporum, foecunditatem terrae et animantium, et curat et servat genus humanum, custodit politicam societatem, imperia, iudicia, iusticiam, punit atrocia scelera pugnantia cum lege naturae, in qua voluntatem suam nobis ostendit, et tandem iniuste oppressos liberat.' *Corpus Reformatorum Philippi Melanthonis Opera quae supersunt omnia*, xiii, 203.

64. I have used the English version: Calvin, *An admonicion against Astrology Iudiciall*, transl. G. G[ylby] (London, 1561), Cvir. (I have modernized the spelling.)

65. Calvin, *An admonicion against Astrology Iudiciall*, Cvijvr.

66. Calvin, *An admonicion against Astrology Iudiciall*, Cvijr.

67. Calvin, *An admonicion against Astrology Iudiciall*, 7r. (My interpolation).

68. Calvin, *An admonicion against Astrology Iudiciall*, Cir, Div.

69. Calvin, *An admonicion against Astrology Iudiciall*, Civ.

70. Calvin, *An admonicion against Astrology Iudiciall*, Ciiiv-iv.

71. Calvin, *An admonicion against Astrology Iudiciall*, Diiv.

72. Calvin, *An admonicion against Astrology Iudiciall*, Dviijr.

73. W.J. Bouwsma, *John Calvin: A Sixteenth-Century Portrait* (Oxford, 1988), 162-7.

74. Although Danaeu also sees the value of natural philosophy as primarily a mode of praise of God the Creator, he understands the Created world as written in the Bible rather than the world he lives in. He also has no place for astrology in his natural philosophy. See Lambert Danaeu, *The Wonderfull Woorkmanship in the World*, trans. T[homas]. T[wyne]., (London, 1578).

75. S. Kusukawa, 'Providence Made Visible: the Creation and Establishment of Lutheran Natural Philosophy', Ph.D. thesis (Cambridge, 1991).

76. G. Buchwald, 'Archivalische Mittheilungen über Bücherbezüge der Kurfürstlichen Bibliothek und Georg Spalatins in Wittenberg', *Archiv für Geschichte des deutschen Buchhandels* 18 (1896), 7-15.

77. C.G. Brandis, 'Luther und Melanchthon als Benutzer der Wittenberger

Bibliothek', *Theologische Studien und Kritiken* 90-2 (1917), 212-7.

78. Belluci, 'Melanchthon et la défense de l'astrologie'.

79. Thorndike, *A History of Magic and Experimental Science*, 178-233.

80. For G. Pico della Mirandola, see B.P. Copenhaver, 'Astrology and Magic', *Cambridge History of Renaissance Philosophy*, ed. C.B. Schmitt, *et al.* (Cambridge, 1988), 267-74 and E. Garin, *Astrology in the Renaissance: the Zodiac of Life*, trans. C. Jackson and C. Robertson (London, 1983), 83-96; for Ficino, see D.P. Walker, *Spiritual and Demonic Magic from Ficino to Campanella* (London, 1975); for the limited influence of Bellantius' defence on Melanchthon's astrology, see Belluci, 'Melanchthon et la défense de l'astrologie'; similarly, for the limited influence of the 1524 debate, see Caroti, 'Melanchthon's Astrology', 110.

81. For Melanchthon's 'Neo-Platonism' and Stöffler's influence, see W. Maurer, 'Melanchthon und die Naturwissenschaft seiner Zeit', *Archiv für Kulturgeschichte* 44 (1962), 199-226; for Melanchthon's 'superstitions', see K. Hartfelder, 'Der Aberglaube Philipp Melanchthon', *Historisches Taschenbuch* (Leipzig, 1889), 233-69.

82. *Urkundenbuch der Universität Wittenberg*, I, 1502-1611, 267; Kusukawa, 'Providence Made Visible: the Creation and Establishment of Lutheran Natural Philosophy', 147f.

83. Although we cannot discern this from statutory prescriptions, it is clear from lecture advertisments by mathematics lecturers at Wittenberg that they taught the basics of astrology with a clear understanding of the goal of the natural philosophy to which that astrology belonged. See for instance: 'Absolutis Theoricis [Purbachii], Deo dante, adiiciam praecepta, de figuris geneseon constituendis, ut syderum positus in qualibet genesi recte computare studiosi possint. . . . Quare doctrina de motibus et de significationibus consideranda est, qua quidem, ut recte utamur, etiam studiosos adhortari debemus, videlicet, quod et motus et significationes de Deo opifice nos admoneant, ut cogitemus, nos ad agnitionem Dei, et ad immortalitatem conditos esse. Significationes vero etiam hortentur nos, ut mores diligentius regamus, et Deum invocemus, ut eventus gubernet, qui praecipue sint in Potestate Dei.' Erasmus Reinhold, 'In lectionem Theoricam Purbachij' (1540), *Scriptorum publice propositorum a professoribus in Academia Witebergensi, Ab anno 1540 usque ad 1553, Tomus Primus* (Wittenberg, 1560), D1v, D2r. My emphasis and interpolation. For some samples of horoscopes used in such mathematical lectures (by Rheticus), see K.H. Baumeister, *Georg Joachim Rhetikus 1514-1574* (3 vols.; Wiesbaden, 1967-8), i, 6f., 30f.

84. For an exhaustive list of Melanchthon's prefaces, see note 1 in Pantin, 'La lettre de Melanchthon à S. Grynaeus: les avators d'une apologie de l'astrologie',

85. For the Ptolemy editions Melanchthon was involved in editing, with the collaboration of his friend Joachim Camerarius, see *Corpus Reformatorum Philippi Melanthonis Opera quae supersunt omnia*, xviii, 1-10. For Melanchthon's interest in editing Pliny, see his letter (9 December 1538) to the University of Prague asking them for a loan of their Pliny manuscript, *Corpus Reformatorum Philippi Melanthonis Opera quae supersunt omnia*, iii, 616. For Melanchthon's interest in Aratus, see Kusukawa, 'Providence Made Visible: the Creation and Establishment of Lutheran Natural Philosophy', 153f. For Camerarius' active interest in astrology, see Baron's article, 'Camerarius and the Historical Doctor Faust' in *Joachim Camerarius (1500-1574)*, ed. F. Baron (Munich, 1978), 200-22.

85. Thus in Wittenberg a medic could claim: ' . . . decrevi . . . explicare libros

Galeni ad tuenda valetudine. Quorum librorum lectio etsi principaliter ad artis Medicae studiosos pertinet; tamen sunt ij libri ita scripti a Galeno, ut a nemine, cuiuscunque[,] sit professionis, sine insigni fructu legi et cognosci possint, praesertim *a Philosophiae et Physices studiosis.*' Iohannes Hermannus (24 November 1560), *Scriptorum publice propositorum a gubernatoribus Witebergensi, Tomus quartus* (Wittenberg, 1561), cvv. (My emphasis.)

86. See Melanchthon, 'Studiosis' (no date), *Corpus Reformatorum Philippi Melanthonis Opera quae supersunt omnia*, x, 82; K.H. Dannenfeldt, 'Wittenberg Botanists During the Sixteenth Century', in *The Social History of the Reformation*, ed. L.P. Buck and J.W. Zophy (Columbus, Ohio, 1972), 223-48.

87. ' . . . Evangelium est doctrina vitae spiritualis et iustificationis coram Deo, Philosophia vero est doctrina vitae corporalis, sicut vides medicinam valetudini servire, navigantibus discrimina tempestatum, more civiles communi hominum tranquillitati. Est autem huiusmodi usus necessarius et a Deo probatus, sicut multis locis docet Paulus, utendum esse creaturis Dei cum gratiarum actione.' *Corpus Reformatorum Philippi Melanthonis Opera quae supersunt omnia*, xii, 695.

88. Cf. Melanchthon's earlier encomium of medicine which is a typical humanist speech of praise centering on Homer's praise of medics in the *Iliad* (xi, 514); 'Laus artis medicinae' (1529/30) and 'Encomium Medicinae' (1529/30), *Corpus Reformatorum Philippi Melanthonis Opera quae supersunt omnia*, xi, 191-202.

89. At least in one instance natural philosophy is known to have been taught in the 'hall of medics'; 'Cum autem hora duodecima nec lectori, nec auditoribus idonea sit, ita iudicavimus distribuendas esse has operas, ut hora tertia in auditorio maximo tribuatur Arithmeticae et Sphaerae doctrinae, quarta vero *in auditorio Medicorum*, doctrinae physicae.' 'Studiosis' (no date), *Corpus Reformatorum Philippi Melanthonis Opera quae supersunt omnia*, xii, 92. (My emphasis.)

90. *Geschichte der Universität Wittenberg*, 212f. For Milich's commentary on Pliny, see B.S. Eastwood, 'Plinian Astronomy in the Middle Ages and Renaissance', *Science in the Early Roman Empire: Pliny the Elder, his sources and influence*, ed. R.K. French and F. Greenaway (London, 1896), 218-20.

91. J. Köstlin, *Die Baccalaurei und Magistri der Wittenberger philosophischen Fakultät 1538 bis 1546 und die öffentlichen Disputationen derselben Jahre . . .* (Halle, 1890), 23. *Scriptorum publice propositorum . . . Tomus Primus*, B5vf., *Geschichte der Universität Wittenberg*, 282. C.G. Nauert, Jr., 'Caius Plinius Secundus', *Catalogus Translationum et Commentariorum* 4 (1980), 402.

92. *Geschichte der Universität Wittenberg*, 282. C.G. Nauert, Jr., 'Caius Plinius Secundus', *Catalogus Translationum et Commentariorum* 4 (1980), 402.

93. *Geschichte der Universität Wittenberg*, 275, 277. See also note 97 below.

94. For Peucer, see *Geschichte der Universität Wittenberg*, 274-7; for an indication of the range of his astrological interests, see R. Kolb, *Kaspar Peucer's Library: Portrait of a Wittenberg Professor of the Mid-Sixteenth Century* (St Louis, 1976), 65-72; and Peucer, *Elementa doctrinae de circulis caelestibus* (Wittenberg, 1563) and *Commentarius de praecipuis divinationum generibus* (Wittenberg, 1553).

95. Medics such as Melchior Fendt (1486-1564) and Johannes Aurifaber (1512-59) also taught natural philosophy at Wittenberg, though I have no direct evidence that they taught astrology. See *Geschichte der Universität Wittenberg*, 214f., 231f. For a further list of Melanchthon's pupils, see Thorndike, *A History*

of Magic and Experimental Science v, 378–405 and R.S. Westman, 'The Melanch-thon Circle, Rheticus, and the Wittenberg Interpretation of the Copernican Theory', *Isis* 66 (1975), 170f.

96. See *Scripta quaedam in Academia Witenbergensi a Rectoribus, decanis et alijs eruditis quibusdam viris publice proposita* (Wittenberg, 1545), Ciir–Ciiir; and see also *Geschichte der Universität Wittenberg*, 259–61.

97. 'Usitatum est in hac Academia repeti enarrationem libri secundi Plinij, et quia elementa quaedam continet doctrinae de coelestium corporum ordine et motibus, et de elementis: Et quia interpreti occasionem praebet multa utilia addendi . . . *Ipsa etiam naturae et ordinis aspectio, testimonium est providentiae divinae. Utilissimum est autem, quam plurima testimonia divinae providentiae in natura saepe contemplari.*' In lectionem secundi Plinii, Sebastianus Theordor-icus (1549), *Scriptorum publice propositorum . . . Tomus Primus*, 283rf. (My emphasis.)

98. 'Ut . . . in medica arte ex cognitone causarum, signorum et effectuum ars extitit tum iudicandi, tum praedicendi multas corporum mutationes, et ea praedictio physica res concessa est, et aliena a superstitione, quia est aspectio divinorum operum, causarum, signorum, et effectuum; ita in hac divinatrice, iudicante ex siderum positu, causae, signa, effectus aspiciuntur, et horum consideratio tantum est divinorum operum aspectio.' Melanchthon, 'Praefatio in libros de iudiciis nativitatum Iohannis Schoneri' (1545), *Corpus Reformatorum Philippi Melanthonis Opera quae supersunt omnia*, v, 819. (My emphasis.)

99. 'Quae si nesciat Medicus, quid praestiturus est quaeso in morbis qui secundum lunae in signis zodiaci cursum, Planetarum nunc hoc, nunc altero accedente aspectu, aut lethaliter incrudescunt, aut mitescunt suaviter . . . Hoc autem asserere ausim, summopere hanc [= scientiam astrorum] omni homini Christiano suspiciendam as suspiciendam esse, nedum Medico, qui, ut Hippocrates inquit, cuiusmodi Medicus est, si Astronomiam ignorat? At Christianus homo nequaquam hanc improbabit, nisi tam lucidam ac caelatam machinam frustra tot splendissimis syderibus ornatam ab opifice omnium rerum Deo Opt. Max. putabit, ac non potius in immensae eius potentiae, ac summae bonitatis certum inditium [sic].' Janus Cornarius, *Quarum artium, ac linguarum cognitione Medico opus sit. Praefatio ante Hippocratis Aphorsimorum initium*, (Hanau, no date), Avir, Aviir. For Cornarius, see O. Clemen, 'Janus Cornarius' *Neues Archiv für sächsische Geschichte und Altertumskunde* 33 (1912), 36–76. I thank Andrew Cunningham for this reference. See also the astrological activities of another Lutheran medic, Achilles Priminius Gasser, K.H. Burmeister, *Achilles Primin Gasser 1505–1577: Arzt und Naturforscher, Historiker und Humanist* (3 vols.; Wiesbaden, 1970–5), vol. i.

100. See for instance the case of an English doctor (Richard Napier) who extensively uses medical astrology in M. Macdonald, *Mystical Bedlam: Madness, Anxiety and Healing in Seventeenth-century England* (Cambridge, 1983), esp. 21–3, 220–2 for Napier's orthodox religious views.

101. This explains why the phenomenon of medics professing quadrivial arts was peculiar to German Protestant universities, as noted in R.S. Westman, 'The Astronomer's Role in the Sixteenth Century: a preliminary study', *History of Science* xviii (1980), 118.

102. See J.V. Field, 'A Lutheran Astrologer: Johannes Kepler', *Archive for the History of the Exact Sciences* 31 (1984/5), 189–272.

103. Cf. Westman, 'The Melanchthon Circle'.

104. See for instance the reference to Copernicus in Bartholomaeus Schönborn, *Oratio de studiis astronomicis* (Wittenberg, 1564), C2v–C3r. Cf. reaction to

Copernicus' work by Italian medics in their commentary on Avicenna's *Canon* I.i, Siraisi, *Avicenna in Renaissance Italy*, 266–79, 282–9.

105. Thorndike, *A History of Magic and Experimental Science*; but see now S. Schaffer, 'Newton's Comets and the Transformation of Astrology', *Astrology, Science and Society*, 219–43, for Newton's commitment to restore true Chaldaean natural philosophical astrology.

106. See for instance the introduction by B. Vickers in *Occult and Scientific Mentalities in the Renaissance*, ed. B. Vickers (Cambridge, 1984), 1–55. Cf. K. Hutchison, 'What Happened to Occult Qualities in the Scientific Revolution?' *Isis* 73 (1982), 233–53.

3

Paracelsus: medicine as popular protest

Charles Webster

The life of Theophrastus von Hohenheim (1493–1541), or Paracelsus as he is generally known, coincides directly with the Reformation. Indeed, at least from the time of his brief official appointment in Basle in 1527 he was sarcastically labelled as the Luther of medicine. Paracelsus occasionally mentioned Luther, and he seems to have taken seriously the parallel between their roles. With the posthumous growth of his reputation, the comparison between Paracelsus and Luther took on a more sober and less pejorative character. Paracelsus had shaken the authority of classical medicine, and Paracelsianism remained a vigorous force for more than a century. As a self-conscious movement of reform Paracelsianism constituted one of the vital ingredients of the so-called Scientific Revolution.

The academic effort has understandably been preoccupied with the natural philosophy and medical theories of Paracelsus, and with their antecedents and subsequent influence. Although Paracelsus was responsible for a not insignificant body of religious, theological, social and ethical writings, these works have attracted relatively little attention.[1] It is therefore timely to consider the relationship of Paracelsus to the movement for religious reform and also trace connections between the medical and non-medical writings. It will be suggested that the two bodies of writing are more intimately linked than is customarily realized. Reassessment of the medical writings in the light of the protest literature of the Reformation explains some of the features which have rendered the medical work of Paracelsus uncongenial, obscure and even incomprehensible to the modern historian of science. Sensitivity to the historical circumstances of the early Reformation and Peasants' War enables us to adopt a more sympathetic response to the mission of Paracelsus. The formula which he evolved for exposition of his ideas matched the aspirations of his contemporaries and guaranteed his work a greater degree of familiarity and acceptability than would have been the case if he had adopted a dry, formal academic presentation. By adopting literary forms familiar to the reading public of his age and by presenting his

57

scientific and medical ideas in the context of a religious and ethical framework which commanded wide assent, Paracelsus elevated the status of his mission. The reader was constantly reminded that Paracelsus was first and foremost prophet and apostle. His first priority therefore lay in defining the moral and ethical guidelines for the science and medicine of the new apostolic age. The specific scientific and technical content was secondary to this purpose, which accounts for the frequently provisional, fragmentary and unsystematic nature of the medical writings. Although Paracelsus undoubtedly sacrificed ease of accessibility to the modern reader, he successfully gauged the aspirations of his contemporaries and determined that medicine would not be excluded from the framework of reformation debate.[2]

The maturity of Paracelsus coincided with the catastrophic decline in the standing of the Church in the German-speaking cultural area. As a young man Paracelsus personally witnessed the overturning of the authority of the Church in Basle, Nuremberg, Salzburg and Strasbourg, and his wanderings during this period familiarized him with the main territory of the peasants' uprisings of 1524 and 1525.[3]

As a marginal figure, from a genteel but impoverished background, of uncertain social status, without firm academic credentials or ascertained civic position, Paracelsus had much in common with the alienated tradesmen, clerks and artisans who led the popular movement of social protest and religious discontent. Important among its products, this movement generated a tide of some 4,000 different pamphlets between 1500 and 1530.[4] Pamphlets and illustrated broadsheets provided a means whereby the substance of learned academic disputations was filtered down to the lay public at large. Equally important, the pamphlets represented a buoyant, independent and heterogeneous force, constituted from a wide variety of elements blended in various combinations, perpetuating older medieval traditions of piety alongside newer influences derived from humanists such as Erasmus. The pamphlet literature became an influential vehicle of propaganda and a stimulus to defiance of authority. The pamphlets confirm the general collapse of authority of the Church hierarchy and priesthood. The Church presented an unfortunate combination of anachronism and exploitation. It was in harmony with the undeservingly affluent rather than the deserving poor. All of this contributed to the general sense of spiritual impoverishment against which the pamphlet literature reacted.

The pamphlets became an influential vehicle for anticlericalism and rehearsal of socio-economic grievances. They echoed the widespread urge for spiritual regeneration based on a return to a simple scriptural piety, modelled on the New Testament. The *lex evangelica* and *vita apostolica* became the watchwords of this assertive lay theology. This movement gave prominence to the idea of the universal priesthood of believers, which reinforced the status of the laity in general, but was especially important in emphasizing the worth of the common people. Hard times added to the urgency of the message of the protest literature and further intensity was provided by the eschatological perspective widely adopted in the tracts. A powerful atmosphere of expectancy was created, in which the multiple traumas of present existence constituted a final test, pending the final day of judgement and return of a beatific age.

Some indication of the intensity of eschatological speculation is provided by the publication in the period 1519-24 of some 160 tracts produced by sixty authors concerned with the conjunction of superior planets in Pisces which took place in February 1524.[5] This literature fuelled hysteria concerning a great flood and possible end of the world. The failure of this cataclysm to materialize produced no disincentive to the prophetic literature. Astrological prognostications were reinforced by works such as the prophecies of Johannes Lichtenberger which infiltrated astrology with Joachimite prophecy. The Lichtenberger prophecies were regularly published from 1488 onwards, and Lichtenberger's prophecies and figures became widely imitated.[6] A parallel Joachimite source came into circulation due to Andreas Osiander, the future editor of Copernicus, who in 1527 issued his commentary on the figures which he claimed to have discovered in the Carthusian library in Nuremberg. Both German and Latin editions of Lichtenberger were produced in the same year under the sponsorship of Luther. Osiander's eschatological taste infected the famous Hans Sachs, who provided verses of the edition of the Nuremberg figures. Osiander and Sachs mobilized the figures as propaganda for the Lutheran Reformation.[7]

Short tracts containing prophecies concerning astrological phenomena were a potent element in the popular pamphlet literature. The title page comprising a lengthy and ominous title, together with a large woodcut burgeoning with lurid symbolism, constituted an instrument of propaganda in itself. Prophecies, prognostications, or *Practicas* brought celebrity to such authors as Johannes Carion, Johannes Copp, Lorenz Fries, Joseph Grünpeck, Pamphilus Gengenbach, Leonhard Reynmann, Georg Tannstetter and Hans Virdung. Paracelsus was following the precedent of Fries, the physician of Colmar, whose dialogue in defence of astrology framed between the author and Luther, was partly instrumental in securing the sympathy of Luther and Melanchthon for astrology.[8] Also such an intervention had the additional virtue of drawing attention to the primacy of astronomy in the medical theory of Paracelsus, which was premised on the idea of unity between the macrocosm and microcosm. The publicity gained by Osiander, Sachs and others engaged in prophecy arguably led Paracelsus to visit Nuremberg in 1529 and use this as the base for his first publications.

The *Practica gemacht auf Europen 1530-1534*, published by Frederick

Practica D. Theo
phrasti Paracelsi / gemacht
auff Europen / anzufahen in dem nechstkunffti
gen Dreyssigsten Jar / Biß auff das Vier vnd
Dreyssigst nachuolgend.

Illustration 4 Title page of Paracelsus: *Practica gemacht auf Europen 1530–1534* Nuremberg, 1529. From Karl Sudhoff (ed.), *Theophrastus von Hohenheim gen. Paracelsus. Sämtliche Werke,* (Munich, 1923), vol. 7, 41. Reproduced by permission of the Syndics of Cambridge University Library.

Peypus in Nuremberg in 1529, arguably constituted the first proper publication produced by Paracelsus and it was the first occasion on which he was described as 'Paracelsus' rather than Theophrastus von Hohenheim on a title page.[9] Judging by conventional standards the *Practica* of 1529 was a success. The appeal of the *Practica* was undoubtedly assisted by inclusion of an elaborate woodcut on the title page (see Illustration 4). Five issues of this *Practica* are recorded for the years 1529 and 1530.[10] Paracelsus was launched into a successful career as pamphleteer. Indeed *Practicas* account for the major part of his published literary output between 1529 and his death in 1541. Prognostications account for 16 out of the 23 titles recorded in Sudhoff's bibliography for this period, which slightly underestimated the prevalence of these writings, because it does not take full account of reissues.[11] To the general public Paracelsus was therefore primarily known as an author of disconcerting prophecies, based primarily on conjunctions, eclipses, and comets, but also incorporating evidence of other kinds. In addition, probably during his stay in Nuremberg, Paracelsus produced commentaries on both the Nuremberg and Lichtenberger figures and prophecies.[12] These commentaries demonstrate the habitual tendency of Paracelsus to set himself at variance with authority. Swimming against the Lutheran tide in Nuremberg, Paracelsus disputed the claim that the Nuremberg and Lichtenberger figures sanctioned the Lutheran Reformation, instead maintaining the view stated elsewhere in his prophetic writings that schismatic reform was a vain enterprise destined to perish at the hands of a radically altered Catholic Church.

The *Practica* of 1529 contains the conventional predictions of political and civil unrest. Compared with other commentators Paracelsus paid less regard to the prospects of environmental catastrophes and more to the likelihood of disintegration of the economy. The infrastructure of the *Practica* introduces many points which were to become recurrent themes in his other writings. The coincidence between a new star and the birth of Christ was seen as evidence that crucial events would be accompanied by astronomical omens, and indeed that the heavens contained the secrets of all manner of terrestrial events. Paracelsus also believed that Christ's miracles, including the healing of diseases, implied knowledge of the powers of the firmament. Therefore in order to fulfil Christ's invocation to care for the needy and the sick it was necessary to recognize the primacy of the power of the firmament. Finally, Paracelsus adopted a strong eschatological framework for his prophecies. He was sceptical about precise prophecies and warned against false prophets. Nevertheless he believed that the Day of Judgement was near and might come at any time. All the evidence suggested that after enduring terrible tribulations the new order of Christ would at last gain ascendancy over the old regimes, which, although entrenched, were at last breaking apart under the weight of their corruption.

Capitalizing on his new position as a prophet, Paracelsus published his first medical writings, two short tracts on syphilis.[13] This represented a further effective piece of opportunism because syphilis was arousing acute anxiety, and this disease seemed totally beyond the control of the medical profession. These two tracts gave Paracelsus his chance to pay back scores against the medical elite, no doubt inspired by the humiliation he had recently suffered at their hands in Basle. He pursued the line that whatever good resided in the medicines then in use was counteracted by the incompetence and greed of medical practitioners, in whose hands all classes suffered, but the poor in particular. These tracts contained a skilful blend of medicine and social propaganda. He intermixed sensible, accessible and practical medical advice, with a strong infusion of the kind of social criticism which struck a chord with his audience and which was consistent with the message stemming from the religious and social tract literature.

Consistency between his medical and prophetic writings was emphasized by the inclusion of a large woodcut on the title page of the first of his tracts on syphilis which, like the *Practica*, was published by Frederick Peypus in Nuremberg in 1529 (Illustration 5). The double-frame woodcut reinforced the polemical message of the tract, by contrasting the traditional and Paracelsian approaches to the sick poor. On the left the sick person crouches in an attitude of dejection, barefoot and clothed only in a shirt. By contrast the doctor's expensive attire signifies his academic status. Following established practice, the patient is being forced to eat some chicken leg before being given a concoction containing guaiacum, which is being prepared in a massive pot by a woman servant. The representative of the sick poor is casting a furtive glance at the illustration on the right which shows a comfortable hostelry scene. The windows are glazed expensively with bulls-eye panes. The anxious patient is being invited by the honest, simply-dressed proprietor, to take wine served in a cut-glass beaker before being offered a fulsome meal at a well-laid table covered by a tablecloth. Paracelsus therefore offers a form of therapy which avoids humiliating the poor with dietary prohibitions and he introduces them to a variety of simple, more effective and economical treatments, including mercurial preparations, which soon became one of the centre-pieces of Paracelsian medicine.

The utilization of a simple but effective cartoon on the title page of his first medical tract indicates the sensitivity of Paracelsus to the technique of propaganda recently developed in the popular protest literature and broadsheets. The cartoon also underlines the close association between the medical outlook and social message of Paracelsus. His medical ideas were formulated against a background of incessant writing on the religious

Durch den hochgeler

ten herren Theophrastum von

hochenheym beyder Artzeney Doctorem.

Vom Holtz Guaiaco gründlicher heylung / Darinn essen vnnd trincken / Saltz vnd anders erlaubt vnd zu gehört.

Auch von den verfürigen vñ Jrrigen büchern artzeten Brauch vnnd ordnung wider des holtz arth vnd natur auffgericht vnd außgangen.

Vom erkantnis was dem holtz zugehört vnd was nicht / aus welchem erstanden dis verderben der kranckheyten.

Dergleichen wie ein almuß aus dem holtz erstanden / dem armen zu gut / Solchs in ein verderben gedyhen / weyter corrigirt / vnd in einen rechten weg gebracht / mehr erspießlich.

Auch wie etlich hölzer mehr seind denn allein Guaiacum / die gleich so wol als Guaiacum dise krafft haben.

Illustration 5 Title page of Paracelsus: *Vom Holtz Guaiaco gründlicher heylung*, Nuremberg, 1529. From Karl Sudhoff (ed.), *Theophrastus von Hohenheim gen. Paracelsus. Sämtliche Werke*, (Munich, 1923), vol. 7, 53. Reproduced by permission of the Syndics of Cambridge University Library.

and social questions which were preoccupying his contemporaries. In addition to producing extensive biblical commentaries, especially on the books of Psalms and Matthew, he wrote a wide variety of shorter works which were broadly compatible in style and content with the lay religious tract literature. The shorter religious, social and ethical writings of Paracelsus involved frequent reference to medicine. These shorter works provide the natural link between the more specifically theological and medical writings. Most of the social and ethical writings comprise brief essays, sometimes divided into sections commenting on biblical texts. These essays usually exist in two forms, one being a slightly abbreviated form of the other. None were published during the lifetime of Paracelsus, but most were widely copied in manuscript form after his death. If published they would have constituted tracts varying in length between ten and twenty pages. Paracelsus produced some thirty titles, although these involve a substantial amount of repetition.

The prevalent anticlericalism of these prospective pamphlets is well-illustrated by the *De septem punctis idolatriae Christianae.*[14] This attack on the corruption of the clerical hierarchy provided a model for his assault on academic medicine and the medical profession.

Paracelsus painted a portrait of a Church almost totally overtaken by idolatry and seemingly vanquished by Satan. Yet even in the prevalent darkness the word of God carried forward the Christian message, and revelation was available to all those amenable to the inspiration of the Holy Spirit. Through this medium Christ himself was an active, living force, rather than merely a past historical example.

The purity of Christ's message, Paracelsus believed, had been undermined by the academic theologians over the centuries. This old learning, embedded in the Old Testament and classical learning, he associated with flattery ('Schmeichelei') and corruption. Christ, he argued, had replaced the Old Testament by the New Testament. The new should therefore sweep away the old. Christ was therefore associated by Paracelsus with spirit, youth, vitality and power. The old religion was dead and earthbound. Paracelsus boldly announced that the tenure of the corrupt priesthood was over and he conducted a fierce diatribe against virtually every aspect of current Church practice, including most of the popular targets, such as indulgences, pilgrimages, religious orders, and taxes. The whole system was condemned because instead of faith springing from the heart it substituted trivial tokens of religious observance, which were exploited by the privileged classes to the detriment of the poor.

The frequency of intrusion of medical subject-matter is well-illustrated by *De summo et aeterno bono* and *Liber de felici liberalitate.*[15] These two short tracts conveniently illustrate a line of argument frequently employed in the other tracts. The following paragraphs briefly summarize the discussion of Christian brotherhood, where relevant referring to parallels from other tracts. Selective identification of biblical quotations shows the extent to which the argument of Paracelsus is constructed from biblical sources, especially from the New Testament, and the gospel of Matthew more than anything else.

The discussion of social obligation contained in *De summo bono* and *De felici liberalitate* is predictably interspersed with calls to renounce the Old Testament in favour of the New Testament order, critiques of beliefs and action reflecting adherence to the letter rather than the spirit of the new law of Christ and the apostles, and appeal to the Holy Spirit and the light of nature as guides to thought and action. In *De summo bono* the principal target of criticism is vanity, whereas in *De felici liberalitate* it is avarice. Vanity and avarice contribute similarly to the syndrome of vice.

Paracelsus opens by stressing the fundamental beneficence of the deity. Notwithstanding our fall from grace in the Garden of Eden, God had endowed the earth with ample resources to satisfy all human needs. These gifts were freely available to those pursuing their vocation in the spirit of genuine liberality.[16]

High among God's blessings were the riches of medicine. The reader is warned not to be misled by the splendour of such Old Testament models as Solomon. The works of the old prophets were merely a trivial foretaste of the powers of Christ and the apostles. Christ undertook to feed the thousands, heal the sick and the insane, restore the sight of the blind, and indeed to raise the dead. These signs and wonders, frequently reiterated in the gospels, were guarantees of the powers allotted to the righteous.[17]

Scientific knowledge was of course universally available, but Paracelsus argued that true insight into nature was restricted to those Christians genuinely subscribing to the apostolic faith. It was not suggested that spiritual enlightenment provided some direct revelation of the truths of natural philosophy. Post-lapsarian men and women were destined to live by hard work.[18] Achievement of higher moral standing constituted a necessary precondition for determining that their labour would be rewarded by genuine knowledge, power over nature, and useful arts. Paracelsus repeatedly contrasted the dead knowledge contained in scholastic sources, signifying no more than the print from which it was composed, with the vital and productive knowledge stemming from the light of nature.

Every person was granted complete freedom, either to make responsible use of God's gifts or to abuse their privileges, by falling victim to such vices as intolerance, false pride or avarice. According to Paracelsus the human constitution contained a mixture of influences, coinciding with the attributes of the planets. The final outcome of character was not predetermined by a particular constellation of planetary attributes because moral choice could overcome any predisposition. True liberality stemmed from positive choice to renounce multifarious temptations to evil, and adoption of a discipline of service and self-sacrifice. Only the most inspired effort would prevent dissipation of precious gifts, as indicated by the scriptural warning against casting pearls before swine.[19]

Fundamental to the expression of liberality was disinterested pursuit of the interests of the least privileged members of the community, the 'poor neighbours' as they were designated. In the eyes of God all were equal, bound together in universal brotherhood.[20] In this context Paracelsus made repeated reference to the injunction of the Psalms: 'blessed is he that considereth the poor'.[21] Also the gospel laid down a firm obligation of Christian duty to feed the hungry, give drink to the thirsty, clothe the naked, or take care of the prisoner, the sick and the stranger.[22]

Paracelsus wrote particularly harshly against those who squandered their liberality on drinking and gaming in low company. He wrote at length on the improper and improvident use of God's bounty. His censure fell just as strongly on those who made signs of outward piety but were not motivated by the true evangelical spirit. They were guilty of cheating the poor by imposition of a double standard. True liberality involved the unrestricted distribution of wealth or medical knowledge according to the needs of the poor. It was for instance inadmissible for the better off to subsist on fine white bread, while consigning the poor to black bread made from coarse rye and oatmeal. The Lord was ever vigilant to detect hypocritical avoidance of Christian responsibility to the poor. Communities guilty of this vice would be deprived of the access to useful medicine, and indeed fresh plagues would be visited on them.

Any doctor taking up a court position or assuming civic office was judged guilty of betraying his obligation to use his knowledge for the common good. Fine dress and social status were regarded as pretentious surrogates for effective practice. The doctor was invited to learn from the sweaty worker or sooty miner, rather than the religious and secular orders, with all their distinctions of dress and obsession with hierarchy. Since academic education, status and wealth led to intellectual sterility and moral corruption, Paracelsus was forced to the conclusion that the greater merit resided in the lower orders, especially the skilled artisans. The common people or handworkers were held up as the model for their social superiors on both vocational and spiritual matters. The apostles were recruited from among the common people. Paracelsus believed that Christ's judgement on this matter could be taken as a sign of the intrinsically superior capacity of the common people to attain apostolic purity.[23]

Hypocrisy served the purposes of the Devil. Neglect of the solemn obligation to serve the poor paved the way for regression into vice and ostentatious living, the ultimate expression of this tendency being relapse into idolatry. This marked the final accomplishment of the cunning wiles of the Devil.

Especially in *De felici liberalitate* Paracelsus concentrated on the Old Testament as a source for recidivism into idolatry. The living and vital images of the New Testament were forsaken in favour of images wrought from wood or silver. At the best statues and icons were minor substitutes for spiritual experience. At the worst they were the equivalent of the idols placed before the Children of Israel to mislead them. The worship of idols was associated with the corruption of values and the persecution of the saints. Corruption was detected by Paracelsus at all levels in the Church. Even the seemingly innocuous hermits wandering about in the forest, or the monks behind the thick walls of their monasteries were chastised for engaging in useless or impoverished works of mercy. Their faith and works were useless because they sprang from authority rather than the heart. Such errors were magnified with ascent in the hierarchy of the Church.

The papacy was attacked for embodying the institution of corruption. Lavish ceremonial feasts, elaborate dress, ornament, jewellery, silver, statues and paintings were castigated as manifestations of pagan idolatry. The papacy had relapsed into worshipping the goddess Diana, whose silver shrine at Ephesus was confronted by Paul.[24] The vices of self-indulgence were intruded into the centre of religious life. Secular elites and church hierarchy had thus become united in a common way of profligate life. Religious and secular organizations were bound by rules and orders which stemmed from humans rather than from God.

In order to sustain their affluent existence the idolaters, like ants, were covetous and avaricious. Thereby they exploited rather than assisted their poor neighbours. Even their acts of charity were without real content. Even when cried up with trumpets and bells, their liberality was inspired by the Devil, as for instance the unction administered by priests, or the salves of the doctor, all of which were worthless to the poor. False prophets, false apostles and false doctors were no better than the Pharisees or Anti-Christs, all of whom would be subject to the eternal damnation at the Day of Judgement.[25] On the other hand those who rejected the Devil, avarice and idolatry and who followed the apostolic faith would be granted fruitful knowledge and be permitted to perform genuine works of benefit, inspired by the example of Christ and the apostles as recorded in the gospels.

In *Ex libro de religione perpetua*, Paracelsus drew out in more detail the relevance of his religious ideas to the theory of medicine.[26] The revival of medicine was presented as a major feature of the process of re-newal which would take place during the final age when the Church was reformed. In the new age of the spirit a general amelioration of life would take place. This would allow fulfilment of God's declared

67

intention that the human race should overcome its sins and enjoy a long life. God had endowed nature with marvellous powers, but this knowledge had become neglected and lost. By following Christ's example it was now within the capacity of doctors to recover these skills and apply them for the benefit of those with the greatest need. By this means the art of medicine would reproduce the miraculous cures recorded in the New Testament.

Paracelsus aimed to replace the prevalent 'theory' of medicine derived from the ancients with a new theory, which he also called the 'religion' of medicine. Galenic medicine is dismissed as a redundant scholastic exercise. The construction of abstract systems and discussion of recondite issues of causation was attacked by Paracelsus as a refuge from the more important priorities of medicine.

The 'highest religion' of medicine required the intensive investigation of stones, roots, plants and seeds, in order to reveal their powers. Paracelsus appealed for diseases to be treated as species with distinguishing characteristics, just as other natural species. Species of disease were to be identified and given an appropriate name. Each disease was then capable of being combated by a specific cure or arcanum.

The search for arcana was by no means to be limited to the investigation of the chemical properties of natural products. Paracelsus attached great importance to the example of the wise men from the east who recognized the call of the star to visit the infant Jesus.[27] These Magi from Saba and Tharshish were designated as ancestral natural magicians, whose experience witnessed the potency of the firmament, not only as a source of astrological omens, but as a more general source of influence on human life. Paracelsus believed that the powers of the firmament could be channelled into the service of medicine, although this was a delicate and potentially dangerous exercise because it carried the risk of trespassing into forbidden magic or superstition.

The writings of Paracelsus conventionally classified as scientific and medical are strikingly different from their counterparts produced by the medical establishment. Paracelsus avoided the commentaries, compendia, consilia, pandectae or systematic expositions beloved by his medical humanist contemporaries. His writings contain few traces of the stylistic conventions cultivated in learned circles. The individual works of Paracelsus are generally short, simple in structure, impressionistic in style and wide-ranging in their coverage. Their titles pronounce bold and radical objectives. Often the title pages include a Latin short-title, sometimes making the connection with some medical classic which Paracelsus aimed to supersede, but the text is entirely in the vernacular, following the vigorous, polemical and sometimes coarse style of the pamphlet literature. Paracelsus made few concessions to humanistic refinement. He was sensitive to criticisms on this point and he conducted a stout defence of his robust and aggressive approach to medical discourse.[28]

Although virtually none of the scientific and medical writings of Paracelsus were published during his lifetime, the works prepared for publication bear many of the hallmarks of the protest literature. It has already been noted that in physical appearance his first medical tract on guaiacum was similar to his first *Practica*. The connection with the protest literature is particularly indicated by the intrusion of religious and social comment into the scientific works. Indeed the entire edifice of his scientific and medical writing is built on an explicit theological infrastructure, and this is emphasized by the frequency with which scientific tenets are linked to biblical quotation. Indeed the Bible is virtually the only literary source acknowledged by Paracelsus. This overt biblicism is a further feature of the protest tracts.

The tendency to infiltrate discussion of medical and scientific issues with religious and social allusions was prominent from the outset and it showed no diminution in the later works. This element of continuity is conveniently indicated by reference to *De pestilitate* and the Carinthian Trilogy, which are works completed shortly before his death.

Notwithstanding its specialized title, *De pestilitate* constitutes a convenient general review of the ideas of Paracelsus.[29] Writings on plague, just as much as on syphilis, were guaranteed eager reception by the reading public. Paracelsus utilized plague to defend his theories concerning the interdependence of celestial and terrestrial events. This system of magical correspondences he identified as the counterpart of ancient biblical magic. The key to this magic lay in the book of Revelation. Among other things, this text contained the secret of plague. John as the author of Revelation was drawing on a tradition of biblical wisdom stretching back through the prophets to Moses. On this occasion Paracelsus was kinder to the Old Testament magi than he was in some of his other writings. These cabalists and prophets had been persecuted and their wisdom was lost. In its place had evolved profane philosophy, which was degenerate because severed from its biblical roots. The result was a system of lies embodied in Galenic medicine and still maintained by exploitative doctors and perpetuated by the medical schools in Paris, Padua, Montpellier, Salerno, Vienna and Leipzig.[30]

The following brief example indicates the manner in which the characteristic Paracelsus argument ranges by free association over the entire subject-matter of his discourse, generating an inextricable admixture of ingredients. He urged that in contradistinction to the corrupt learned doctor, the natural doctor or theologian would understand that the sun possessed a hidden Evester, or 'night' spirit, which possessed powerful hold over the Evester determining the physical processes of human existence. Through this correspondence God was able to punish man by infection of plague, just as the father could punish an errant child. Planetary bodies were the hand or rod through which the father punished humans on earth by inflicting diseases on them. The title page of the *Practica* of 1529 (see Illustration 4) provided iconographical expression of this idea. Paracelsus went on to suggest that everything undertaken by humans, whether good or bad, was marked down by the Evester of the sun, which acted as a chancellor or secretary. The Lichtenberger prophecies were applauded for making it clear what the Book of Revelation had proclaimed, drawing attention in the very first figure to the power of the sun. Sectarian misinterpreters should be warned that the moon is subservient to the sun and its seven 'lights', a point also evident from the *Practica* woodcut. Anyone believing that the star over Bethlehem can only be seen from Wittenberg, or the Cross of Christ only in Rome, was guilty of leaving buried the pearl of wisdom and thereby failing to understand the Apocalypse. It was essential to take note of the biblical pronouncement that there would be great signs in the heavens (Revelation 12: 1). Therefore, Paracelsus warned, ignore the prattle of the schools, or the Pharisaical pronouncements of the accursed pulpits concerning plague. Plague is not simply an act of God, but it strikes suddenly, like a burning glass or the reflection of light, the sun using planets as its agent, each releasing a chemical poison according to its character. Such actions strike with suddenness and deadly effect, like the fatal glance of the basilisc.[31]

De pestilitate contained a particularly concentrated attack on polypharmacy as practised by Galenic physicians. Paracelsus disputed the claims of the herbals that particular plants possessed 50 or over 100 virtues. He ridiculed the elaborate theoretical basis and grotesque calculations used for determining compositions and concluded that recipes, often containing as many as 40 or 50 ingredients, were useless. This approach to therapy was caricatured as an elaborate and useless religious ritual, comparing unfavourably with the simplicity of his own application of mineral remedies.[32]

This theme provided Paracelsus with an opportunity to extol the virtues of the simple form of medicine practised by the laity. In Saxony and the towns of Braunschweig, Hildesheim and Goslar, for instance, townspeople and peasants were more skilful than all their doctors.[33] Paracelsus acknowledged having learned from more than 80 peasants how to identify the signatures of plants and perform remarkable cures with them.[34] This respect for the collective medical knowledge of the common people was an echo of the theme of the common people in the protest literature. The folk healers of Paracelsus were the counterpart of Karsthans, the idealized wandering labourer, carrying hoe, flail or scythe, who symbolized the virtues of commonsense and simple piety.[35] Paracelsus believed that God had chosen the simple folk, and even animals,

70

to teach the right course of therapy. When this knowledge was guided by light, (or understanding possessed by the angels, 'Engelsvernunft', equivalent to the instinctive understanding of animals, 'tierische Vernunft'), then the common people and those of low social status were capable of attaining the highest skill. Such knowledge collected into a little book would be better than all the commentaries on Galen and Avicenna. The doctors, by depending on books of print ('Bücher der Buchstaben'), had neglected the true books of nature. They were merely purveyors of secondhand information learned from unreliable sources. They merely retailed phantasies derived from Pliny, Aristotle, Avicenna or Galen, rather than utilizing the grace of God to overtake these ancient authorities.

Whereas *De pestilitate* was a miscellaneous jumble, the Carinthian Trilogy was one of Paracelsus' most polished works, prepared with the expectation of imminent publication in 1538, but left unpublished because of interruption by his visit to Salzburg, where his premature death occurred in 1541.[36] The most substantial part of the trilogy was an exposition of his theory of the role of tartar in the formation of disease. Significantly this long, technical treatise was introduced by three shorter items, a short historical chronicle about Carinthia, the *Defensiones septem* and the *Labyrinthus medicorum*.[37] The latter two tracts contain some of the most sustained and effective polemics by Paracelsus against the medical establishment, and they draw upon social and religious themes prevalent in the protest tract literature. The Carinthian Trilogy therefore underlines the manner in which Paracelsus utilized his most technical presentations as a vehicle for his wider social and religious message.

The *Defensiones septem* contains a particularly passionate defence of the direct and combative style of his writings. Paracelsus boasts that his manner is rooted in the habits and customs of the simple country people among whom he has lived and journeyed. Self-consciously Paracelsus identified himself with the tradition of Karsthans. He aligned himself with the itinerant journeyman, dressed in coarse homespun cloth, fed not on figs, mead or wheaten bread, but on cheese, milk and oatcakes.[38] Journeys among the fir-cones in the relentless search for knowledge was the only sound way to experience. The only way to understand nature was to tread its books with one's feet.[39] This unpretentious and humble path to learning was repeatedly contrasted with the bankruptcy of the learned doctors whose culture was inimical to sound learning and effective medical practice. Academic physicians were caricatured on account of their fine dress, fondness for jewellery, and effete habits. They were presented as weaklings, inhabiting dark chimney corners, or women's chambers, and cosseting themselves with expensive luxury foods.[40] Such manners were inimical to effectiveness as scholars or practitioners. In fact, the physicians surrounded by their books were

71

captives of the Ship of Fools.[41] Instead of following the example of Christ and the apostles and practising out of love for their poor neighbour, the learned practitioners practised for selfish gain.[42] The physician was casting away his pearl and turning aside from the field in which the treasure of medicine resided.[43] Their practice could not be fruitful unless they gave away their wealth and abandoned practising for profit. Then their needs would be taken care of, and they would flourish like the lilies of the field or birds of the air.[44] Although Paracelsus made few overt comparisons, both from style and content of the critique of the medical profession, the reader would readily have made the connection with the anticlericalism of the protest tracts.

Readers would also have recognized the strong apocalyptic overtones of the *Defensiones septem*. Paracelsus opened his first defence by stating the conflict between the new and old theories of medicine. The old theory was discredited, not only because it was corrupted by generations of scholastics, but also because it was in principle irrelevant to different geographical circumstances and the special characteristics of the new age or latest monarchy, which was characterized by unprecedented social and economic change, greater population pressure and new diseases, all of which called for a new form of knowledge and much greater level of inventiveness than had previously existed.[45]

God provided for the cure of diseases and other human needs in each preceding monarchy, but corrupt manners prevented exploitation of the abundance of nature. The example of Christ, which had itself hitherto been disregarded, provided renewed guarantee of reaping the full benefits of the light of nature.[46] Having followed Christ's dictum: *Perscrutamini Scripturas*, practitioners in medicine should by analogy commit themselves: *Perscrutamini naturas rerum*.[47] But this teaching had been corrupted by false prophets and false apostles, who were in league with the Devil. Only the regenerate would be endowed with the full gifts of knowledge, which were implicit in the system of Paracelsus, and which constituted a 'new medicine appropriate to the present Monarchy'. For those guided by the precepts of humility and love for their neighbour, God would provide a cure for every disease, even diseases which the learned physicians claimed were incurable.[48]

The eleven short chapters of the *Labyrinthus medicorum* elaborated the theory of the light of nature, which was central to the epistemology and methodology of Paracelsus. Predictably, Paracelsus included a further diatribe against the classical and Arab medical authorities and modern academic medicine as cultivated by the humanist medical establishment. The result of this vast exercise in paper and ink was to produce worthless tomes, filled with dead knowledge, worth no more than the type from which it was composed. Academic medicine was of no more value than the prattle of priests.[49]

The epistemology outlined by Paracelsus was modelled on the empirical procedures of craftsmen. This form of knowledge was called *Experience, Experiment* or *Erfahrenheit*. The *Labyrinthus* outlined the way in which empirical methods could be pursued on an organized basis, to embrace all aspects of nature. The total system was called Magic, the descendant of the knowledge possessed by the wise men who travelled from the East to pay homage to the infant Christ.[50] By contrast with the fictitious entities and dead knowledge of the academics, letters, words, sentences, etc. of empirical data could be constituted into living books, giving an insight into the real elements and species of nature. This system would reveal the whole course of disease and enable cures to be matched with diseases. In searching for appropriate analogies, Paracelsus concluded that the seeds of plants, their growth and development, provided a model for the understanding of disease, which should replace humoral theory. Therefore the medical practitioner should follow the wisdom of the farmer and abandon the fictions of the Galenists.[51] The system of magic would reveal signatures which would appropriately link cures and diseases. This form of magic was possessed by the peasant rather than the physician.

The above body of knowledge based on sound precepts of theology was called the 'theology' or 'religion' of nature. While the knowledge through the light of nature was ascertained empirically, Paracelsus emphasized that acknowledgement of faith through the light of the Holy Ghost was a necessary precondition for the proper realization of the light of nature.[52] The Doctors who lacked faith in God, the Trinity, and who failed to imitate the example of Mary and the saints, were destined to fall into vice and neglect their duty to the poor. Only those who loved God and followed the path of righteousness would be granted their share of the benefits of nature.[53] If this duty was neglected no benefits would be forthcoming.[54] At the Day of Judgement those who had failed to abide by the injunction of Christ to help the needy and who had cherished their treasure on earth would face their punishment.[55] Paracelsus appealed to the academic physicians to abandon their vices and turn to the light of nature. Otherwise there would be no escape from the labyrinth in which they were entrapped.

Although the treatise on tartar, which concludes the Carinthian Trilogy, is largely technical in nature, the first two chapters recapitulate the major points of emphasis in the *Defensiones septem* and the *Labyrinthus*.[56] Consequently, religious and social comment was intruded prominently into this technical treatise, and a similar impression is derived from most of the other medical and scientific writings of Paracelsus. As indicated above, similar themes echo throughout his writings and they are supported by the same biblical sources. It is impossible to avoid the conclusion that the religious framework and social criticism were essential and integral. Paracelsus linked his critique of the medical establishment with the anticlericalism of his time, and he self-consciously presented his own alternative system as a natural extension of the form of scriptural piety which commanded wide assent in reforming circles. By drawing on the modes of expression developed in the vernacular tracts, Paracelsus evolved a formula capable of appealing to a wide audience. The mood of social protest and apocalyptic tone cultivated by Paracelsus induced a sense of the heightened urgency of his message. His tracts therefore directed a potent blend of religious and technical argument against the medical establishment. His success as a propagandist is confirmed by the intense efforts made by the medical elite to suppress his work. Consequently, a variety of adverse circumstances prevented the immediate publication of the majority of his writings. Nevertheless his editors discovered a remarkable level of continuing demand for these works. Thereby Paracelsus succeeded posthumously in his mission to draw medicine into the centre of the Reformation stage. The relevance of the Reformation as a religious and social context to the genesis and reception of the ideas of Paracelsus must be taken into account in the evaluation of his location in the history of medicine. It is arguable that underplaying of the immediate context has resulted in greater emphasis on purely scientific factors or on more distant erudite sources of influence than is warranted by the evidence. Any realistic assessment of Paracelsus must recognize the unity of his vocation as apostle, prophet and healer.

Notes

1. For recent work, mainly concentrating on the internal examination of the theology of Paracelsus, see: R. Dilg-Frank (ed.), *Kreatur und Kosmos. Internationale Beiträge zur Paracelsusforschung* (Stuttgart, 1981), especially, H. Rudolph, 'Schriftauslegung und Schriftverständnis bei Paracelsus', 101–24; K. Goldammer, *Paracelsus in neuen Horizonten. Gesammelte Aufsätze* (Vienna, 1986); idem, *Der göttliche Magier und die Magierin Natur. Religion, Naturmagie und die Anfänge der Naturwissenschaft von Spätmittelalter bis zur Renaissance* (Stuttgart, 1991); E. Kämmerer, *Das Leib-Seele-Geist Problem bei Paracelsus und einigen Autoren des 16 Jahrhunderts* (Wiesbaden, 1971).

2. For relevant studies of major contemporaries of Paracelsus, see, M. Brecht, *Martin Luther. Sein Weg zur Reformation 1483–1521* (Stuttgart, 1981); R. van Dülmen, *Reformation als Revolution. Soziale Bewegung und religiöser Radikalismus in der deutschen Reformation*, second edition (Frankfurt-am-Main, 1987); T. Nipperdey, *Reformation, Revolution, Utopie. Studien zum 16 Jahrhundert* (Göttingen, 1975); S. Wollgast, *Der deutsche Pantheismus im 16 Jahrhundert. Sebastian Franck und seine Wirkungen auf die Entwicklung der pantheistischen Philosophie in Deutschland* (Berlin, 1972).

3. P. Blickle, *Die Revolution von 1525* (Munich, 1981); idem, 'Thesen zum Thema "Die Bauernkrieg" als Revolution des gemeines Mannes', in P. Blickle

(ed.), *Revolte und Revolution in Europa*, Historische Zeitung, Beiheft 4 (Munich, 1975), 127–31; H. Buszello, P. Blickle, R. Endres (eds), *Der Deutsche Bauernkrieg*, second edition (Paderborn, 1991).

4. H.J. Köhler (ed.), *Flugschriften als Massenmedium der Reformationszeit* (Stuttgart, 1981); S. Ozment, 'The Revolution of the Pamphleteers', in A. Rotondo (ed.), *Forme e Destinazione del Messaggio Religioso. Aspetti della Propaganda Religiosa nel Cinquecento* (Florence, 1991), 1–18; P.A. Russell, *Lay Theology in the Reformation. Popular Pamphleteers in Southwest Germany 1521–1525* (Cambridge, 1986); R.W. Scribner, *For the Sake of Simple Folk. Popular Propaganda for the German Reformation* (Cambridge, 1982); idem, *Popular Culture and Popular Movements in Reformation Germany* (London, 1987).

5. P. Zambelli, 'Fine del mondo o inizio della propaganda? Astrologia, filosofia della storia e propaganda politico-religiosa nel dibattito sulla con-giunzione del 1524', in *Scienze, credenze, occulte livelli di cultura: Convengo Internationale di Studi (Firenze, 26–30 giugno 1980)* (Florence, 1983), 291–367; G. Hellmann, 'Aus der Blütezeit der Astrometeorologie: Johannes Stöfflers Prognose für das Jahr 1524', in *Beiträge zur Geschichte der Meteorologie, I, Veröffentli-chungen der Königlichen Preussischen Meteorologischen Instituts*, No. 273 (Berlin, 1914), 5–107; P.A. Russell, 'Astrology as Popular Propaganda. Expec-tations of the End in the German Pamphlets of Joseph Grünpeck (+1532)', in A. Rotondo (ed.), *Forme e Destinazione*, 165–96.

6. D. Kurze, 'Prophecy and History, Lichtenberger's forecasts of events to come (from the 15th to the 20th century); their reception and diffusion', *Journal of the Warburg and Courtauld Institutes* 21 (1958): 63–85; idem, *Johannes Lichtenberger* (Lübeck and Hamburg, 1960); M. Reeves, *The Influence of Prophecy in the Later Middle Ages* (Oxford, 1969), 347–52.

7. In 1527 Osiander produced editions of both the Nuremberg figures and the prophecies of Hildegard of Bingen: *Eyn wunderliche Weyssagung von dem Babstumb, wie es yhm biss an das endt der welt gehen sol* (Nuremberg, 1527); *Sanct Hildegardten Weissagung uber die Papisten und genanten Geystlichen* (Nuremberg, 1527). See R. Bainton, 'The Joachimite Prophecy: Osiander and Sachs', in *Studies on the Reformation* (London, 1964), 62–6.

8. C. Ginsburg, *Il Nicodemismo* (Turin, 1970), 30–2; S. Caroti, 'Cometi, portenti, causalità naturale e eschatologia in Filippo Melantone', in *Scienze, credenze, occulte livelli di cultura*, 393–426. Lorenz Fries was author of the popular *Spiegel der artzney* (Strasbourg, 1532), which contains a defence of vernacular medicine. Fries was also a chronicler of the Peasants' War.

9. K. Sudhoff, *Versuch einer Kritik der Echtheit der paracelsischen Schriften*, 2 vols. (Berlin, 1894–1899), vol. 1, 6; J. Huser (ed.), *Paracelsus. Bücher und Schrifften* 10 vols. (Basle, 1589–1591) vol. 10, fasc. 5–12; K. Sudhoff (ed.), *Paracelsus: Sämtliche Werke. 1. Abt.: Medizinische, naturwissenschaftliche und philosophische Schriften*, 14 vols. (Munich, Berlin, 1922–1933), vol. 7, 459–64.

10. Sudhoff, *Paracelsus*, vol. 7, 40–9.

11. Sudhoff, *Versuch*, vol. 1, 4–36.

12. *Ein Ausslegung der Figuren so zu Nürnberg gefunden seindt worden geführt in Grundt der Magischen Weissagung*, in Huser, *Paracelsus*, vol. 10, Appendix, 139–89; Sudhoff, *Paracelsus*, vol. 12, 509–85; *Ausslegung über ettliche Figuren Jo. Lichtenbergers*, in Huser, *Paracelsus*, vol. 10, Appendix, 230–75; Sudhoff, *Paracelsus*, vol. 7, 475–530. See Goldammer, *Paracelsus in neuen Horizonten*, 87–152.

13. *Vom Holtz Guaiaco gründlicher heylung* (Nuremberg, 1529), in Sudhoff,

Versuch, vol. 1, 4–5; J. Huser (ed.), *Paracelsus. Chirurgische Bücher und Schrifften* (Strasbourg, 1605), 323–7; Sudhoff, *Paracelsus*, vol. 7, 51–65. *Von der Frantzösichenkrankheit. Drey Bücher*, (Nuremberg, 1530), in Sudhoff, *Versuch*, vol. 1, 10–11; Huser, *Paracelsus. Chirurgische Bücher*, 149–89; Sudhoff, *Paracelsus*, vol. 7, 67–181.

14. Sudhoff, *Versuch*, vol 2, 333–40. This short polemical work seems to have been a product of the first visit of Paracelsus to Salzburg in 1524 at the height of peasant unrest, see H. Rudolph in Dilg-Frank, 110. Although extreme in style, Paracelsus was in substance only marginally less critical of many of the defects of the Church than Erasmus in his *Enchiridion* (1503) and *Moriae encomium* (1511). For prevalent anticlericalism, see H-J. Goertz, 'Aufstand gegen den Priester. Anti-klerikalismus und reformatorische Bewegung', in P. Blickle (ed.), *Bauer, Reich und Reformation* (Stuttgart, 1982), 182–209.

15. *De summo aeterno bono*, in Goldammer (ed.), *Religiose und Sozialphiloso-phische Schriften in Kurzfassungen* (Wiesbaden, 1973) 9–18; *Liber der felici liberalitate*, ibid., 83–92.

16. II Cor. 9: 7–8.

17. See also, *De ordine doni*, in Goldammer, *Paracelsus Sozialethische und sozialpolitische Schriften* (Tübingen, 1952), 119.

18. See also, *De honestis*, in Goldammer, *Religiose und Sozialphilosophische Schriften in Kurzfassungen*, 94.

19. Matth. 7: 6.

20. Matth. 22: 39.

21. Ps. 41: 2.

22. Matth. 5: 6; 25: 42–3.

23. See also, *De honestis*, in Goldammer, *Religiose und Sozialphilosophische Schriften in Kurzfassungen*, 94.

24. Acts 19: 24.

25. See also, *De honestis*, in Goldammer, *Religiose und Sozialphilosophische Schriften in Kurzfassungen*, 94–5.

26. *Ex libro de religione perpetua*, in W. Matthiessen (ed.), *Paracelsus: Sämtliche Werke*, vol. 1, (Munich, 1923), 87–107.

27. Matth. 2: 1–2.

28. *Defensiones septem*, in Huser, *Paracelsus*, vol. 2, 182–6.

29. *De pestilitate*, in Huser, *Paracelsus*, vol. 3, 24–107; Sudhoff, *Paracelsus*, vol. 14, 597–661.

30. *De pestilitate*, in Huser, *Paracelsus*, vol. 3, 79.

31. *De pestilitate*, in Huser, *Paracelsus*, vol. 3, 73–6. See Goldammer, *Paracelsus in neuen Horizonten*, 250–62.

32. *De pestilitate*, in Huser, *Paracelsus*, vol. 3, 65–8.

33. *De pestilitate*, in Huser, *Paracelsus*, vol. 3, 67–8.

34. *De pestilitate*, in Huser, *Paracelsus*, vol. 3, 37–40, 57–9.

35. For representative discussions of the common man, see, C. Gilly, *Die 'Gelehrten die Verkehrten'. Oder der Verrat der Intellectuellen im Zeitalter der Glaubensspaltung*, in A. Rotondo (ed.), *Forme e Destinazione*, 229–378; R. Lutz, *Wer war der gemeine Mann? Der dritte Stand in der Krise des Spatmittelalters* (Munich, 1979); E. Muschke, *Stadte und Menschen* (Wiesbaden, 1980); B. Otwinoska, 'Der "gemeine Mann" als Adressat in der volkssprachlichen Literatur in der Renaissance', in R. Weimann *et al.* (eds.), *Renaissance Literatur und frühburgerliche Revolution* (Berlin, 1976), 194–202.

36. *Drey Bücher . . . des Ertzhertzogthumbs Karnten*, in Huser, *Paracelsus*, vol. 2, 143–342; Goldammer *et al.* (eds), *Paracelsus, Die Kärtner Schriften*, (Klagenfurt, 1955).

37. *Das erst Buch die verantwartung uber etzlich verunglimpfung seiner Missgünner [Defensiones septem]*, in Huser, *Paracelsus*, vol. 2, 158–901; Sudhoff, *Paracelsus*, vol. 11, 123–60. *Das ander von dem Irrgang und Labyrinth der Artzten [Labyrinthus medicorum]*, in Huser, *Paracelsus*, vol. 2, 191–243, in Sudhoff, *Paracelsus*, Vol. 11, 161–220.

38. *Defensiones septem*, in Huser, *Paracelsus*, vol. 2, 183.

39. *Defensiones septem*, 177.

40. *Defensiones septem*, 168, 177, 179–80, 183.

41. *Defensiones septem*, 175. *Das Narrenschiff* (1494), section 55 criticises current practices in medicine.

42. *Defensiones septem*, 177–8.

43. Matth. 12: 46.

44. Luke 12: 22–7.

45. *Defensiones septem*, 160, 167, 172–3.

46. Among the representative texts quoted by Paraclesus, Matth. 9: 12; 11: 29; 13: 52; John 6: 45.

47. John 5: 39.

48. *Defensiones septem*, 160–4.

49. *Labyrinthus medicorum*, in Huser, *Paracelsus*, vol. 2, 191–3, 194–5, 200–1, 224–8. See Goldammer, *Paracelsus in neuen Horizonten*, 229–49.

50. *Labyrinthus medicorum*, 228–32.

51. *Labyrinthus medicorum*, 224–41.

52. *Labyrinthus medicorum*, 228–32, 236–41.

53. Matth. 6: 33.

54. Matth. 13: 12, 22, 29.

55. Matth. 25: 41–6.

56. *Das Buch von dem Tartarischen Krankheiten*, in Huser, *Paracelsus*, vol. 2, 244–340; Sudhoff, *Paracelsus*, vol. 11, 15–121. See especially, Huser, *Paracelsus*, vol. 2, 246–56.

4

Caspar Bartholin and the education of the pious physician

Ole Peter Grell

The Reformation not only replaced the rituals of the Catholic Church with faith as the only avenue to salvation, but it also introduced Scripture, instead of the authority of the Church, as the guiding principle for all true Christians. However, this conviction that the ordinary pious Christian was capable of reading and understanding the Bible evaporated quickly among Luther and his associates due to the challenge of the 'radical reformation' in the 1520s. By 1530 the Lutheran leaders realized that ordinary Christians needed instruction by learned ministers in order to avoid the pitfalls and dangers of heterodoxy. Consquently, catechising of the laity and education of the clergy became major concerns for the reformers. Furthermore, since good works were no longer relevant to salvation a new role and significance had to be allocated to such potentially important social activities. They had to be redirected away from their original focus on the Church – there was no longer any need for lighting candles or paying for masses – towards society, where pious Protestants would demonstrate their godliness through charity towards their neighbours. According to Melanchthon, Protestants should show a 'sincere desire and a good will to give honest useful service to human society'.[1] By spiritualizing everyday work, the Reformation helped promote the concept of 'calling', whereby ordinary secular activity came to be seen as a moral and religious duty.[2] At the time of Caspar Bartholin's birth this early Reformation emphasis on 'calling' and personal piety had, however, disappeared as a consequence of the doctrinal preoccupation of orthodox Lutheranism. But this obsession with doctrinal purity eventually led to a strong reaction within German Protestantism (as can be seen from the writings of Johann Arendt, Johann Gerhardt and many others) which, towards the end of the sixteenth century, led to a call for a full 'reformation of life' to follow Luther's 'reformation of teachings'.[3] This revivalist movement, which wanted to complete the Reformation Luther had begun, not only achieved considerable influence in Denmark, but, as I shall argue, it also came to determine not only Caspar Bartholin's theology, but also his medicine.

First and foremost, therefore, I commend to you piety, an unblem-
ished life, daily prayers, love of the Word of God and heed for it:
If God is not present and pours strength into herbs, what use, I ask, is
dittany and panacea?[4]

These are the introductory words to a manual for the study of medicine
which Caspar Bartholin wrote for a young relation, who was no other
than a grandson of the famous Royal physician, the Paracelsian, Petrus
Severinus. The author described his work, *De Studio Medico* written in
1626 and published two years later, as a 'brief and improvised advice
concerning the study of medicine aimed at the well-prepared, future
physician who will rise above the mass'.[5] These expectations mirrored
those expected of the Protestant clergy who were supposed to rise above
the level of their flock.[6]

Caspar Bartholin was convinced that only medicine based on Protestant faith and practised by a godly physician would be effective. Thus he
wrote:

Some people seem to themselves perhaps to want to or to be able to
undertake the study of medicine without piety, after the fashion of
Heathens and Jews. But either success lasts only for a while as the
love of vice stains everything in the mind and in the hand, or creates
a dangerous melancholy. And for those who do not suffer from this
disease, their consciences generate anxiety and worry either when
they treat dangerous cases, or if their treatment fails. Prayers and
consolations in accordance with the Word of God most powerfully
dispel all these things. Therefore, anyone who is a student of this art
will count it as a gain every single morning, after prayers, to read one
or two chapters from Holy Scripture, not superficially but carefully
and reflectively; and in such a way that each and every year he runs
through the whole Bible and completes it.[7]

There was, in other words, no doubt in Caspar Bartholin's mind about
what was needed in order to become a good Protestant physician. Only
through the continued personal study of the Bible could faith and piety
be obtained. It was exclusively on this basis that the physician could
properly comprehend God's Creation – the Book of Nature – and thereby
truly understand his own métier. Bartholin practised what he taught, and
presided over a pious household. Psalms were sung and Caspar Bartholin
would read chapters of the Bible to the assembled household, emphasizing the obligation to lead an active and pious life; and when public
commitments prevented him from fulfilling these domestic activities his
wife replaced him.[8] For him, it must have been only a natural progression
when in 1624 he took the unusual step, even for a period characterized by
considerable academic mobility between different subjects, of exchanging

Illustration 6 Caspar Bartholin: print by Simon de Pas, 1625. Reproduced by permission of Det kongelige Bibliotek, Copenhagen.

his Chair in medicine for one in theology at the University of Copenhagen.

More than anyone else Caspar Bartholin was to be instrumental in the plans for a major restructuring of the study of medicine in Copenhagen. Like his first post-Reformation predecessor, Christian Torkelsen Morsing, Bartholin was prompted by Protestantism. He drew his inspiration from the pre-pietist, Lutheran revival with its strong emphasis on godliness and eschatological urgency, which in Denmark was inspired by Caspar Bartholin's noble patron, Holger Rosenkrantz.[9]

Before considering the practical medical consequences Bartholin drew from his Lutheran piety, it will prove helpful to take a closer look, not only at the medical faculty of the University of Copenhagen in the post-Reformation period, since this was the institution Bartholin inherited, but also at the life and career of Caspar Bartholin himself.

The University of Copenhagen, founded in 1479, had only incorporated a medical faculty in name before the Reformation. When it was closed down by the Catholic Bishop of Sealand in 1531 as a dangerous hot-house of evangelical sedition, only one professor, the Scotsman, Alexander Kynghorn, who also served as Royal physician, had ever been appointed to the faculty.[10] Doubt about the value of university education had been prevalent among leading Danish reformers as late as 1530. The University was perceived as being dominated by Aristotelian scholasticism and therefore seen as opposed to true Scripture-based knowledge. Such ideas had, of course, already been voiced by Luther in his work, *To the Christian Nobility of the German Nation*, ten years earlier, but by 1536 the Danish reformers' opinions had changed, as had attitudes in Wittenberg under the influence of Melanchthon. Consequently, the Danish reformers petitioned the King, Christian III, to have the University of Copenhagen reopened as a Protestant seat of learning.[11] With the support of their new Lutheran ruler they saw the University reopened the following year. Significantly, the Reformation and the refoundation of the University in 1537 brought the medical faculty from the world of possibilities to within the realm of reality. Thus the first Protestant Vice-Chancellor of the University was the Professor of Medicine, Christian Torkelsen Morsing, who had established his evangelical credentials back in 1520 when, according to tradition, he recruited Martin Reinhardt and Matthias Gabler, from Wittenberg – the first Protestant preachers to arrive in Denmark.[12]

According to the lecture-list of 1537, which was put together by Christian Torkelsen Morsing in his capacity as Vice-Chancellor, the medical faculty should have two professors. One would lecture on theoretical medicine, especially the original Greek texts by Galen and Hippocrates, the other would lecture on practical medicine and more recent Latin authors. Lectures would also be provided on some of the more difficult authors of physics, mathematics and cosmography. Finally it was emphasized that anatomy should not be neglected.[13] Evidently, Christian Torkelsen Morsing wanted a considerable change from the traditional medieval curriculum in medicine. Gone were authors and textbooks, such as those by Rhazes and Avicenna; instead students were to return to the original Greek texts of Galen and Hippocrates, while the importance of anatomy was underlined. This obsession with a return to the original texts was, of course, humanist in origin, but the Reformation most certainly helped to reinforce it. That Morsing saw the reform of the study and practice of medicine within the general context of the Reformation can be seen from the introduction he wrote to Henrik Smith's herbal in 1556:

> And as Paul states, that among those chosen for the holy office of preacher, only few are powerful and noble, similarly not many wealthy and mighty, but only poor and simple people, are chosen to become physicians, thereby serving Man's bodily needs, as his soul is served through the preaching of the Gospel.

Both ministers and physicians were considered part of the apostolic tradition and recruited from the common people. Morsing went on to stress the physician's obligation:

> To know the herbs and other healing plants which God allows to grow on Earth for the use and benefit of Man, and to see several human bodies dissected, part by part, in order better to understand how the inner parts of Man are created, in order to know what remedies are needed for that part of Man's body which is found to suffer from want and damage.[14]

Two years later the newly founded University received its Statutes drawn up under Luther's friend and collaborator, Johannes Bugenhagen's supervision. Bugenhagen, who had already been responsible for framing the Danish Lutheran Church Ordinance of 1537, opted for a more traditional and conservative approach to medical education than Morsing had suggested in 1537. In drafting the Copenhagen Statutes, Bugenhagen probably used the Melanchthonian Statutes from Wittenberg as a model, which specifically included Avicenna and Rhazes, while making no mention of the need to consult the original Greek texts by Hippocrates and Galen. Bugenhagen might, of course, also have realised the impracticality of trying to introduce Greek texts into the medical curriculum in Denmark at this stage. To judge from the complaints which materialized early in the seventeenth century, very few Danish students would have had the necessary knowledge of Greek by the time they commenced their university education. Like the lecture-list, the Statutes specified that the new medical faculty should have two professors. They should lecture on Avicenna and Rhazes, authors favoured in the traditional, medieval curriculum, while also paying attention to practical and newer authors. Bugenhagen, however, must have had Morsing's exclusion of Avicenna from the lecture-list of 1537 in mind, when he specifically stated in the Copenhagen Statutes that 'the best medical doctors are of the opinion that Avicenna should not be thrown out of the universities'.[15] Furthermore, the Statutes emphasized that lectures on useful works by Galen and Hippocrates should be provided, but no indication was given whether or not they should be based on the original Greek texts, while lectures in physics should be concerned with the works of Aristotle. Astrology was also considered an important part of the new medical curriculum in Copenhagen, on a par with Melanchthon's reforms in Wittenberg. The significance of anatomy, however, was only stressed to the extent that the introductory lectures on this subject ought to be attended by all students of the University.[16] This emphasis on the general value of anatomical knowledge should undoubtedly be seen within the context of the Reformation. Knowledge of God's most important creation, Man, was not only useful to Man himself, but served to glorify God and emphasize the significance of true religion, i.e. Protestantism.[17]

As mentioned above, the new professor of medicine, Christian Torkelsen Morsing, considered both botany and anatomy of paramount importance to the Protestant physician. Morsing, who dominated the medical faculty in Copenhagen from 1537 till his death in 1560, further demonstrated his botanical interests in the Seal he had designed for the faculty in 1537 (see illustration 7). It shows a crown, symbolizing the Danish Monarchy, out of which grow flowers and herbs. These useful plants have all been created thanks to God's Providence, which is implied by the hand stretching down from heaven. Thus the seal served to underline the significance of Reformation theology for the study of medicine in Copenhagen.[18]

It was undoubtedly Morsing's *peregrinatio academica* in the early 1530s, when he studied at the Universities of Montpellier and Basle, which had drawn him towards applied anatomy and botany. In Basle, where he received his MD, the study of medicine was transformed during the 1530s on the instigation of Basle's reformer, Johannes Oecolampadius, who had emphasized practical medicine in general and botany in particular in his suggestions for a reform of the University, *Iudicium de schola*. The influence of Paracelsus on Oecolampadius' *Iudicium* is generally recognized, and it was on Oecolampadius' invitation that Paracelsus had taken up the post of city-physician in Basle in 1527. Less than a decade later these ideas had found their way into the official curriculum in Basle when the medical faculty suggested that the

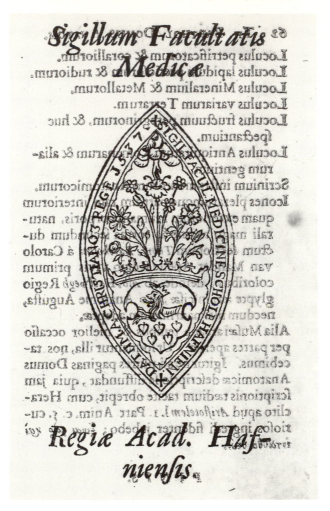

Illustration 7 Seal of the Medical Faculty of the University of Copenhagen, 1537. Reproduced by permission of Det kongelige Bibliotek, Copenhagen.

course ought to include public dissections and teaching of botany which would make it possible for students to compound their own medicines.[19]

Apart from the important inspiration Morsing personally received in Basle, by taking his MD there he also established what can only be described as the most important foreign institutional connection for the medical faculty in Copenhagen in the next ninety years. Of the twelve professors of medicine who served the medical faculty in Copenhagen from 1537 to 1623, no less than seven received their MDs from Basle.[20] And more importantly, these seven, including such famous names as Thomas Fincke, Caspar Bartholin and Ole Worm, were by far the most

84

influential and innovative forces within the medical faculty, except for possibly Hans Frandsen, who had studied under Leonard Fuchs in Tübingen and received his MD in France.[21] This Basle connection was established at a time when serious confessional splits within European Protestantism had yet to occur but, remarkably, not only did the connection between the two medical faculties survive the growing confrontation between Lutherans and Calvinists, it actually intensified in the years of inter-confessional rivalry within Protestantism from the second half of the sixteenth to the first quarter of the seventeenth century. This period happened to coincide with the most flourishing period of the medical faculty in Basle, when such leading lights as Theodor Zwinger, Jacob Zwinger, Felix Platter and Caspar Bauhin taught there. These were the years when subjects such as Ramist philosophy, modified Paracelsianism, botany, and human anatomy flourished within the Calvinist University of Basle.[22]

Apart from Morsing, however, it proved difficult to find other candidates for the professorships in medicine in Copenhagen. There was a distinct shortage of local talent in this field; and even if Christian III was keen on recruiting the best people from Wittenberg and other Protestant seats of learning in Germany, few could be tempted, not least because of the lack of economic incentives and the financial constraints imposed on the Kingdom following the civil war (1534–6). Thus Leonard Fuchs refused the offer and a second professor of medicine was not appointed until 1547, when the Wittenberg-based Dutchman, Peter Capiteyn, accepted the position while simultaneously becoming Royal physician.[23]

The new University remained a parochial institution during the reign of Christian III (1536–59). It was in constant need of funds and only managed to attract few students. Consequently, only a small portion of the intentions laid down in the Statutes was realized.[24] However, the University's situation improved dramatically during the reign of Christian's son, Frederik II (1559–88). Denmark in particular appears to have benefited from the general economic boom in Europe during the second half of the sixteenth century, not least thanks to a growing demand for Danish agricultural products. Consequently, more money became available for the University. Salaries of professors improved dramatically making these posts more attractive to talented and ambitious individuals. These improvements gathered pace when the Seven Years' War with Sweden (1563–70) drew to a close, liberating finances which had hitherto been swallowed up in the war effort. Thus, in 1569 a Royal Trust was founded, providing stipends for 100 students, which was modelled, as was more often than not the case in Copenhagen, on a similar institution in Wittenberg. That year also saw the creation of four Royal stipends, which were to finance studies abroad for one medical and three theological students.[25] Likewise, the number of Danish students matriculating abroad saw an explosive growth in the decades after 1570. Numbers more than doubled in the period 1571–1600, reaching 1095, compared with the period 1536–70, when only 528 students matriculated abroad.[26]

Medical students in particular benefited from the willingness of Frederik II to allow salaries tied to vacant Chairs to be spent on stipends for students studying abroad. Among those who enjoyed the fruits of this policy were the two Paracelsians and close friends, the later Royal physician, Petrus Severinus and the later professor of medicine, Johannes Philip Pratensis. Between 1566 and 1571 they shared the salary from the vacant Chair in medicine, while in 1579–80 another future professor of medicine, Anders Christensen, received half the salary tied to the vacant Chair in law.[27]

Likewise, the lack of money and the difficulties in recruiting and retaining two professors of medicine meant that the medical faculty in Copenhagen had not been able to develop along the lines its first post-Reformation professor, Christian Torkelsen Morsing, would have wished. It was not until 1571, when Morsing's successor, Hans Frandsen, was joined by the Paracelsian, Johannes Philip Pratensis, and the faculty acquired two professors on a permanent basis, that things started to improve.[28] Frandsen, who had been appointed in 1561, when both Chairs in medicine were vacant, had been a close friend of the Heidelberg professor of medicine, Peter Lochitius, and had studied under the famous Lutheran, botanist/anatomist Lenoard Fuchs in Tübingen. Fuchs' teaching, however, does not appear to have inspired Frandsen to take any specific interest in natural history or the more practical aspects of botany and anatomy, which might have been expected from a Protestant physician. He became a close friend of Tycho Brahe, who admired him as a poet, but described him as a Galenist physician – not exactly a positive attribute, coming from Brahe. Frandsen's friendships with Tycho Brahe and the well-known professor of theology, Niels Hemmingsen, combined with his interest in mathematics and astronomy, not to mention his concern for education, would indicate that he was influenced by Ramist philosophy and crypto-Calvinism, as was a growing number of his colleagues within the University of Copenhagen.[29] His translations into Latin of works by Galen and Hippocrates demonstrate his commitment to the improvement of education. In the introduction to his translation of Galen's *On the Bones* (1579), he states his intention to bring greater organization and clarity to his own teaching of medicine. Instead of random lecturing on specific doctrines, Frandsen wants to start from the beginning of 'medical science' and to focus on the basic elements, such as the bones in the human body. Most fittingly, Frandsen included a print of a skeleton in his translation of the Galen text.[30]

It was during the 1570s that a modified Paracelsianism acceptable to the more 'liberal' Lutherans made its entry in Copenhagen.[31] Thus, it was Frandsen's friend and colleague, the theologian Niels Hemmingsen, who in his capacity as Vice-Chancellor of the University was instrumental in recruiting the Paracelsian physician, Johannes Pratensis, for the vacant Chair in medicine in 1571. Pratensis had recently returned to Denmark with his travelling companion, Petrus Severinus, who had been recalled in order to take up the position of Royal physician to Frederik II, to whom Severinus very appropriately had dedicated his work, *Idea Medicinae Philosophicae*, published in Basle 1571. While wanting Pratensis for the Chair, Hemmingsen evidently had some reservations about his Paracelsianism. It was on Hemmingsen's suggestion that the University imposed restrictions on Pratensis' teaching, forcing him to teach only Hippocratic and Galenic medicine in accordance with what was taught at the Universities of Wittenberg and Leipzig.[32] Hemmingsen's attempt to try to keep Paracelsian teachings out of the University can, however, hardly have been seriously meant, and should rather be seen as a prudent move, which served to make Pratensis' appointment generally acceptable. Hemmingsen's predecessor, as the Kingdom's leading theologian, Peder Palladius (1537–60), had, as a true Melanchtonian Aristotelian, been strongly opposed to Paracelsianism and alchemy.[33] Both Palladius and Hemmingsen were pupils of Melanchthon, which in itself goes a long way to explaining why Hemmingsen might have been willing, at least, to pay lip-service to such views. Had he been determined to stop Paracelsian teachings from entering the University, his involvement in Pratensis' appointment would have been strange. Neither would such an attitude have been in harmony with Hemmingsen's known humanist and irenic views, not to mention his crypto-Calvinism, which eventually forced his resignation from the University in 1579.[34] Likewise, if such views had truly been Hemmingsen's, why would he only six years later, in 1577, have suggested that Tycho Brahe be elected Vice-Chancellor of the University, when it was common knowledge that Brahe held Paracelsian opinions? Similarly, Severinus' sympathy for Hemmingsen, when the theology professor found himself accused of crypto-Calvinism in the mid-1570s, becomes incomprehensible if Hemmingsen was an antagonist of Paracelsianism.[35] Whatever motives caused the restrictions to be imposed on Pratensis in 1571, they proved spectacularly unsuccessful. In a letter to Severinus written a couple of years later, Pratensis joked about his enforced promise to teach Galenic medicine only:

> While I conscientiously followed the teaching of Galen and placed each of his claims on the anvil of truth, which, after all, was my duty, something strange and surprising happened, even against my intention. Often I was forced to correct his boring and incomplete

explanations about natural conditions, sometimes also his mistaken claims on second thoughts, which I could give proof of through rich experience. From the beginning I was quietly happy, when through the secret and clever art of Proteus I could fetch such beautiful and splendid flowers from foreign gardens, which I planted in place of Galen's weeds to the great astonishment of worthy men, because for a long time it had escaped our teachers, that considerable obscurity was hidden in Galen. But now, when they too have had the chance to explore foreign gardens, I cannot keep quiet any longer, after the delusion has been unmasked by some inventive new philosophers.[36]

Evidently, Pratensis had taken the opportunity to introduce his Paracelsianism to the students via the backdoor, through his criticism of Galen, rather than by the more controversial way of directly using Paracelsian texts. In the process he claims to have converted some of his conservative, academic colleagues. That this was not just boasting can be seen from the pamphlet published by the University in connection with his death in 1576. Here Pratensis was officially praised for his exposition of both medical systems, 'the Galenic and the Paracelsian', in which 'his ingenuity, fortune and enterprise was famous and divine'.[37] Furthermore, in 1602, when Petrus Severinus was given a Chair in medicine, which his sudden death prevented him from occupying, the University sought no assurances that he would abstain from teaching Paracelsian medicine. Even if the Statutes remained unchanged, it can safely be assumed that a gradual change of what was taught within the medical faculty in Copenhagen took place during the last three decades of the sixteenth century. But such reforms were restricted to theory, while a more empirical and practical approach to medicine had yet to make an impact within the faculty.

By the turn of the century, however, the official attitude in Lutheran Denmark to modified Paracelsianism, as originally promoted by Petrus Severinus, had totally changed. In 1609 King Christian IV had built a distillation house in the garden of Rosenborg and employed the Paracelsian physician, Peter Payngk, who had worked at the Court of Emperor Rudolph II. Furthermore, in 1620 serious attempts were made, at the request of Christian IV and his Chancellor, Christian Friis, to have Petrus Severinus' manuscripts edited and published.[38]

Meanwhile the Basle connection was strengthened through the friendship which had been established between Theodor Zwinger and Petrus Severinus, through the latter's visit to Basle in 1569. This visit may, by the way, account for the Ramist influences which have been found in Severinus' work, since this was exactly the year Ramus sought refuge in Basle and stayed with Theodor Zwinger.[39] Furthermore, from 1577 until Simon Paulli was made extraordinary professor of anatomy, botany and surgery in 1639, all new professors of medicine in Copenhagen had Basle MDs. Among these, especially Anders Christensen and Thomas Fincke are of interest here.

Anders Christensen, who received his MD in 1583, was appointed professor of medicine in Copenhagen in 1585. While professor he managed to develop a considerable practice among the nobility, but he is probably best remembered for his attempt to introduce anatomical dissections at the University. Public hostility towards such acts, however, quickly forced him to stop. His interest in botany, another important discipline within the medical faculty in Basle, is in evidence from his offer in 1600 to establish a botanical garden within the University. His promotion in 1602 to the Directorship of the new Academy in Sorø, for sons of the nobility, prevented him from executing these plans, but his continued interest in practical and investigative medicine later resulted in his establishment of a pharmacy in Sorø.[40]

Thomas Fincke became professor of medicine in 1603, immediately taking over the leading professorship in medical theory, due to the sudden deaths of Anders Lemvig and Petrus Severinus. Since 1577 he had spent fourteen years abroad, studying for five years under Johannes Sturm in Strasbourg before attending a number of German universities. He briefly returned to Denmark in 1582 where he attended his cousin's wedding to Petrus Severinus. This new family connection helps to explain why Severinus recommended him warmly to his friend, Theodor Zwinger, in Basle, as an excellent mathematician. Fincke, who appears to have been taught and befriended by all the leading physicians in Basle, including Thomas Erastus, Felix Platter, Caspar Bauhin and Theodor Zwinger, under whose tutelage he obtained his MD in 1587, initially seems to have concentrated on mathematics.[41] In 1583 he published the only major work he ever wrote, *Geometria Rotundi*, in Basle. Considering that Fincke wrote a preface to this book which was extremely flattering to Tycho Brahe, the later animosity between the two, which began while Fincke was professor of mathematics in Copenhagen, is something of an enigma. Most likely it was caused by a clash of personalities – Tycho Brahe is known to have been a difficult man – rather than conflicting philosophies. Even if Fincke is probably best described as an Aristotelian, his schooling by Sturm and long stays at Calvinist universities would have made him tolerant, if not sympathetically inclined towards Ramism, with its emphasis on practical 'common sense', educational reform and mathematics, and possibly even towards a moderate form of Paracelsianism. Thus Fincke appears to have had excellent relations with colleagues in the University who espoused such ideas, many of whom were former assistants to Tycho Brahe, such as his colleague in the medical faculty, Gellius Sascerides, the professor of physics, Anders Kragh, and the later professor of theology, Cort

Aslaksen.[42] It was, however, Thomas Fincke's dynastic contacts rather than his medical qualifications which made him a pivotal character within the University of Copenhagen. Of his four daughters, one married Caspar Bartholin, another Ole Worm, both of whom became highly influential members of the medical faculty, while the remaining two married a professor of theology and a leading Copenhagen physician, Jørgen Fuiren, respectively.[43]

In 1603, when Caspar Bartholin matriculated at the University of Copenhagen, it was, in spite of the pressure from orthodox Lutherans, especially in Germany, which had forced the theology professor Niels Hemmingsen to resign in 1579, a fairly flexible, humanist institution. The University had no difficulties in tolerating the Ramist philosophy which was espoused by several of its professors.[44] Such irenic, 'liberal' attitudes had, as we have seen, also made it possible for Paracelsian ideas to be taught within the medical faculty. However, the aspiration that medicine should be concerned with experimentation and direct observation of the natural world – a hands-on approach to the Book of Nature reinforced by the reformers' concern for pure and unadulterated Scripture – which found its clearest expressions in the fields of anatomy and botany, had in spite of Morsing's intentions seen only little progress in Copenhagen. Initially, this had undoubtedly been caused by lack of money. Later, the urgency and single-mindedness which had characterized that generation of scholars who lived through the Reformation period had waned and the medical curriculum had remained largely unchanged.

Like so many of his contemporary Danish students, Bartholin came from a clerical family. His father had been a minister in Copenhagen and later in Malmø where Caspar had attended the Latin school.[45] Initially Caspar Bartholin seems to have aimed at an ecclesiastical career. He spent three years studying philosophy and theology in Wittenberg, eventually also teaching philosophy to younger students. During the spring of 1606 Bartholin visited a number of universities and academies in Germany before spending the summer in the United Provinces, where interest in medicine attracted him to the University of Leiden. In spite of spending less than a month in the city, Bartholin managed to get nearly all the famous professors to sign his *album amicorum*.[46] While in Leiden Bartholin must have decided to concentrate on medicine and accordingly travelled via Giessen, Heidelberg, and Strasbourg to Basle in order to benefit from the teaching of Jacob Zwinger, Felix Platter and Caspar Bauhin. In Basle, Bartholin came into contact with the practical and empirical approach to medicine, especially in the fields of anatomy and botany, but also in Paracelsian, chemical medicine, which had characterized that University since the days of Theodor Zwinger. Before receiving his MD in 1610, under the supervision of Caspar Bauhin, Bartholin spent some time in Padua, practising human dissections.[47] Jersin's claim that Bartholin, in spite of better offers of employment in Catholic Naples and Calvinist Sedan, preferred a more modest position at home, for the sake of true religion, may well have been correct. It is supported by the fact that Bartholin dedicated his famous anatomical textbook, *Institutiones Anatomicae*, published in 1611, to the pious and influential Danish nobleman, Holger Rosenkrantz, who, he admitted, was personally unknown to him but whom he had heard praised as the most pious and learned man in Denmark, being the owner of a large medical library and a herbarium and possessing substantial knowledge of pharmacy.[48] Rosenkrantz's reputation and power among the Lutheran intelligentsia in Denmark made him an obvious choice for a dedication from a young scholar in search of a sponsor and a position. It seems to have paid off immediately, because hardly had Bartholin returned to Denmark when he was offered the vacant Chair in Latin at the University of Copenhagen. The following year he improved his career prospects by marrying the daughter of the leading professor of medicine in Copenhagen, Thomas Fincke. Three years later his friend Ole Worm became his brother-in-law, when Worm married another Fincke daughter. Since Caspar Bartholin had been made professor of medicine in 1613 and Worm succeeded him when he moved on to theology in 1624, while Thomas Fincke occupied his Chair in medicine for more than fifty years, the Fincke/Bartholin clan was to remain in total control of the medical faculty in Copenhagen for most of the seventeenth century.

Of far greater importance, however, was the growing friendship between Holger Rosenkrantz and Caspar Bartholin. From at least 1617 until Bartholin's death in 1629, they corresponded regularly and collaborated closely on several projects. Holger Rosenkrantz, who had abandoned the orthodox Lutheran theology he had been taught as a student in Wittenberg, became the leading exponent of a pre-Pietist variety of Lutheranism in early seventeenth century Denmark. He rejected the doctrinally-centered and controversy-orientated orthodox Lutheranism which had become a dominant force in Germany during the last quarter of the sixteenth century. Like Arendt and Gerhardt in Germany, Rosenkrantz wanted to return to a Scripture-based theology, in his case with an emphasis on double justification through faith and acts.[49] Rosenkrantz and his followers, among whom were Caspar Bartholin, wanted a return to the basics of the Reformation. They wanted to bring to completion what had been forgotten or left unfinished by the first generation of Protestants. Like them they focussed on education. It was therefore no coincidence that when Rosenkrantz was made a Councillor to the King in 1617, he concentrated all his efforts on the reform of education in Denmark. That his influence in this field proved considerable and was recognized abroad can be seen from Samuel

Hartlib's *Ephemedires*. Here Hartlib states that Rosenkrantz was 'framing by Education and learning a New Commonwealth being the father of every one in particular'.[50] Religiously Rosenkrantz most certainly inspired, if not totally shaped, the theology of Caspar Bartholin, who, on his mentor's instigation and in some cases with his assistance, wrote the new textbooks and manuals in logic, rhetoric, ethics, and metaphysics for the elementary schools as well as the new 'Gymnasiums', which the King had ordered to be issued in 1619.[51] The influence of Rosenkrantz and Bartholin is also detectable in the Instruments of Foundation which a number of Latin schools/Gymnasiums received in the early 1620s. In the case of the school in Odense the Instrument of 1621 stated that the school's physician should take the pupils on botanical excursions while during the winter he should give them lessons in anatomy *ex scheleto*. The purpose was obviously to provide pupils with a comprehensive and direct experience of God's creation, especially Man, the crown of the achievement. For Bartholin it was yet another avenue, apart from the study of the Bible, which would lead to true Protestant piety. Bartholin and Rosenkrantz may well have inspired the King to promote anatomy dissections in 1639, when he employed and personally funded a third professor of medicine, who was to concentrate on these subjects. That no initiatives were taken earlier was undoubtedly due to Christian IV's disastrous involvement in the Thirty Years' War. Meanwhile, however, an order had been issued to the effect that anyone who wanted to become a country parson ought to have a basic knowledge of human anatomy.[52]

While professor of medicine in Copenhagen, Caspar Bartholin – together with his Basle-educated brothers-in-law Ole Worm and Jørgen Fuiren – retained an interest in botany and botanical excursions, which undoubtedly had its roots in the teaching he had received from Caspar Bauhin.[53] Bartholin's interest in the empirical and practical aspects of medicine had undoubtedly been awakened during his time in Calvinist Basle. His decision actively to further the new experimental medicine in areas such as anatomical dissection, applied botany and iatrochemistry is, however, more closely connected with the religious revival, which his association with Holger Rosenkrantz brought about around 1620. According to his funeral sermon, it was on the instigation of God, 'as someone whom God would use *in better medical practice* to heal the souls of many people with the sound and true reason and teaching of salvation, like he had restored the bodily health of so many people with healing drugs', that Caspar Bartholin made the decision to abandon medicine for theology. Instead, he wanted to concentrate with all his *Meditationes, Studia et Labores* on the Word of God, which is the soul's true medicine, nourishment and cause'.[54]

Having come to the same conclusion as his mentor Rosenkrantz that a return to an unadulterated scriptural theology was urgently needed,

Bartholin must have concluded that a similar reformation of the study of medicine in Copenhagen was called for. Bartholin's belief in double justification through faith and acts could only help generate an active piety which concerned itself with social and educational issues, which were made so much more urgent through the inherent eschatological expectations within the Rosenkrantz circle.[55] Together with another Rosenkrantz pupil, Jesper Brochmand, professor of theology, Bartholin drafted new Statutes for the University in 1621. They were primarily concerned with the study of theology and medicine and aimed at radically changing the curriculum. In medicine, the traditional hierarchical order of the two professors of medicine should be changed. The leading professor should in future lecture on practical medicine and cover the whole subject in a year's lectures. (Bartholin added in an appendix that it would be useful if he would concentrate on botany for half a year and on *rebus metallicis et mineralibus* for the other half.) As far as possible the first *Medicus* should gear his botanical instruction *ad domestica remedia*. Likewise he should take the students on botanical excursions during the summer and have responsibility for a botanical garden which should incorporate rare and exotic plants. The professor should have an *adjunctum pharmacopaeum* who for an hour a day should teach the medical students the *Pharmacopaea* and *Chymica, vulgaria et rariora*, which belonged in a well-stocked pharmacy.

The second professor of medicine should lecture on medical theory, covering the whole topic in one year's lectures. Every winter he should give anatomical instruction through dissections or demonstrations from a skeleton. This professor should have an assistant who could help him in his dissections and instruct the medical students in surgery for an hour every day, teaching them all the techniques used by barber-surgeons.

Apart from the intended improvements of the medical curriculum the draft evidently aimed at reform and control of the way surgery and pharmacy were practised in Denmark, guaranteeing that such practitioners received some basic education in the vernacular at the University. When the so-called *Novellae Constitutiones* for the University were issued by Christian IV in May 1621 very little of the original and extensive draft was included. Instead, the *Constitutiones* were primarily concerned with securing doctrinal orthodoxy among future ministers and schoolmasters. Thus, students of theology who wanted to study abroad were to be restricted to universities which corresponded in doctrine with Lutheran Denmark, if, as was to be expected, they wanted to become ministers or schoolmasters. Students of medicine, however, together with sons of the nobility were expressly excluded from these restrictions because they had to visit foreign universities 'for *Excercicia* and other reasons'.[56]

Why did Caspar Bartholin's plans for a reformation of the study of medicine, and for that matter Brochmand's for theology, come to nothing in 1621? Were they too dramatic and therefore unacceptable to the more conservative and orthodox wing within Church and University who, under the leadership of Bishop Hans Poulsen Resen, had recently purged the country of a number of suspected crypto-Calvinists?[57] In the case of medicine, however, it is more likely to have been a simple question of money. A reorganization of the medical curriculum as envisaged by Bartholin would have meant the employment of additional staff, the building of new auditoria, not to mention an anatomical theatre and a botanical garden. By 1621 Christian IV was already toying seriously with the idea of entering the Thirty Years' War as the leader of the Protestant party, having been constantly encouraged by Maurice of Nassau, Stadholder of the United Provinces, and James I of England. With such expensive military plans the King would not have been tempted to spend large additional sums on the University.[58]

Despite the fate of his draft, which must have been a personal disappointment, Caspar Bartholin continued to develop his ideas about an improved medical education. This was a natural consequence and integral part of his pre-Pietist Protestantism, as can be seen from a comparison between his *De Studio Medico* and his *De Studio Theologico* published simultaneously in 1628. In his manual for the study of theology Bartholin complained that letters from the Apostles, which had been fully comprehensible to all the original recipients, could nowadays only be understood through commentaries and interpretations, and even then people were often more confused when they had finished reading than when they began, because of the conflicting views of the commentator. All the theological commentaries had to be abandoned in favour of an exegetical study of Scripture alone. True godliness depended on such a change. It determined the study of theology as much as the study of medicine. Both subjects were firmly anchored in the continuous study of Scripture which through faith and grace generated piety. For Bartholin this personal religious experience was a necessary precondition for ministering to the body as well as to the soul.[59]

In *De Studio Medico* Bartholin specified what was needed of the godly physician apart from personal piety. He should have adequate knowledge of Latin and Greek in order to be able to determine what was good and bad in Hippocrates and Galen. Only the original texts could be relied on! This was the same anti-authoritarian, Protestant quest for truth which had taken him back to a rigorous and regular study of Scripture. In this connection Bartholin also took the opportunity to point out that the Arabic authors had borrowed their most valuable information from the Greeks, but in the process often missed even more important stuff. On these points, he proved himself in total accordance with Morsing's lecture-list of 1537 which had excluded Avicenna and Rhazes.

In rejecting rhetoric as useful for physicians Bartholin emphasized that 'the patient is not cured by words, but by herbs'. This emphasis on an empirical approach to medicine dominated his manual. When mentioning the importance of botany for the physician, Bartholin stressed the need for the physician to collect plants and make herbariums, rather than reading extensively in the botanical literature. Similarly, in anatomy Bartholin placed the emphasis on dissections, pointing out that students ought to 'dissect animals and parts of their bodies privately and, as often as possible, to attend public dissections of humans'. His advice about pharmacy and surgery corresponded neatly with this. Students ought to obtain a solid practical knowledge of how drugs were made in pharmacies, while a direct experience of surgery, especially from France and Italy, where the best surgeons were to be found, was considered absolutely essential.[60] For an Aristotelian, Caspar Bartholin was surprisingly positively inclined towards iatrochemistry. He warmly recommended the works and arcana of Paracelsians such as Joseph du Chesne, Petrus Severinus, John Bannister and Johannes Hartmann to his students, referring them to his own considerable alchemical library. He acknowledged the negative attitude among some physicians, who preferred traditional Galenic medicine to chemical medicine, but he stressed that 'while one should be pursued the other should not be neglected'. In this connection, Bartholin once more underlined the need for direct empirical experience of the subject, stating that students should always personally practise alchemy 'with its charcoal and glass flasks'. He added that 'no-one should be ashamed to seek information from old wives and barbers about their remedies, as long as they had been successfully tested'. These words were identical to similar statements by Paracelsus and can hardly have been the opinion of a strict Aristotelian.[61]

When Bartholin died in 1629 his proposals for reform had yet to be officially introduced in Copenhagen. The realization of at least some of his plans eventually fell to his brother-in-law Ole Worm and his son Thomas Bartholin in the 1640s.[62] Like Christian Torkelsen Morsing before him, Caspar Bartholin's scheme for a radical reform of the study of medicine in Copenhagen foundered on primarily economic grounds. Morsing's more modest plans had been a product of the dramatic years which saw the Reformation introduced in Denmark, while Bartholin's far-reaching reforms resulted from his Lutheran pre-Pietism. For Bartholin, the Reformation still remained an unfinished business by the early seventeenth century, which had to be addressed with eschatological urgency. It was this concern which more than anything else was the motivation behind both the many textbooks and manuals he produced in the 1620s and his ideas for a reform of the study of medicine in Copenhagen, including his manual for the education of the pious, Protestant physician.

Notes

I should like to thank the Humanities Research Council in Denmark for a travel grant in 1991 and the Royal Library in Copenhagen for assistance and permission to reproduce the pictures in this chapter.

1. Cited in G. Strauss, *Luther's House of Learning: Indoctrination of the Young in the German Reformation* (Baltimore, 1978), 242.
2. For these aspects of the Reformation, see E. Cameron, *The European Reformation* (Oxford, 1991), 389–408.
3. See R. Po-Chia Hsia, *Social Discipline in the Reformation* (London, 1989), 23.
4. Caspar Bartholin, *De Studio Medico* (Copenhagen, 1628), f.2r. I should like to thank Dr John Henderson, King's College, Cambridge for helping me in translating this text.
5. *De Studio Medico*, f.1r. The manual was dedicated not only to his relation, Jonas Charisius, but also to Caspar Bartholin's six sons.
6. Cameron, *The European Reformation*, 395–6.
7. *De Studio Medico*, f.2r-3r.
8. C.E. Brochmand, *Vita et Mors Caspari Bartholini*, (Copenhagen, 1629), fol. B2ff.
9. J.O. Andersen, *Holger Rosenkrantz den Lærde*, (Copenhagen, 1896), 98–112.
10. For medicine in Denmark before the Reformation, see P.L. Panum, *Vort medicinske Fakultets Oprindelse og Barndom* (Copenhagen, 1879), 14–23. For the University of Copenhagen during the Reformation years, see M. Schwarz Lausten, 'Die Universität Kopenhagen und die Reformation', in L. Grane (ed.), *University and Reformation* (Leiden, 1981), 103–5.
11. For the negative attitude towards universities, see Peder Laurentsen, *Malmøbogen* (Malmø, 1530), reprinted and edited by H.F. Rørdam (Copenhagen, 1864). For the petition, see W. Norvin, *Københavns Universitet i Reformationens og Orthodoxiens Tidsalder*, II (Copenhagen, 1940), 1–3. Norvin has mistakenly given the date 1537; it should be 1536, see M. Schwarz Lausten, *Christian den 3. og Kirken 1537–1559* (Copenhagen, 1987), 110, note 1.
12. H.F. Rørdam, *Kjøbenhavns Universitets Historie fra 1537 til 1621*, I-IV (Copenhagen, 1868–74), 435.
13. The lecture-list of 1537 is reprinted in Norvin, *Københavns Universitet*, II, 4–8, see especially 5.
14. Reprinted A.E. Brade (ed.), *Henrik Smiths Lægebog*, I-IV (Copenhagen, 1976). For Morsing's introduction, see Aij 1556 edition. See also V.Ingerslev, *Danmarks Læger og Lægevæsen*, I-II (Copenhagen, 1873): I, 80–81 and Panum, *Vort medicinske Fakultet*, 33–6.
15. 'Doctissimi enim medici non sustinent, ut Auicenna è Scholis explodatur', see Norvin, *Københavns Universitet*, II, 26.
16. The Statutes of 1539 are printed in Norvin, *Københavns Universitet*, II, 9–70, see especially 26–7. See also Ingerslev, *Denmarks Læger og Lægevæsen* I, 72–3.
17. Bugenhagen has been seen as the driving force behind both the lecture-list of 1537 and the Statutes of 1539. This may well have been the case in theology, but the difference between what is laid down for medicine in the lecture-list and the Statutes would indicate that the wider changes of 1537 were inspired by Morsing while the more conservative/traditional approach, which corresponded with the Wittenberg Statutes of 1536, was the responsibility of Bugenhagen, Compare W. Norvin, *Københavns Universitet*, II, 26 with W. Friedenburg (ed.), *Urkunden*

buch der Universität Wittenberg, Magdeburg 1926, 176. For the view that Bugenhagen was responsible for both lecture-list and Statutes, see M. Schwarz Lausten, *Biskop Peder Palladius 1537–1560* (Copenhagen, 1987), 225–36, 239.

18. The Seal has recently been reproduced in the new history of the University of Copenhagen. Here the authors have mistakenly interpreted the hand as coming from above to pick the flowers, see V. Møller-Christensen and A. Gjedde, 'Det lægevidenskabelige Fakultet', in S. Ellehøj (ed.), *Københavns Universitet 1479–1979*, I-XIV, VII (Copenhagen, 1979), 1–49.

19. For Basle, see K.M. Reeds, *Botany in Medieval and Renaissance Universities* (London, 1991), 96–104. See also A. Burckhardt, *Geschichte der medizinischen Fakultät zu Basel 1460–1900* (Basle, 1917).

20. The following seven professors of medicine received their MDs from Basle: (1) Christian Torkelsen Morsing, Professor 1537–1560, MD 1530s; (2) Anders Lemvig, Professor 1577–1602, MD 1576; (3) Anders Christensen, Professor 1585–1602, MD 1583; (4) Thomas Fincke, Professor 1603–1656, MD 1587; (5) Gellius Sascerides, Professor 1603–1612, MD 1593; (6) Caspar Bartholin, Professor 1613–1624, MD 1610; (7) Ole Worm, Professor 1624–1654, MD 1611. Of the other five, Johannes Philip Pratensis visited Basle together with his friend and travel-companion, Petrus Severinus in 1569, while other influential professors in the arts faculty in Copenhagen, such as Jon Jacobsen Vinusinus, Anders Kragh and the later professor of theology, Cort Aslaksen, studied there in the 1580s and 1590s. I have not included the five professors of medicine in Copenhagen who served the University for brief periods only: Thomas Zeger, Johannes Pomerius, Johannes von Freudenburg, Elias Rempold and Hadrianus Junius. See Panum, *Vort medicinske Fakultet*, 37–8, Ingerslev, *Danmarks Læger og Lægevæsen*, I, 75–7, F. Bastholm (ed.), *Petrus Severinus og hans Idea Medicinæ Philosophicæ*, (Odense, 1979), 5, and V. Helk, *Dansk-Norske Studierejser fra Reformationen til Enevælden 1536–1660* (Odense, 1987).

21. See Rørdam, *Kjøbenhavns Universitet*, II, 543–56.

22. See Reeds, *Botany in Medieval and Renaissance Universities*, 110–11. In the forty years between 1581 and 1620 around 100 Danish students matriculated in Basle, see Helk, *Dansk-Norske Studierejser* 42–3.

23. For Fuchs, see Ingerslev, *Danmarks Læger og Lægevæsen*, I. 75. For Peter Capeteyn, see *Dansk Biografisk Leksikon*, 3rd edition.

24. L. Grane, 'Teaching the People – the Education of the Clergy and the Instruction of the People in the Danish Reformation Church', in L. Grane and K. Hørby (eds.), *Die Dänische Reformation vor ihrem internationalen Hintergrund*, (Göttingen 1990), 166.

25. Rørdam, *Kjøbenhavns Universitet*, II, 74–98.

26. Figures from Helk, *Dansk-Norske Studierejser*, 44, Table 2.

27. Rørdam, *Kjøbenhavns Universitet*, II, 576–7 and Helk, *Dansk-Norske Studierejser*, 14–15.

28. See Panum, *Vort medicinske Fakultet*, 37–8.

29. The number of Danish students who matriculated at Calvinist universities such as Basle, Franeker, Geneva, Heidelberg, Herborn and Leiden, and the Lutheran/Ramist University of Giessen between 1571 and 1620 was considerable. Of a total of 1520 matriculations abroad for this period, more than a third, 567, matriculated at the above-mentioned universities, see Helk, *Dansk-Norske Studierejser*, 42–4.

30. For Frandsen, see Rørdam, *Kjøbenhavns Universitet*, II, 543–56 and Panum, *Vort medisicinske Fakultet*, 44–5. See also Thomas Bartholin, *Cista*

Medica Hafniensis, in N.W. Bruun and H.O. Loldrup (eds) (Copenhagen, 1982), 69–70.

31. For the way Paracelsianism made itself acceptable to different types of Protestantism, see O. Hannaway, *The Chemist and the Word. The Didactic Origins of Chemistry*, (London, 1975).

32. See Bastholm, *Petrus Severinus og hans Idea Medicinæ Philosophicæ*, 6.

33. Palladius gave his verdict in his *Formula Visitationis Provincialis*, (Copenhagen, 1555). The relevant sections are quoted in Panum, *Vort medicinske Fakultet*, 24–5.

34. For Niels Hemmingsen, see *Dansk Biografisk Leksikon*, 3rd edition. See also J. Glebe-Møller, 'Socialetiske aspecter af Niels Hemmingsens forfatterskab', *Kirkehistoriske Samlinger* (1979), 7–56.

35. For the suggestion to make Brahe Vice-Chancellor, see Rørdam, *Kjøbenhavns Universitet*, II, 174. For Severinus's letter, see Bastholm, *Petrus Severinus og hans Idea Medicinæ Philosphicæ*, 40. Here Severinus stated that 'Nature loves silence and God curses the quarrelsome', adding, while undoubtedly with Hemmingsen in mind, 'I feel sorry for the theologians in these times'.

36. Letter in Bastholm, *Petrus Severinus og hans Idea Medicinæ Philosophicæ*, 41–4, quotation from 42–3.

37. Quoted in Bastholm, *Petrus Severinus og hans Idea Medicinæ Philosophicæ*, 6–7.

38. For Peter Payng, see A. Fjelstrup, *Dr. Peter Payngk, Kong Kristian IV's Hofkemiker* (Copenhagen, 1911). For the plans to publish Petrus Severinus's MSS, see *Breve fra og til Ole Worm*, (ed.) H.D. Schepelern, I–III (Copenhagen, 1965–8), nos. 73–4. That Ole Worm should have been unwilling to edit the unpublished works by Severinus in order not to be associated with Paracelsianism, as claimed by Schepelern (H.D. Schepelern, *Museum Wormianum* (Odense, 1971), 128), is a misinterpretation of Worm's politeness towards Severinus's son, the physician, Frederik Sørensen. Worm, in fact, ends his letter to Sørensen by declaring his willingness to undertake the task if Frederik Sørensen would agree to it, see no. 73.

39. See Bastholm, *Petrus Severinus oq hans Idea Medicinæ Philosophieæ*, 5, for letters exchanged between Zwinger and Severinus, 45–58. For Ramus's stay with Zwinger in 1569, see A. Burckhardt, *Geschichte der medicinischen Fakultät zu Basel*, 90.

40. Rørdam, *Kjøbenhavns Universitet*, II, 653–9. A contemporary described him, 'in perscrutandis et investigandis simplicium et herbarum naturis omnium facile suæ ætate sagacissimus' 658.

41. See Rørdam, *Kjøbenhavns Universitet*, III, 550–62. See also E. Bartholin in *Cista Medica Hafniensis*, 73, For Severinus's letter recommending Fincke to Zwinger, see Bastholm, *Petus Severinus og hans Idea Medicinæ Philosophicæ*, 48.

42. For Sascerides, see *Dansk Biografisk Leksikon*, 3rd edition. For Anders Kragh, see Rørdam, *Kjøberhavns Universitet*, III, 508–22. For Aslaksen, see O. Garstein, *Cort Aslaksen* (Oslo, 1953).

43. See Bartholin, *Cista Medica Hafniensis*, 74.

44. See the complaints by Holger Rosenkrantz, who saw the University of Copenhagen as totally dominated by Ramists and crypto-Calvinists in the 1590s, J.O. Andersen, *Holger Rosenkrantz den Lærde*, 31, 34, 36, 39, 45, 46 and 75.

45. See the funeral sermon by Jens Dinesen Jersin, *Enochs Leffnit oc Endeligt* (Copenhagen, 1632), Eijv-Eiijr. In Malmø Bartholin's father served as a minister

to one of the city parishes, as well as a chaplain to Malmø Castle. He was never associated with the Court, as stated by E. Snorrason in *Dictionary of Scientific Biography*, I (New York, 1970), 479.

46. See The Royal Library Copenhagen MS, Ny Kgl. Sml. 359 (8), *Thesaurus fautorum et amicorum Caspari Bartholini*. The signatories from Leiden are Joseph Justus Scaliger, Bonaventura Vulcanius, Pieter Paaw, Rudolph Snellius, and Daniel Heinsius; more surprisingly we also find entries by the Reformed theologians Franciscus Gomarus, Lucas Trelcatius, Jacob Arminius and Petrus Bertius, see fols. 91, 99, 137, 171, 173, 217, 225, 271, 367. Jersin mentions in his funeral sermon that Bartholin 'experienced the Reformed theology of Arminius and Trelcatius' while in Leiden, see Jersin, *Enochs Leffnit oc Endeligt*, fol. Eviijr.

47. Felix Platter, Caspar Bauhin and Jacob Zwinger all signed Caspar Bartholin's *album amicorum*. Zwinger added what eventually proved a most characteristic proverb for his student, 'Pietas ad omnia utilis' *Thesaurus fautorum et amicorum Caspari Bartholini*, 359 (8), fols. 73, 271 and 279. See Reeds, *Botany in Medieval and Renaissance Universities*, 18, 110-33. For Caspar Bartholin's studies at Padua, see Jersin, *Enochs Leffnit oc Endeligt*, fols. Exr-XIv; for Caspar Bartholin, see also *Dansk Biografisk Leksikon*, 3rd edition.

48. See preface to Caspar Bartholin, *Institutiones Anatomicæ*, (Wittenberg 1611) and Andersen, *Holger Rosenkrantz den Lærde*, 127.

49. For the friendship between Rosenkrantz and Caspar Bartholin, see Andersen, *Holger Rosenkrantz den Lærde*, 112, 176, 195-8. For Rosenkrantz's theology, see J. Glebe-Møller, *Doctrina Secundum Pietatem. Holger Rosenkrantz den Lærdes Teologi* (Copenhagen, 1966). For letters exchanged between Rosenkrantz and Bartholin, see H.F. Rørdam, 'Breve fra og til Holger Rosenkrands', *Kirkehistoriske Samlinger*, III Rk., V (1884-6), 757-61; VI (1887-9), 40-43, 47, 53-5, 62, 69-70, 297, 307-8, 315-16.

50. Sheffield University Library MSS. Samuel Hartlib MS 29/3/15A.

51. Andersen, *Holger Rosenkrantz den Lærde*, 176-7. These textbooks, which were published during the 1620s, were abbreviated versions of his philosopical textbooks for undergraduates, published from 1608 onwards, see *Dansk Biografisk Leksikon*, 3rd edition.

52. N.D. Riegels, *Små Historiske Skrifter*, 3 Parts (Copenhagen, 1796), I, 143.

53. *Breve fra og til Ole Worm*, I, no.24. The close contact between members of the medical faculties in Basle and Copenhagen can be seen from the correspondence between Worm and Bauhin, see ibid., nos. 24, 34, 42, 46, 51, 58, 62, 65, 77. When Worm received the news of Bauhin's death in 1625, he wrote: 'I mourn the death of this man, who was the leading light of botany and anatomy in our era and who showed me great friendship. Basle has lost an immense light, and I cannot see what excellency within the field of medicine can now be expected from there,' see no.175.

54. Jersin, *Enochs Leffnit oc Endeligt*, fol. Fiiijr. J.O. Andersen has shown that Caspar Bartholin was already contemplating a move away from medicine to theology in 1619, see Andersen, *Holger Rosenkrantz den Lærde*, 242. Bartholin's religious revival has traditionally been connected with his unexpected recovery from the serious illness he suffered in 1623, see Jersin, fol. Fiiijv.

55. See for example C. Bartholin, *Underviisning af Guds Ord om Krijg* (Copenhagen, 1628), fols. Avjv-Aviijv.

56. The draft for the new statutes of the University and the so-called *Novellæ Constitutiones* of 1621 were published by H.F. Rørdam, 'Aktstykker til Universitets Historie i Tidsrummet 1621-60', *Danske Magazin* 5, Rk. I, 1887-8, 37-47; for

medicine, see especially 38, 43 and 44. See also Andersen, *Holger Rosenkrantz den Lærde*, 189–198.

57. See B. Kornerup, *Biskop Hans Poulsen Resen*, I-II (Copenhagen, 1928 and 1968), I, 373–491.

58. See E. Ladewig Petersen, 'The Danish Intermezzo', in G. Parker (ed.), *The Thirty Years' War*, (London, 1984), 71–81, especially 73.

59. For *De Studio Medico*, see note 4 above. For theology, see Caspar Bartholin, *De Studio Theologico*, (Copenhagen, 1628), fols. Alr-A3v.

60. Bartholin, *De Studio Medico*, fols. 3r, 4r, 6r-v, 7r.

61. See Bartholin, *De Studio Medico*, 7v-8r; the nearly identical phrase by Paracelsus is mentioned in Reeds, *Botany in Medieval and Renaissance Universities*, 102. Bartholin has traditionally been portrayed as a strict Aristotelian, see for instance Snorrason in *Dictionary of Scientific Biography*.

62. See Schepelern, *Museum Wormianum*, 134.

5

Spiritual physic, Providence and English medicine, 1560–1640

David Harley

The early reformers gave an Augustinian emphasis to the doctrine of Providence, following late mediaeval voluntarism, which had asserted the unconstrained nature of God's will, but they stressed its implications for personal piety. Rather than the sacraments or good works, they emphasized preaching, Bible study and self-examination as the keys to a Christian life. Providentialism and lay piety created a distinctive attitude towards medicine and a repertoire of religious metaphors which reflected that attitude.[1] Calvin's doctrine of Providence was undoubtedly the most respected in England during the late Reformation period. He insisted that all events were governed by the will of God, differentiating three forms of divine Providence. General providence guided all God's creatures and was indistinguishable from the order of nature. Special providence concerned Man, the most eminent of God's creatures for whom heaven and earth were created. Finally, there was a particular providence that governed the faithful.[2]

This view of Providence was generally adopted by most English Protestants, despite disputes about the scope of human will, so it was necessary to combat the tendency to blame circumstances for misfortunes. 'All men for the most part will confesse the world to be gouerned by the Lord: but when it comes to their owne particular case in affliction, few doe acknowledge it . . .'[3] For God there were no accidents; sickness did not come by chance but was sent as a fatherly correction by God either to punish human wickedness or as a trial of faith. One should give thanks as much for afflictions as for blessings, all God's works being good.[4] The business of the godly was to scrutinize the workings of Providence, in their own lives and in the world.[5] Bodily healing, like that of the soul, lay with God although the sick should use all legitimate means. 'Physicke is good, if we intreat God by Prayer to giue a blessing to it.'[6] Medicine was the means ordained for use in sickness by God who usually acted through second causes, 'So that the neglect of ordinarie means is a contempt of Gods ordinance, and a sin of presumption.'[7]

This was the attitude of most literate men and women in England so there was a broad consensus about the relationship between religion and medicine. No medical means were forbidden by Calvinist theology, apart from sorcery. The 'experimental religion' of English Protestants, seeking experience of God's Providence to confirm assurance of salvation, was decidedly sympathetic to the empirical augmentation of medical knowledge. George Hakewill, for example, cited improvements in anatomy, herbalism and chemistry as evidence of the continuing Providence of God.[8] Preventative medicine was especially respected by the godly, who saw it as akin to the diligent care they took of their souls' welfare. Prompt repentance was prophylactic, 'the vomit of the soule'.[9] The godly had to take care of their bodies, 'that our souls be not annoyed with the filth and stincke of our corruptions, while we abide in the same'.[10] A temperate way of life was seen as consonant with true religion; nature itself punished immoderation with diseases. As the Manchester physician Thomas Cogan wrote, 'no doubt but that meane and temperate dyet, in the feare of God, is more commendable than all the delicate fare in the world, and ought of the godly to be esteemed as a thing which best contenteth nature, and preserveth health.'[11] Hippocratic dietary medicine was compared to the renouncing of sin, although natural or medicinal abstinence was clearly distinct from religious fasting.[12] However, the strictest observation of the six non-naturals would be in vain unless coupled with thankfulness for health and the fear of God, who might choose to distemper the humours.[13] Sickness and weakness should teach the godly to make better use of their health. Those who failed to keep the rules of health would be troubled with the thought, 'I am accessary to my own death, I have been an intemperate man, I have shortened my days.'[14]

The afflictions of the godly bore a different meaning to the punishments of the wicked, although 'afflictions are common to the godly and vngodly, they suffer alike'. Whereas the wicked were cursed whatever their condition, the children of God were 'blessed in sicknesse: blessed in health'. Among the godly, afflictions were no matter for reproach. They were to be regarded as tokens of God's fatherly love rather than as signs of reprobation or God's hatred. 'By affliction and sicknesse, God exerciseth his *children*, and the *graces* which hee bestoweth vpon them.'[15] In the absence of severe persecution after 1558, such apparently mundane troubles as scorn, sickness and poverty had to be emphasized. Since heavy affliction had 'euer beene the portion of Gods Children', the godly might expect to suffer: 'By dying to Christ, we lose perhaps Health, but we gain it in strength, we may lose countenance, and Friend, we gain it in spirituall things.' Regular affliction was the best way for the soul to remain healthy. Ill health could be seen as 'a sort of *spiritualizing* our bodily life', keeping the Christian from sinful works, spurring devotion and preparing the soul for death. Moreover, it was in the pious fortitude of the godly during severe sickness, which exceeded their own strength, that the power of Christ was revealed to the world.[16]

The task was to sanctify afflictions, rather than simply to seek their removal, since they would only be inflicted for the benefit of the afflicted individual. 'A soul that is sanctified had rather have pardon of sin, and strength against corruption, than to have recovery.' Sanctified affliction would further true conversion, encourage compassion towards others, and act as an example.[17] God would renew his afflictions, like a physician repeating his treatment on a desperate case, until a broken and contrite heart resulted, so to suffer without contrition was 'a greater plague than the plague itself'. Not to repent thoroughly was like following a doctor's orders for only a day or two.[18] As a consequence, the godly tended to embrace afflictions as a sign of grace. Joseph Hall, early in his career, held that 'Not to be afflicted is a sign of weakness . . . when I am stronger, I will look for more.'[19] Archbishop Ussher had been prone to this view, 'which some might have gathered out of certain unwary passages in Books, and which he himself had met with in his *Youth*, and which wrought on him so much that he earnestly prayed God to deal with him that way, and he had his request.' Regretting his youthful enthusiasm, he counselled others not to tempt God but to wait on his will.[20]

The reverse of this coin was a tendency to judge others on the basis of afflictions since nothing was so effectual a warning as the sudden death of the ungodly.[21] A Cambridge baker returned after the 1630 plague and 'instead of giving thanks to God fell to revelling, dancing, and drinking, but in the midst of his jollity he fell down suddenly and died, not of the plague, but some other stroke of God.' A Cheshire woman, twice married bigamously, was aptly stricken when 'a secret judgement of God befel her in her secret parts, which rotted away'.[22] Parishioners who abused ministers and their families were apt to be struck down, as were patients who abused medical practitioners.[23] Such comments by the godly verged on a vulgar providentialism that was all too widespread among the ungodly. 'The world is ready to passe their verdict presently upon a man. Oh, such a one, you see what a kind of man he was, you see how God follows him with crosses.' This tendency was condemned by ministers as worthy only of the papists.[24]

Bodily diseases, like all other afflictions, were God's 'seuerall potions of heauenly physicke', sent to treat spiritual diseases through the mortification of the flesh. As natural evils, these medicinal diseases might be 'gall in the mouth' but they would be found to be 'honey in the bellie'. Just as the man whose humours were unbalanced might feel at ease until the doctor purged him, so God's remedies made the afflicted feel worse for a time: 'the Physicke must make vs sicke, that doeth vs any good.' God's bitter medicines of affliction were sent to purge out corruptions, as the doctor purged peccant humours.[25] In seeing affliction as medicinal, however, it was not suggested that in itself it could heal the soul, any more than medicine could heal the body without the blessing of God. Affliction 'is like an eating or a fretting corrasiue which cannot cure, yet it is profitable to make the way for the healing medicine.'[26] Diseases were sent by God to benefit the soul by preparing it for the healing grace of God so 'when God visits us with sicknes, wee should thinke our worke is more in heauen with God than with men, or physicke.'[27]

Sickness had always been regarded as an especially suitable time for prayer and meditation. As Thomas Becon had pointed out, 'Would Ezechias haue prayed for health and long lyfe, if he had not felte himself sycke & at the poynte of death?' English prayers intended for the use of the sick generally depicted disease as a scourge sent by God for the benefit of the afflicted, grateful for such 'gentle chastisement'. The cure of sickness was at God's disposal: 'when I am sicke, thou makest my bed, and curest my disease.'[28] Some writers, however, preferred to attribute specific ailments to 'the frawde and malice of the diuell' or the 'carnall will and frailty' of the sick person. God was seen by such authors as forgiving sin and assuaging pain.[29] The need to ascribe evils to the providence of God was to become a major stumbling block. In orthodox thought, however, even demonic afflictions were only inflicted with the permission of God and the Devil operated through natural causes to accomplish his apparent miracles.[30] Satan was used by God's providence as 'a helpfull instrument, setting forward our perfection'.[31] Demonic afflictions had to be treated with the same combination of prayer and medicine as any other affliction. Stephen Bradwell the elder was appalled by a physician who briefly relieved Mary Glover's bewitchment 'by some extraordinary & unlawfull means'.[32]

Providential doctrine had several implications for patients and their friends, principally in the realm of meaning. Lady Margaret Hoby saw her ailments as useful, although she does not appear to have ascribed their causation to God. She wrote in 1605, 'This day I tooke somethinge for my Shoulder, which had a paine in it by reason of Could, w[ch], I praise god, did me good: afflictions draw one nearer to god.'[33] Thankfulness for afflictions was to become one of the most familiar elements of spiritual autobiographies. Jane Turner, a Newcastle Baptist, for example, wrote that 'being under a bodily affliction, the Lord was pleased to visit me with his loving kindness, that I can truly say, it was a time of great joy to my soul. . .'[34]

The godly were very eager to offer advice to their friends on how to make the best use of suffering. How welcome some of this comfort was is difficult to gauge. As Paul Baynes wrote, 'it is easier to counsel others, and see them take their physicke, than ourselves to enter such courses'.[35] A serious visiting of the sick was enjoined upon the godly, partly to do good to the afflicted and partly for the benefit of their own souls by contemplation of the spectacle of mortality, even though 'many people deeme such like courses to savour of melancholicke madness, and too much puritanical austeritie'. Although they were expected to encourage the sick 'to a Christian carriage in sickness', this was not to the exclusion of compassion and charity. Indeed, even the poorest Christian could perform acts of mercy by visiting the sick, if only by watching the sickbed or bringing an apple. It was not given to all the godly to be apt visitors of the sick, only to 'some sons of *Consolation* . . . such as can comfort the sicke, and pray for him'. Those who visited the sick especially needed to beware of the twin dangers of harming themselves, by falling into either complacency or false comparisons between the seemingly comfortable deaths of the wicked and 'the violent death and sicknesse of many good men', and harming the sick, by making sport of their weakness or giving them false confidence of recovery.[36] While it might sometimes serve a useful purpose to encourage the sick, 'to make the means to work the better', it was 'a corrupt atheistical course' to mislead them about their prospects, thus preventing them from putting their spiritual affairs in order. Physicians needed to be 'Divines in some measure'.[37]

Criticism of physicians was widespread in early modern Europe, from a variety of standpoints. The early reformers often echoed humanist criticisms that physicians were avaricious. Thomas Becon, for example, explicitly stated that it was not lawful for a physician to pray 'that many might fall sycke or that they that are sycke, might so contynue longe, that he myghte haue the more auantage'.[38] John Robinson, the pastor of the English congregation in Leyden, noted that not only were regular physicians far more expensive than empirics, they were also 'many times supercilious, and neglective of meaner persons'. Moreover, there was among the common people a reluctance to consult physicians based upon 'a superstitious presumption of Gods speciall help, where mans is neglected'.[39] John Woolton felt constrained to defend physicians 'because of some men, that both think and speake amysse of Physitions. . . . For by the Physition, as by a mynister, God expelleth disseases, and by Physicke as by an instrument, he conserueth health, and restoreth the same againe being lost.' Medicine was given a bad name both by incautious patients and by inexpert or ungodly practitioners.[40]

So, for the godly, the means employed by the physician were to be respected but not relied upon:

> the more we depend on a wise Physitian, the more wee will observe his *directions*, and be carefull to use what hee prescribes; yet wee must use the meanes as meanes, and not set them in Gods roome, for that is the way to blast our hopes.[41]

Means could only be expected to work if they had God's blessing, which would not be forthcoming if they were seen as independently efficacious, let alone if they were habitually consumed for pleasure, like tobacco.[42] Those who took their medicine as if it were their daily sustenance could expect a miserable life and an early death, noted Joseph Hall.[43] Just as it was the physician's application of a drug and not the drug itself that cured, so all means were effective only insofar as they were applied by God to his ends, something that was as true of Holy Communion as of a loaf of bread.[44] A familiar *topos* was the sin of Asa, who was guilty of placing too much faith in physicians, as opposed to Hezekiah, who first looked to God and then used the means. 'Let us not do like Asa, to trust in the Physitian, or in subordinate meanes, but know, that all Physicke is but dead meanes without him.'[45]

The first priority in time of sickness had to be the repentance of sin. 'When therefore God summons thee, do not as the common course is, send first for the bodily physician, and when thou art past natural care, then for the divine; but contrarily let the divine begin.'[46] According to Robert Bolton, it was actually worse to appear to be saved by secondary causes alone than to suffer affliction, since all punishments came only from God. He reproved 'all those, who affect a stoicall apathy and insensibilitie this way . . . they look no higher than to the hand of the Physitian, they depend onely upon the power of physic for their deliverance and recovery' instead of seeing God's hand in their afflictions.[47] Nevertheless, the godly did not in any sense demote the physician, they merely insisted that there was a danger of idolatry if mere means were seen as causing recovery. The physician had to be used 'as Gods *Instrument*, and *Physicke*, as Gods *meanes*'. In the most frequently republished manual of domestic piety, Lewis Bayly provided pages of prayers and meditations for the sick that stressed this point: 'O Lord, in this my necessitie, I haue, according to thine ordinance, sent for thy seruant (the *Physitian*) who hath prepared for mee this *Physicke* which I receiue, as *meanes sent* from thy fatherly *hand*.'[48] This attitude was reflected in the self-examinations of the godly. Bulstrode Whitelocke, remembering his youth and childhood, attributed his recovery from various mishaps to God's blessing on the means applied by his mother or physicians.[49] Sometimes, however, even the best of means did not receive the blessing of God. Paul Baynes wrote to his brother-in-law, 'My most christian Wife (your Sister) hath since Easter last been very ill, and it hath not pleased God to blesse any meanes which shee hath attempted here or elsewhere.'[50]

The prescribed response to any kind of adversity was a combination of repentance, patient waiting upon the will of God, and the use of legitimate means. The clergy were not always the most docile of patients, however, having other concerns than their own bodily welfare. It was notorious that, in the final illness of Calvin, 'the Physicians did what they could, and hee was very observant of their rules, but yet hee would by

106

no means intermit the labors of his minde.' The scholar John Rainolds died as a result of 'his exceeding great pain in his studie (whereby hee brought his bodie to a very *Sceleton*)'. Robert Bolton, 'beeing advised by Physicians, for his health's sake, to break off the strong intentions of his studies, hee rejected their counsel, accounting it greater riches to enjoie Christ by those fervent intentions of his minde, then to remit them for his health's sake.'[51]

Affliction was a rehearsal for death and the godly were expected to 'Study and exercise daily the Art of dying'.[52] Since it was the duty of the godly to set a good example in sickness as in death, their attitude towards medicine became part of the Protestant *ars moriendi*. John Preston suffered a long illness, consulting doctors in London, Oxford and Bury St Edmunds. Finally, he was fatally misdiagnosed as having scurvy. 'When this dream and fancy of the Scorbute failed, and Dr. *Ashworth* was gone, he resigned up himself to God alone, and let all care of Physick and the Doctors go.'[53] When Robert Bolton was dying of a quartan ague, 'by the judgement of the best Physitians . . . ever deemed mortall unto old men', he decided that he was not strong enough to survive and so 'patiently submitted to indure, what by strugling hee could not overcome'.[54] In the funeral sermon of a Devon gentleman who had diligently prepared his soul for death, the mourners were reminded that 'as often as hee receiued any Phisicall help (for no meanes was neglected for his preseruation and life, if God would) he neuer receiued any ayde, but he prayed vnto God to giue it a blessing'.[55]

Since healing was in the gift of God, he might choose to cloud the physician's judgement: 'If a skilfull Phisician doth us no good, it is because it pleaseth God to hide the right way of curing at that time from him'.[56] When Lady Margaret Hoby's doctor died of a sleeping draught in 1599, she reflected on

> the mercie and power of god shewed in openinge his eies touchinge me, and shuttinge them against him selfe . . . therefore I may truly conclude it is the Lord, and not the phisision, who both ordaines the medesine for our health and orderethe the ministring of it for the good of his children.[57]

God might also suspend the action of medicine if he saw fit. When sin was being punished, 'Physicke ministred doth often lose his working'.[58] Paradoxically, this led to greater confidence in the ministrations of physicians, since their remedies were not expected to have automatic efficacy. A funeral sermon for the High Sheriff of Suffolk insisted that the physician was not to be blamed for that worthy's demise, whatever 'the ignorant multitude' might say, since nothing could be done 'if God shooteth his arrow'.[59]

Collective afflictions, such as war, plague and famine, were obviously sent to warn the whole nation to repent from their sins, however much 'irreligious persons, who look no farther then into second causes, doe fondly imagine this or that eclipse' to be responsible. 'The sin was general, and God's visitation was general . . . Is it a spreading sin? Take heed of a spreading and contagious punishment.' Such general afflictions were brought upon the nation by conspicuous sinners, 'where is lying, swearing, stealing, &c . . .'[60] Outbreaks of plague had to be addressed by both collective prayer and appropriate sanitary and medical responses, all of which were the God-given 'meanes to preserue vs from the infection of this contagious sicknesse'. As in cases of individual sickness, however, it was God's prerogative 'to work for the good or euil of the whole, aboue, and beside, yea & against nature' so he might 'punish a nation beyond all the rules of second causes', as the Dean of Worcester told James I during the 1603 plague.[61] There was no conflict between the sense that epidemics were sent by God and the understanding of the natural means by which the disease was transmitted or controlled although, among medical writers, clerical physicians and the Paracelsians were the most explicit about the divine origins of plague.[62]

Before the 1625 plague reached Cambridge, Samuel Ward was concerned that the nation should repent, 'desiring the Lord to mitigate this grievous Judgment which hath seized our Mother-City, and from thence is diffused to many other Towns in the Land', but he reassured correspondents that he was 'careful that the Letter be conveyed by Persons safe from all Infection'. Speedy repentance could ward off the outbreak of plague or promptly banish it, as Joseph Hall told the King in a 1628 sermon and Edward Burghall noted in Cheshire in 1631, 'where were many public fasts kept, for the turning away of God's hand'. During an outbreak in Cambridge during the spring of 1630, Ward wrote that it had been brought by a soldier dismissed from the Swedish army. The students had been sent home and the magistrates were taking appropriate measures, although the burden of supporting the sick and the poor was becoming heavy. As in 1625, Ward's interest in practical measures did not conflict with his desire for public humiliation: 'I pray God we may be sensible of our Sins, and his heavy Hand, and may by serious Repentance meet him, that so he may forgive our Sins, and heal our Town and Land.'[63]

The clergy and magistrates were expected to stay at their posts in time of plague, for the good of the community, although they were not expected to visit the bedside of plague victims.[64] Others might reasonably flee the contagion, however, since God required Christians to use means to avoid disease and 'the chiefest meanes to preuent the plague is to auoide the place infected'. However, those who fled without leaving anything for the abandoned poor or who put their trust in flight rather than in God, would be justly punished if they were mistreated by 'sordid

Rusticks'.[65] In general, the authorities experienced little conflict between the duty of public humiliation and the need to avoid spreading the disease. The Mayor and Corporation of Norwich wrote to the Bishop during the plague of 1603, requesting a day of fasting and prayer, but this was refused in view of the behaviour of 'the unruly multitude' and 'the danger of infeccion'. The rest of the diocese was instructed to pray on behalf of the towns.[66] It was not respectable among English Protestants to suggest that appropriate measures should not be taken or that God would only strike the ungodly during an epidemic. A puritan weaver in Norwich wrote a bitterly critical invective to a negligent curate after he had preached a funeral sermon which suggested that only the wicked died of plague: 'Doe yow thinke that they are greter sinners then the rest that are not yet touched?'[67]

Plague and other contagious or infectious diseases supplied an ample repertoire of metaphors for sin, popery and atheism as ailments of the individual and the commonwealth, to be remedied by Christ's spiritual physic.[68] The English Church should separate itself from 'Churches *mortally sicke* of *heresie*, or *idolatry*, as it were of a *contagious plague* or *leprosie*'. England might be fortunate that its cold climate did not encourage the hot frenzies of Continental heresy but there were plenty of 'cold Epilepsies, and dead Apoplexies and slumbering lethargies' among lukewarm Christians.[69] Both medical practitioners and clergy made frequent reference to Christ or God the Father as the good physician.[70] Dedicating her translation of Calvin's sermons on Hezekiah to the Dowager Duchess of Suffolk, Anne Locke drew an extended comparison between medicine and spiritual physic: 'This receipte God the heauenly Physitian hath taught, his most excellẽt Apothecarie master Iohn Caluine hath compounded, & I your graces most bounden & humble [servant] haue put into an Englishe box, & do present vnto you.' The papists, with their works of supererogation, she compared to a wicked practitioner who destroyed the patient 'by faulte of ill diet and throughe poisonous potions'.[71] Christ's word was physic freely dispensed at the parish church. Christ had taken sinful flesh so that 'he was as sicke among the sicke, that hee might be a most familiar and acceptable Physician'. Christ was no papist quack but 'good at all kind of diseases, and will not endure the reproach of disabilitie to cure any'.[72]

Godly ministers were also described in medical terms, despite some initial reluctance lest this comparison should detract from the absolute power ascribed to God. In the cure of hardheartedness, for example, Robert Harris insisted that 'It is proper to God to doe this, it is his sole worke. To him therefore must you haue recourse, for recouery, apply your selues diligently to the vse of all his meanes, for all his medicines are curing.' Nevertheless, the preacher was charged with the application of the medicine.[73] Thomas Taylor insisted that the sufferer must go to

109

Christ, 'the onely Physician of this Leprosie of sinne', but he dedicated his *Davids Learning* to Lord Knollys for having favoured him as 'a soules Physician'.[74] 'The Minister is the Surgeon of mens soules, who must heale wounds, but not make them, except for cures sake.' If their own spiritual physic failed in the task of subduing bodily corruption, the godly should turn to 'Gods skilfull Surgeons to be handled'.[75] As with bodily physic, the application of spiritual remedies required a knowledge of the causes of disease, the appropriate season and the fittest medicine.[76] The medicine that they distributed came from God and was no more affected by their own spiritual condition than was the physician's prescription by the character of his messenger.[77]

In part, such images reflect the commonplaces of the day. The writers of pious letters and moral tracts used comparisions with medicine because the eagerness of the patient for the wise practitioner's advice, his willingness to reveal his symptoms frankly, and his respect for the directions, however unwelcome, were familiar to their readers: 'The use of *trust* is best known in the worst times, for naturally in sickness we trust to the Physitian.' The trouble was that patients, like sinners, could not be persuaded to follow the rules of health thereafter.[78] Nevertheless, the repetition of such analogies influenced the very relationship they described. The intention of the writers was to encourage their readers to behave in ways that might seem melancholy or puritanical by reminding them that they willingly did unpleasant things for the good of their bodies but, in doing so, they created a stronger image of the ideal practitioner than medical writers had ever produced. Godly practitioners reinforced the image by stressing their role as God's instruments when they gave thanks for the recovery of patients.[79]

The comparisons made by religious writers inevitably tended to enhance the authority of medical practitioners, at least ideally, since the earthly physician was assumed to be better able to judge what would promote his patient's bodily welfare just as the divine physician knew better than the sinner: 'that befalleth vs which is obserued in vnskilfull Patients, wee misse the marke often when wee coniecture the grounds of our owne griefes.' Like doctors, God carefully suited his treatment to the constitution of his patients: 'A physician loves all his patients alike, but he does not minister sharp potions alike to all; but out of the same love there is a different carriage of the same, according to the exigent of the party. So doth the wise God.' Like the ideal Galenic physician, God prescribed his medicines carefully, so that nothing in the mixture would 'exceed the quantity any whit which is fit for his patients'.[80] Faith, repentance and confession were the necessary posture towards God although these were not the cause of salvation. So too the physician 'would haue his patients haue a good perswasion of him, be thankfull to him, be sorrie if they rudely provoke him', although these were not the cause of the cure.[81]

The providential doctrine of vocation required Christian medical practitioners to take their work very seriously, as part of their religious duty rather than as a means to earn their living, a point stressed in a study guide for surgeons. Unqualified competitors were execrated, since they were straying from their God-given callings, 'having neither conscience, learning, art, nor Feare of God; nor never had good Tutor to instruct them'.[82] Impatience and the failure to keep within one's calling were intimately linked with the urge 'to vse any indirect & vnlawful meanes to come out' from under affliction. Since it was sent by God, one should be in no hurry to escape affliction, especially if evil means were involved.[83] Few things vexed the godly more than the tendency of the sick to consult cunning folk, 'that vile and damnable practise of many, who for the curing of themselues . . . will presently forsake God, & haue recourse vnto the diuell by his seruants the Witches'. Unlike the means employed by regular practitioners, those used by cunning folk had been forbidden by God. The sick were warned that they should 'bee sure that God will neuer giue a blessing by those means which he hath accursed'. Since affliction was intended to be profitable there could be no excuse for employing illicit means, especially since they derived their efficacy from the Devil. Even if God allowed such means to succeed, it was only as a curse on those who had failed to repent. The refusal to seek reconciliation with God before the removal of afflictions, which led to the use of forbidden means, could only increase God's anger.[84]

No medical texts in this period can have had a readership as wide as that of some of the moral tracts cited above. Lewis Bayly's *Practice of Piety*, for example, went through scores of editions. Such books were to be found as heirlooms in the humblest households. John Bunyan's first wife, for example, brought to their marriage in 1649 the works of Dent and Bayly as her only dowry.[85] Although it is beyond the scope of this essay to assess the extent to which the prescribed ideals were fully internalized, and by what proportion of the population, it is clear that they were available to a great many English men and women. The early reformers had felt the need to capture the hearts and minds of a populace little acquainted with Protestant theology. Their successors, marginalized by the state's support for an anti-puritan campaign that increasingly opposed even mainstream Calvinism, wrote a flood of works of popular piety to counter the influence of the bishops. The failure of the formalist clergy to address the question of private piety until after their setbacks of the 1640s, concentrating as they did on the public rituals of the Church, meant that Calvinist moral theology dominated the field. Even those who supported the bishops had no other religious source for their code of conduct.[86]

111

The Calvinist view of suffering as medicinal, when visited upon the elect, was in marked contrast to the sacramentalism of English formalists, such as Hooker, and Catholic writers who described the sacrament of Holy Communion as God's medicine, curing corruption in body and soul.[87] Although some early reformers had described baptism in medicinal terms, they stressed that the real medicine was God's offering of the remission of sins. Baptism was 'as it were a consortatiue, vsed to be gyuen vnto the syk after purgations'.[88] English Catholics were perhaps too concerned to ensure the survival of their rituals to develop a providentialism like that of the Jesuits, who insisted on God as 'the author of all the euils of punishment and affliction' but who took all necessary measures to control disease.[89] Jesuits do not seem to have attempted to inculcate such attitudes in the laity, however, unlike the Jansenist clergy of Northern France and the Low Countries, who benefited from their creative interaction with Dutch Calvinism.[90]

The providential view of medicine adopted by English Calvinists was not unique among early modern Christians but it was unusually well developed. The afflictive hand of God, although it was widely rejected in favour of a more benevolent view of the deity during the eighteenth century, did provide believers with an explanation for the most distressing of personal disasters. It also provided an active role for them in seeking their own cure through prayer and repentance, while providing a crucial role for regular medical practitioners. However stern and demanding a creed it might have been, Calvinism invested the whole of life with religious meaning.

Rejecting the miraculous efficacy of the sacraments and relics, Calvinists saw God as operating almost exclusively through second causes, a view that was very favourable to the advance of medical knowledge and the medical professions. All regular practitioners might lawfully take pride in the dignity of their calling. The moral approval of godly practitioners, and the constraints placed on them, helped to justify campaigns against irregular competitors by freeing medical men from the humanist accusation that they were only concerned to line their own pockets. Although Providentialism was significantly eroded after 1660, when English Calvinism went into its terminal decline, many of the associated moral attitudes survived among non-conformists and pious Anglicans, forming an important foundation for medical ethics.

Notes

I am grateful for the comments on this essay at seminars in Oxford and Rotterdam early in 1992. All the works cited were published in London, unless otherwise specified, and most of their authors belonged in the

Calvinist mainstream of English Protestantism. No attempt will be made to distinguish between tendencies.

1. For different views and further examples, see A. Wear, 'Puritan perceptions of illness in seventeenth-century England', in *Patients and Practitioners*, ed. R. Porter (Cambridge, 1985), 55–99; D. Evenden-Nagy, *Popular Medicine in Seventeenth-Century England* (Bowling Green, 1988), 35–42.

2. John Calvin, *Institutes*, ed. J.T. McNeill, 2 vols. (London, 1961), see I, 16, 1 and 4; see also Calvin, *Treatises against the Anabaptists and against the Libertines*, transl. B.W. Farley (Grand Rapids, 1982), 242–8. For English Calvinism, see also R.T. Kendall, *Calvin and English Calvinism to 1649* (Oxford, 1979).

3. E. Elton, *An Exposition of the Epistle of Saint Paul to the Colossians* (1620), 71; J. Hall, *Contemplations upon the Principal Passages in the Holy Story* (1634), 834, 995; S. Crooke, *TA DIAPHERONTA, or Divine Characters* (1658), 24 [posthumous work, probably written in the 1630s]; T. Pierson, 'The Churches Exercise under Affliction', in *Excellent Encoragements against Afflictions* (1647), 94 [Pierson died in 1633].

4. R. Sibbes, *The Sovles Conflict with it selfe* (1635), 351; L. Bayly, *The Practise of Piety*, 3rd edn (1613), 792–3, 818; T. Granger, *A Looking-Glasse for Christians* (1620), sig.C3r; *idem, A Familiar Exposition . . . on Ecclesiastes* (1621), 73; J. Hall, *Holy Obseruations* (1607), 26; J. Yates, *A Modell of Diuinitie*, 2nd edn (1623), 164–75.

5. Sibbes, *The Sovles Conflict*, 367; A. Dent, *The Plaine Mans Path-way to Heauen* (1601), 111.

6. F. Bunny, *A Gvide vnto Godlinesse* (1617), 12.

7. Calvin, *Against the Libertines*, 320–3; T. Bright, *A Treatise wherein is decleared the Sufficiencie of English Medicines* (1580), 9–10, 33–5; R. Walker, *A Learned and Profitable Treatise of Gods Prouidence* (1608), 46–7, 55; J. Woolton, *The Christian Manuell, or, Of the life and maners of true Christians* (1576), sig.H6v–7r; T. Cogan, *The Haven of Health* (1584), sig.¶3r, 270. Medicine was frequently likened to the outward 'means' of religion such as preaching, the sacraments and prayer: H. Mason, *Hearing and Doing* (1635), 42, 162–3, 388, 402–3; A. Maxey, *The Sermon Preached before the King at Whitehall* (1605), sig.B3v–4r; L. Wright, *A Display of Dvty* (1614), f.19.

8. G. Hakewill, *An Apologie of the Power and Providence of God* (1627), 226–31; cf. R. Sibbes, *The Retvrning Backslider* (1639), 143; *idem, A Learned Commentary . . . upon the first Chapter of the second Epistle of S.Paul to the Corinthians* (1655), 129 [Sibbes died in 1635].

9. Sibbes, *The Retvrning Backslider*, 138–9; P. Baynes, *Holy Soliloqvies: or, a holy helper in God's building*, 2nd edn (1618), 14; *idem, A Caveat for Cold Christians* (1618), 21; T. Taylor, *Davids Learning* (1620), sig.¶2r–4r, 112; W. Whateley, *The New Birth* (1618), 129–30; *idem, Mortification* (1623), 153. For a discussion of preventative medicine, see A. Wear, 'Making sense of health and the environment in early modern England', in *Medicine in Society*, ed. A. Wear (Cambridge, 1992), 119–47.

10. J. Norden, *A Progresse of Pietie* (1596), f.81r.

11. T. Taylor, *Circumspect Walking* (1631), 164; Cogan, *Haven of Health*, sig.¶2v.

12. R. Bolton, *The Saints Soule-exalting Hvmiliation; or Soule-fatting fasting* (1634), 9–10; A.L[ocke], transl., *Sermons of John Calvin, upon the songe that Ezechias made after he had bene sicke, and afflicted by the hand of God* (1560), sig.A7r; Woolton, *Christian Manuell*, sig.M2v–3r; Bayly, *Practise of Piety*,

624-9; P. Baynes, *Christian Letters* (1620), sigs.A3R, O4r; Baynes, *Caveat*, 20; *Two Elizabethan Puritan Diaries by Richard Rogers and Samuel Ward*, ed. M.M. Knappen (Chicago, 1933), 104, 108-11, 113-14, 117-18; H. Hall, *A Sermon Preacht to his Maiestie on the Sunday before the Fast* (1628), 92-5; S. Crooke, *The Gvide vnto Trve Blessednesse* (1613), 175; H. Mason, *Christian Humiliation* (1625), 15, 156-63.

13. J. Hooper, *A Declaration of the Ten Holy Comaundementes of Allmyghthye God* (Zurich, 1548), 43-4; *ibid.* (1550), f.18r-v; S. Crooke, *Death Subdued, or, the Death of Death* (1619), sig.F11v; R. Sibbes, *2 Corinthians 1*, 202-3; Taylor, *Davids Learning*, 78; *Two Elizabethan Puritan Diaries*, 104-5.

14. R. Sibbes, 'Ivdgements Reason', in *The Saint's Cordials* (1629), 38, 59; P. Baynes, *A Commentarie vpon the First and Second Chapters of Saint Paul to the Colossians* (1634), 294-5; cf. J. Sym, *Lifes Preservative against Self-Killing* (1637), 12-16.

15. W. Attersoll, *A Commentarie vpon the Epistle of Saint Paule to Philemon* (1612), 12-13, 19; Dent, *Plaine Mans Path-way*, 134; Bayly, *Practice of Pietie*, 829, 840; Elton, *Colossians*, 92-3.

16. Baynes, *Christian Letters*, sigs.A1r, N12v; R. Sibbes, *A Learned Commentary . . . upon the fourth Chapter of the second Epistle of Saint Paul to the Corinthians* (1656), 139, 156, 193; W. Struther, *Christian Observations and Resolutions* (1629), 238-41; cf. R. Sibbes, *Divine Meditations and Holy Contemplations* (1638), 155. Contrast the writings of Huguenots: J. Taffin, *Of the Marks of the Children of God*, transl. A. Prowse (1590), ff.56r-74v, 78v, 82r; P.du Moulin, *A Preparation to Svffer for the Gospell of Iesus Christ*, transl. A. Darcie (1623).

17. Dent, *Plaine Mans Path-way*, 125; Sibbes, 'Ivdgements Reason', 38, 59; Bayly, *Practise of Pietie*, 815-16, 818, 832-7; H. Mason, *The Cvre of Cares* (1627), 36-9.

18. Baynes, *Christian Letters*, sig.A2r, C11v, P4v-5r; Baynes, *Colossians*, 28; O. Sedgwick, *Christs Counsell to his languishing Church of Sardis* (1640), 151.

19. J. Hall, *Meditations and Vowes, Diuine and Morall* (1605), 46-7.

20. R. Parr, *The Life of . . . James Usher, Late Lord Arch-Bishop of Armagh* (1686), 90.

21. Woolton, *Christian Manuell*, sigs.K2v-4v.

22. E. Burghall, 'Providence Improved', in D. King (ed.), *The History of Cheshire* (Chester, 1778), vol. 2, 895-7.

23. Burghall, 'Providence Improved', 946; W. Clowes, *A Right Frutefull Treatise for the Artificial Treatment of the Struma* (1602), sigs.H2v-I3r.

24. Sibbes, *2 Corinthians 1*, 129; *idem*, 'Of the Providence of God', in *Works*, ed. A.B. Grosart, 7 vols. (Edinburgh, 1862-4), 5: 41-2; Pierson, 'The Churches Exercise', 39; Elton, *Colossians*, 70.

25. Baynes, *Christian Letters*, sigs.A1v-2r, A7r, D2r, M10r-v, N3r; *idem, A Helpe to Trve Happinesse* (1618), 243; Walker, *Gods Prouidence*, 192; J. Northbrooke, *A Treatise wherein Dicing, Dauncing, Vaine playes or Enterluds are reproued* (1577?), sig.A2v; Sibbes, 'Ivdgements Reason', 38; *idem*, 'Of the Providence of God', 44; Baynes, *Holy Soliloqvies*, 28, 87; Bolton, *Soule-exalting Hvmiliation*, 2, 36; Bayly, *Practise of Pietie*, 824; H. Scudder, *The Christians Daily Walke* (1627), pt.1, 191.

26. Attersoll, *Philemon*, 207.

27. Sibbes, 'Ivdgements Reason', 38; cf. *idem*, *Divine Meditations*, 130.

28. T. Basille [i.e. Thomas Becon], *The Righte Pathwaye vnto Prayer* (1543) f.48r-v; A. Wheathill, *A Handfull of Holesome (though homelie) Herbs . . .*

(1584), ff.43v–45r; [T. Wallis] *The Pathway to Please God* [1617], sigs.E7v–F2v; Bayly, *Practise of Pietie*, 792–809, 815–42; Norden, *Progresse of Pietie*, ff.70v–74r, 95r–v. Catholic prayers for the use of the sick, by contrast, tended to consist of the rehearsal of the articles of faith: *A Manvall of Godly Prayers* [1616], 450–4. There was some nostalgia for such devotions among English formalists: W. Crashaw, *Manvale Catholicorum: A Manuall for True Catholics* (1611), 86–102.

29. e.g. R.W., *A Castle for the Soule, Conteining many godly Prayers, and diuine Meditations* (1578), sigs.E8v–Flv, F4v–7v.

30. J. Mason, *The Anotomie of Sorcerie* (1612), 16–19, 37–8, 69–70; Scudder, *The Christians Daily Walke*, pt.2, 4–8.

31. P. Baynes, *A Commentarie vpon the First Chapter of the Epistle of Saint Paul, written to the Ephesians* (1618), 24, 121.

32. M. MacDonald, *Witchcraft and Hysteria in Elizabethan England* (1990), 6.

33. *The Diary of Lady Margaret Hoby, 1599–1605*, ed. D.M. Meads (1930), 220.

34. J. Turner, *Choice Experiences of the kind dealings of God* (1653), 1.

35. Baynes, *Christian Letters*, sig.Flv, F6r; *idem*, 'Lectvres Preached Vpon these Texts of Scripture', bound with *Colossians*, 207.

36. Crooke, *Death Subdued*, sig.Clv; Harris, *Way to True Happinesse*, 202, 208; J. Bentham, *The Saints Societie* (1636), 170–1; Smith, *Christs Preparation*, 23.

37. M. Day, *Comfortable Considerations* (1621), 1–3; Sibbes, *2 Corinthians 1*, 136; cf. Baynes, *Christian Letters*, sig.G7r; Bayly, *Practise of Pietie*, 909–10. For the English deathbed, see *Death, Ritual and Bereavement*, ed. R. Houlbrooke (1989).

38. Becon, *Pathway vnto Prayer*, f.99v. For the humanist critique, see S. Brant, *The Shyp of Folys of the Worlde*, transl. A. Barclay (1509), sigs.t5r–vlv; T. More, *Epigrammata* (Basel, 1518), 32, 43, 47, 70, 92, 99; N.G. Siraisi, 'Medicine, physiology and anatomy in early sixteenth-century critiques of the arts and sciences', in *New Perspectives on Renaissance Thought*, ed. J. Henry and S. Hutton (1990), 214–29.

39. J. Robinson, *Observations Divine and Morall* (n.p., 1625), 174; cf. E. Philips, *Certaine Godly and Learned Sermons*, ed. H. Yelverton (1605), 194.

40. Woolton, *Christian Manuell*, sigs.H6v–7r; T.W[alkington]., *The Optick Glasse of Hvmors* (1607), f.22.

41. Sibbes, *The Soules Conflict*, 429–30.

42. Taylor, *Circumspect Walking*, 162, 168–9.

43. Hall, *Holy Obseruations*, 30; Walkington, *Optick Glasse*, ff.53–5.

44. Baynes, *Christian Letters*, sig.D5r; Dent, *Plaine Mans Path-way*, 119. More autonomous efficacy was sometimes ascribed to medicine than to the sacraments or the Word of God: Elton, *Colossians*, 190; Baynes, *Trve Happinesse*, 346–7.

45. Sibbes, 'The Life of Faith', in *The Saint's Cordials*, 426; cf. Woolton, *Christian Manuell*, sig.H6r–v; Bayly, *Practise of Pietie*, 816–17, 819; P. Baynes, *The Christians Garment* (1618), 14–16; Sibbes, *The Soules Conflict*, 501–2; *idem*, 'Of the Providence of God', 41; Hall, *Contemplations*, 1188, 1294–9; *idem*, *Meditations and Vowes*, 81; S. Wastell, *A Trve Christians Daily Delight* (1623), 53.

46. Sibbes, 'Of the Providence of God', 43–4.

47. Bolton, *Soule-exalting Hvmiliation*, 32–5.

48. Bayly, *Practise of Pietie*, 817, 819.

49. *The Diary of Bulstrode Whitelocke, 1605–1675*, ed. R. Spalding (Oxford, 1990), 44, 45–6, 53, 80, 88–9.

50. Baynes, *Christian Letters*, sig.F2r.

51. S. Clarke, *The Marrow of Ecclesiastical Historie* (1650), 239, 447, 491.

52. R. Bernard, *A Weekes Work* (1640?), 19–20; *Two Elizabethan Diaries*, 104–5, 114; Crooke, *Death Subdued*, sig.B3r–v; Smith, *Christs Preparation*, 5–7.

53. S. Clarke, *The Lives of Two and Twenty English Divines* (1660), 140–1.

54. [R. Bolton] *Mr Boltons Last and Learned Worke of the Foure last Things* (1633), sig.C4r; cf. *Two Elizabethan Diaries*, 130.

55. W. Miller, *A Sermon Preached at the Fvnerall of the Worshipfull Gilbert Davies, at Christow in Deuon* (1621), sig.D3v.

56. Sibbes, *The Sovles Conflict*, 355.

57. *Diary of Lady Margaret Hoby*, 68.

58. Philips, *Sermons*, 57; Walker, *Gods Prouidence*, 44.

59. T. Oldman, *Gods Rebuke in Taking from vs that worthy and honourable Gentleman Sir Edward Lewkenor Knight* (1619), 43–4; cf. Sym, *Lifes Preservative*, 16.

60. R. Eedes, *Six Learned and Godly Sermons* (1604), ff.37v–38r, 50r, 53r; Sibbes, 'Ivdgements Reason', 38; *idem, The Retvrning Backslider*, 196; Baynes, *Christian Letters*, sig.O11r; Pierson, 'The Churches Exercise', 39; Bunny, *Gvide vnto Godlinesse*, 73.

61. [T. Thayer] *An Excellent and best Approoued Treatise of the Plague* (1625), sig.A3v–4r, 1; Bayly, *Practise of Pietie*, 658–61; *Two Elizabethan Diaries*, 116, 122; Eedes, *Six Sermons*, f.49v.

62. T. Brasbridge, *The Poore Mans Iewel, that is to say a Treatise of the Pestilence* (1578), sigs.A5r–7r, B2v–5v; W. Boraston, *A Necessarie and Briefes Treatise of the Contagious Disease of the Pestilence* (1630), sig.A3r–6r, 1–2.

63. Ward to Ussher, 3 August 1625 and 25 May 1630, in Parr, *Life of Usher*, 330, 435; Hall, *Sermon Preacht to his Maiestie*, 96–7; Burghall, 'Providence Improved', 897. Formalists preaching plague sermons tended to emphasize faith rather than repentance: [T. Hastler] *An Antidote Against the Plague* (1625), 54.

64. Sibbes, 'Of the Providence of God', 52; J. Hall, *Works* (1625), 351.

65. Cogan, *Haven of Health*, 266; J. Taylor, *The Fearefull Summer*, 2nd edn (1636), sig.C1v–2r.

66. *The Registrum Vagum of Anthony Harrison*, pt.1 (Norfolk Record Society 32, 1963), 36–8.

67. *Registrum Vagum of Anthony Harrison*, 163–6.

68. A major source for this imagery was the work of the cleric and physician William Turner, *A Newe Booke of Spirituall Physik for dyuerse diseases of the nobilitie and gentlemen of Englande* (Basel, 1555); for further examples, see W. Turner, *A Preseruatiue, or Triacle, against the Poyson of Pelagius* [1557], sig.M1r; J. Pilkington, *Aggeus the Prophete declared* (1560), sig.B3v; Crooke, *Death Subdued*, sig.D11v; Walker, *Gods Prouidence*, sig.A7r; R. Bolton, *The Carnall Professor* (1634), 194–5; Bayly, *Practise of Pietie*, 867; Dent, *Plaine Mans Path-way*, 6, 34–7, 42, 220, 411; Elton, *Colossians*, 62, 290; W. Symonds, *A Heavenly Voyce* (1606), sigs.B2v, D3r; T. Taylor, *A Commentarie vpon the Epistle of S.Pauls written to Titus* (Cambridge, 1612), 156, 269; J. Welles, *The Sovles Progresse to the Celestiall Canaan* (1639), 64, 157.

69. Crooke, *Gvide vnto True Blessednesse*, 69; T. Sutton, *Englands Second Summons* (1615), 91–3, 99–100, 104, 106.

70. Catholics too could use such imagery, of course: R. Bellarmine, *A Most Learned and Pious Treatise . . . wherby our mindes may ascend to God*, transl. T.B. (Douai, 1616), 443–4, 495, 527–8.

71. Locke, *Sermons of John Calvin*, sig.A3r, A5r–v; cf. J. Woolton, *A Newe Anatomie of the Whole Man* (1576), f.29; Baynes, *True Happinesse*, 109–11.

72. Northbrooke, *Dicing, Dauncing, Vaine playes*, 3-4; T. Taylor, *The Kings Bath* (1620), 26; Sibbes, *The Soules Conflict*, 455; cf. Bayly, *Practise of Pietie*, 804, 818; Welles, *The Soules Progresse*, 86, 98, 152, 164, 169, 174, 177.

73. Harris, 'Of Newnesse of Heart', 50-1, 55; cf. R. Welsthed, *The Cure of a Hard-heart* (1630), 41-2, 72-3.

74. Taylor, *Davids Learning*, sig.¶3v-4r.

75. Taylor, *Titus*, 146, 268-9.

76. Harris, 'Of Newnesse of Heart', 59-61.

77. Taylor, *Davids Learning*, 171-2.

78. Sibbes, *The Soules Conflict*, 435; Becon, *Physike of the Soule*, sig.A2v; M. Day, *Meditations of Consolation* (1621), 47; Baynes, *Caveat*, 17; Becon, *Pathway vnto Prayer*, f.54v; Taylor, *Davids Learning*, 132; Taylor, 'Newnesse of Heart', 49-50; T. Hooker, *Foure Learned and Godly Treatises* (1638), 251, 276; Philips, *Sermons*, sig.A1r, 398, 419.

79. J. Hall, *The Courte of Vertu* (1564), ff.158v-161v.

80. Sibbes, 'Ivdgements Reason', 37; Walker, *Gods Prouidence*, 189, 205, 308-9; Baynes, *Christian Letters*, sigs.D3r, F4v, N11r-v; cf. Sibbes, *The Soules Conflict*, 471; Mason, *The Cure of Cares*, 37; *idem, Hearing and Doing*, 338.

81. Baynes, *Two Godly and Frvitfvll Treatises*, 215-6.

82. E. Edwards, *The Analysis of Chyrurgery* (1636), sig.A2v, 3; *idem, The Cvre of all Sorts of Fevers* (1638), sigs.A2r-4r; Hall, *The Courte of Vertu*, f.80v; Taylor, *Circumspect Walking*, 66-7.

83. Smith, *Christs Preparation*, 126; Elton, *Colossians*, 31; Taylor, *Circumspect Walking*, 77, 140-1.

84. Walker, *Gods Prouidence*, 239, 332-7; Bayly, *Practise of Pietie*, 816; Mason, *Anatomie of Sorcerie*, 50-4, 69-70; Elton, *Colossians*, 175; Pierson, 'The Churches Exercise', 36, 44; J. Yates, *Gods Arraignement of Hypocrites* (Cambridge, 1615), 192-7; S. Clark, 'Protestant demonology: sin, superstition and society (c.1520-c.1630)', in *Early Modern European Witchcraft*, ed. B. Ankarloo and G. Henningsen (Oxford, 1990), 45-81.

85. J. Bunyan, *Grace Abounding to the Chief of Sinners*, ed. R. Sharrock (Oxford, 1962), 8.

86. The Calvinist theology of affliction was accepted as orthodox by formalists such as George Herbert: T.G. Sherwood, *Herbert's Prayerful Art* (Toronto, 1989), 100-20.

87. F. Arias SJ, *The Litle Memorial, Concerning the Good and Frvitfvll Vse of the Sacraments* (Rouen, 1602), 8.

88. Turner, *Poyson of Pelagius*, sig.L4r.

89. Arias, *The Litle Memorial*, 26; A.L. Martin, *The Jesuit Mind: the Mentality of an Elite in Early Modern France* (Ithaca, 1988), 127-41, 153-71.

90. Marc Wingens of Erasmus University, Rotterdam, is currently working on Dutch Catholic attitudes towards healing and pilgrimages.

6

Physicians and the Inquisition in sixteenth-century Venice

The case of Girolamo Donzellini

Richard Palmer

In sixteenth and seventeenth century Italy, a much favoured metaphor described heresy as a plague. Heresy might be spread by personal contact. The Protestant physician Guglielmo Gratarolo was thus described in 1551 as a plague on the faith wherever he went.[1] Equally heresy might be spread through the medium of infected books. In 1614, for instance, Cardinal Bellarmine spoke of a plague of books, spawned above all from the presses of Frankfurt.[2] Just as the Italian Health Boards strove to control plague, so the Inquisition sought to stamp out heresy within Italy, and to prevent it being imported from across the Alps.

In the Republic of Venice an important step towards the repression of heresy was taken in 1547, when the Venetian government appointed a new magistracy of *Tre Savii sopra Eresia*. These were three laymen, who were to join the Inquisitor, the Patriarch of Venice and the papal nuncio to form the tribunal of the Holy Office of the Inquisition.[3] An increasing volume of trials from this time onwards testifies to the burgeoning activity of the tribunal in investigation and sentencing, and in the seizure of books. In 1557 the physician Agostino Gadaldin spoke of a time ten or twelve years earlier when almost everyone was discussing questions of faith and when 'suspect books' were freely available. He, too, had read works by Luther and Melanchthon, but, he implied, that time had passed, and in a voluntary appearance before the Holy Office he recanted eleven reformed beliefs.[4] The change of mood as the Counter-Reformation progressed was felt throughout Italy, and there were many, including the natural historian Ulisse Aldrovandi and the anatomist Gabrielle Falloppio, who were suspected or convicted of heresy in the 1540s, but who lived regular Catholic lives thereafter.[5]

The sixteenth century records of the Venetian Inquisition document the trials of a substantial number of physicians, including the medical and alchemical author Guglielmo Gratarolo, the Paduan anatomist Niccolò Buccella, the Paduan professors Bernardino Tomitano and Fabio Nifo, and doctors practising in Venice such as Agostino Gadaldin, Teofilo

118

Panarelli, Ludovico Abbioso, Girolamo Donzellini and Pier Paolo Malvezzi.[6] Others, such as Giuseppe Moscardo and Giovanni Battista Peranda, fled before a case could be formed.[7] Others still, such as Decio Bellebuono, were investigated at length to assess the reliability of their evidence in trials not their own.[8] Many more physicians, both in Venice and elsewhere, were implicated during trial proceedings. Gadaldin, for instance, named as his former co-religionist Giovanni Battista Susio from Mirandola,[9] while the Ferrarese humanist Nascimbene Nascimbene implicated a whole group of physicians at Ferrara, including Marc' Antonio Florio, Francesco da Argenta Francesco Severi, (subsequently burned at Ferrara), and Pietro Giudici, who was later burned at Mantua.[10]

That doctors were strongly represented in reformed circles in Italy, for instance in Milan, has sometimes been a matter for comment.[11] The Venetian evidence points to the same conclusion, and it would not be difficult to name fifty or more sixteenth century Italian physicians associated in various degrees with non-Catholic beliefs. Their convictions, however, were by no means homogeneous, ranging from common tenets of Lutheranism concerning purgatory or prayers to the saints to the strict Calvinism of Gratarolo, the anabaptist beliefs of Buccella, or the more exotic opinions attributed to Malvezzi, who was accused of atheism and incest.[12]

A number of factors may have drawn Italian physicians towards the Reformation, and may explain the concern which they aroused in the Holy Office. Physicians were, for instance, likely to encounter Protestant views from an early age. In the sixteenth century the University of Padua was at the height of its fame as the leading centre of medical education in Europe.[13] Protestant students from northern Europe attended in large numbers, tolerated by the government of Venice which welcomed the influx of their foreign currency into the Paduan economy. Although Venetian policy towards the University was a source of constant friction between Venice and Rome, Venice was steadfast in protecting foreign students, provided that they lived quietly and without causing scandal.[14] Italian medical students were therefore likely to spend formative years alongside Protestants and sometimes formed long-lasting friendships. Teofilo Panarelli admitted that his life as a student at the University of Padua from 1551 onwards had revolved around religion. There he was able to borrow books from his fellow students, including a copy of Calvin's *Institutes* brought from Germany.[15] So, too, in 1576, when Fabio Nifo had knotted together the sheets from his bed and escaped from imprisonment in the Bishop's palace at Padua, it was the German students who came to his aid, providing the funds which enabled him to make good his flight to Vienna.[16]

Physicians emerged from their long education, in philosophy as well as medicine, as men of learning, accustomed to academic debate. Many became prominent not only in medicine, but in fields such as botany, zoology, mathematics and astronomy, and they were used to an international exchange of ideas and information. Above all they were bookmen: Venice was one of the greatest centres of medical publishing, and many doctors were active as authors, editors, or simply as book collectors. Agostino Gadaldin, for instance, whose father was in the book trade, began his medical career working for the Giunta press on the Latin edition of the works of Galen (Venice, 1541–2). His love of books brought about his second encounter with the Inquisition in 1565, after he was found to possess a heterodox work in Hebrew, a unique surviving copy from an edition consigned to the flames.[17]

The Index of Prohibited Books came to have a general impact on men of learning after 1554, when a new type of index was introduced which banned not only individual titles, but the complete works of a range of Protestant authors, including books on medicine and the humanities. In protesting against the index of 1554, the Venetian booksellers pointed out that it banned the works of Conrad Gesner, including his zoological masterpiece *Historia animalium*, his popular textbook on medical distilling, *Thesaurus Evonymi*, and even his bibliography, *Bibliotheca universalis*. Other banned authors included Otto Brunfels, who had written medical works as well as the herbal which revolutionized botanical illustration, and Janus Cornarius, medical author and translator of Hippocrates and Galen.[18] The works of these three authors also appeared on the Tridentine Index of 1564, the first which was rigorously enforced in Venice. The three decades which followed were the period when the book trade was subject to maximum control, with pre-publication censorship, checks on imported books at customs houses, raids on bookshops, and a high level of prosecution.[19]

It was not, however, only as men of learning that physicians became a source of concern to the Inquisition. Physicians enjoyed a position of influence in society not only through their intellectual training but through intimate contact with their patients, whom they were free to visit privately at home day and night. That they attended patients on their deathbeds also gave them a role at a critical moment in the life of the soul. Hence the bull of Pius V of 1566, which required doctors to withhold treatment from any sick man who had not confessed to a priest within the space of three days.[20] In a case in 1571 a Venetian parish priest denounced doctors in general to the Inquisition, following the death of one of his parishioners without confession and communion.[21] The physician whose patient had died was Gian' Antonio Secco, and it is significant that in his book *De optimo medico* he had argued, in a Galenic tradition, that the doctor's role at the bedside was to inspire optimism, to banish anxiety and, when necessary, to promise recovery.[22] The physicians of Venice had no wish to remind their patients of mortality, and through their College they sought to resist the demands of the Inquisition.[23] The gravest source of danger, from the point of view of the Inquisition, was the Protestant physician. In 1572, for instance, Teofilo Panarelli confessed that at the deathbed of his fellow physician and co-religionist Giuseppe Moscardo he had encouraged his patient to die happily in the reformed faith, without confession or communion.[24]

The case of Teofilo Panarelli was particularly instructive for the Holy Office, since it demonstrated how the medical market place in Venice had been harnessed for the dissemination of reformed beliefs. Investigations in 1567 and 1568 revealed the existence of a full scale Protestant conventicle, in which Panarelli took a leading part. Evidence was given of regular meetings at the pharmacy at the sign of the *Do colombine*, at the German warehouse (*Fondaco dei Tedeschi*), and in gardens on St Giorgio and the Giudecca, where Panarelli read and interpreted the Psalms, the New Testament, the sermons of Ochino and the catechism of Calvin. Almost a dozen physicians were in some way involved in the case, either named as friends and co-religionists of Panarelli (including Francesco Pegolotto and Giovanni Gatta, both from Reggio, Giuseppe Moscardo and Ludovico Abbioso, the latter of whom was also tried and forced to recant), or as taking part with Panarelli in suspect conversations on religion, or, as the Holy Office seems to have believed, in providing free medicine to members of the group. Pharmacies had regularly been the setting for conversations on religion, especially those at the signs of the *Do colombine*, the *Sperone* and the *Elmo*. Not only had pharmacists been involved, but evidence was also given of the shop of a barber at the sign of the *Corona*, where a portrait on the wall proved to be that of Martin Luther. The case was treated with the utmost seriousness by the Holy Office. It was one of the few in the sixteenth century which were remitted to Rome, where Panarelli was hanged in 1572.[25]

For Italians sympathetic to the Reformation, the growing strength of the Holy Office posed urgent questions concerning flight, martyrdom, or the need for accommodation with Catholic religious practice. For physicians flight was often the solution, especially as the high reputation of Italian medicine readily found them employment outside Italy. Giulio Borgarucci, for instance, found a place in London at the court of Elizabeth, while Niccolò Buccella was but one of the Italian doctors at the Polish court.[26] Others considered flight, only to reject it. Ludovico Abbioso, for example, could not bring himself to abandon his mother in Venice.[27] For them the only options were to abjure or to conceal. The Nicodemite view that it was legitimate to conceal true faith in the face of persecution had its advocates, amongst them the physician Otto Brunfels, to whom the first formulation of the doctrine has been attributed.[28] Panarelli also took the view that it was necessary to go to mass and to confession as a pretence in order to escape death.[29]

The dilemma of the Italian Protestants is vividly illustrated in the life of the physician Girolamo Donzellini, since at various moments in his career he fled, abjured, and lived as a secret Protestant. It may be said, unfortunately, that he did not choose his options in the right order, and he was eventually executed in Venice as a relapsed heretic. Early in 1587 he was rowed out to sea at night and dropped overboard, the silent end which the Venetian government preferred to the spectacle of a public burning. The case of Donzellini is interesting not merely because of his reputation – for with at least twelve books to his credit he was one of the most distinguished defendants – but because it reveals attitudes which might motivate a physician to defy the Inquisition.[30]

The birth of Donzellini in the country town of Orzinuovi occurred only a few years after the beginning of the Reformation. He went to school in the provincial capital Brescia, before beginning an eight year association with the University of Padua. He graduated there in 1541, a fortnight before his contemporary John Caius, and he stayed on for a further year as a minor professor of medical theory.[31] His years at Padua corresponded with the period of enthusiasm for medical humanism which followed the publication of the Greek Galen in 1525. There he became a disciple of the luminary of that movement, Giovanni Battista da Monte. He emerged with a mastery of Greek, a profound knowledge of the literature of antiquity, and a commitment to medical progress through the recovery of Greek manuscripts, the emendation and editing of texts, and the production of elegant Latin translations. His earliest publications were a translation of the *De ptisana* of Galen, and editions of works by Da Monte.[32] He was nothing if not bookish, and already at Padua his library appears to have included Lutheran books.

After his graduation, Donzellini spent two years, 1543–4, in Rome, part of the time as doctor to Cardinal Durante. He also moved in Protestant circles, and it was after he was named to the Roman Inquisition in 1544 that he fled to Venice. He remained in Venice for the next nine years, practising medicine, mixing with Protestants at the house of the English ambassador Edmund Harvel, and helping in the clandestine distribution of Protestant literature.[33] He was in contact with Pietro Perna, an Italian Protestant exile who had settled as a bookseller and publisher in Basle and who specialized in sending prohibited books into Italy.[34] Donzellini helped at the Venetian end of his network, and several bales of books are known to have passed from Perna to Donzellini for distribution between 1550 and 1552, amongst them a Protestant work on the epistles of St Paul by Cornelio Donzellini, a brother of Girolamo.[35] This activity came to an end in 1553, when Donzellini was implicated in the case of a fellow humanist from Brescia, Vincenzo Maggi.[36] Summoned to appear before the Holy Office, Donzellini packed up his physician's gown and fled at midnight, first to the notoriously Protestant court at Ferrara of the

Duchess Renée of France, and eventually to Germany. Banished *in absentia* from the Republic of Venice, he spent the next six years in such towns as Nuremberg, where he enjoyed the friendship of the Camerarius family, Augsburg, where he used the Fugger Library, and Tübingen, where he stayed with Vergerio, formerly Bishop of Capodistria and one of the early leaders of the Reformation in Italy.[37] He also developed his contacts with Pietro Perna, who published his editions of the *Opuscula* of Da Monte and of the orations of Themistius.[38]

Despite such unmistakably Protestant associations, in 1560 Donzellini was able, with the help of the Emperor Ferdinand, to obtain a safe conduct to return to Venice, where he appeared voluntarily before the Inquisition. In a carefully prepared defence he admitted that he had begun to read prohibited books before his flight, especially the works of Erasmus, and that he may have spoken against abuses in the Church such as absenteeism, pluralism and simony. He denied, however, that he had ever held Protestant beliefs and argued that he had always lived as a Catholic, going to confession at the Frari, and receiving the sacraments in the parishes of St Benetto and St Lio. He had even tried to reconvert his brother Cornelio to the Catholic faith. As to his numerous contacts with heretics (including the physicians Agostino Gadaldin, Giovanni Battista Susio, Angelo Odoni and Matteo Fabri), this did not mean that he shared their opinions. He also claimed that there was nothing incriminating about his flight to Germany; it was only fear of prison and the ignominy of imprisonment for a man of his position which had brought it about. Impressed by the voluntary appearance of Donzellini, the tribunal appears to have accepted his statement. He was made to abjure only minor heresies: that it was legitimate to converse with heretics in person or by letter, to read prohibited books, and to criticize the authority of the Pope. He was given a mild sentence – confinement for a year in the Venetian monastery of Sts Giovanni e Paolo. Even this sentence was served only in part. By special concessions Donzellini was allowed trips to the Bresciano and to Verona to cultivate a rich uncle who wished to adopt him.[39]

Before the end of 1561, Donzellini was freed to begin a new life, this time in Verona. He was granted citizenship, married, and lived there for the next thirteen years, joining the College of Physicians and serving for a time as its Prior.[40] He also built up a substantial library of works on theology, philosophy, medicine and literature, which was even the subject of a poem published by the humanist Publio Francesco Spinola in 1563.[41]

Outwardly at least, Donzellini lived in Verona as a Catholic, confessing and taking communion, and enjoying the friendship of the Bishop, Agostino Valier.[42] It is probable, however, that he lived as a Nicodemite or secret Protestant. Despite his abjuration he continued to correspond with Protestants in Switzerland and Germany, including Theodor Zwinger in Basle and Joachim Camerarius in Nuremberg.[43] He also remained in contact with Perna, who, as the leading printer responsible for the Paracelsian revival, probably supplied the Paracelsian works which Donzellini owned in the 1560s, although as a humanist Donzellini despised Paracelsianism and later wrote a book against it.[44] Perna was certainly the publisher of the edition prepared by Donzellini of the commentary of Leonardo Giachini on Rhazes, which was published at Basle in 1564.[45]

A medical controversy brought this period of tranquillity to an end. Between 1570 and 1573 Donzellini published three polemical works against the Brescian physician Vincenzo Calzaveglia, two of them issued under the pseudonym Eudoxus Philalethes.[46] The subject was the use of the ancient remedy theriac in the treatment of an epidemic of pestilential fever which affected Brescia and northern Italy in 1570. In the course of the controversy Donzellini claimed to have the edge over his opponent through his long experience in Rome, Venice and Germany. Calzaveglia replied that the travels of Donzellini were no matter for pride, but the result of his enmity to the true religion.[47] In response Donzellini was driven to write a long autobiographical defence of his conduct in which he sought to put a favourable gloss on his sojourn in Germany, and to associate himself with exiles from the past such as Cicero and Aristotle.[48] This seems to have been too much for his opponent. There was an attempt on the life of Donzellini, although he escaped with a single wound,[49] and worse was to follow. The controversy, Donzellini wrote later to Joachim Camerarius, was the cause of great misfortune: in 1574 he was again denounced to the Inquisition.[50]

This time the Inquisition had in its hands damning evidence, including letters written by Donzellini to his father and others on the eve of his flight to Germany in 1553. To his father, for instance, he had written that he was being forced by the enemies of God into a position such that to remain in Italy he would have to renege on Christ and to say that the teaching which he brought from heaven was heresy. It was the holy truth which was being persecuted and defamed.[51] The Inquisition now had proof that Donzellini had lied throughout his previous trial in 1560. Demonstrating the value of archives, the records of those proceedings were dusted down and annotated throughout with telling marginalia. A search of Donzellini's study in Verona also revealed works by banned authors, such as the *Historia animalium* of Gesner, with the name of the author covered up with paper, and a book by Joachim Camerarius on anatomical nomenclature.[52]

Donzellini was therefore driven to alter his earlier defence. He now admitted that he had once held to the Augsburg Confession. He had not believed, for instance, in the intercession of saints, or the authority of the

Pope, and he had accepted communion in both kinds as a memorial and not a sacrifice. He claimed, all the same, that he had been reconverted to Catholicism whilst in Germany by reading the *Enchiridion* of Johann Eck and another work with the title *Concilio Coloniese*. His Protestantism was therefore in the past.[53] As a known perjuror, Donzellini was an appropriate candidate for torture, according to the strict rules followed by the Holy Office. However, a brief session of torture, on 12 April 1575, produced no new information, but only the words 'Oh Signori pity; Oh Jesus, Oh blessed Jesus, Oh Jesus I am dying . . . Oh Signori I am dead'.[54] At the end of a long trial which continued until the summer of 1575, Donzellini was sentenced to imprisonment for life. During the proceedings he had complained of his cell-mate, a clock-maker from Augsburg, whose charcoal fire, drunkenness and snoring at night were unbearable. By the end of the year he protested that the prison made him ill; the darkness blinded him, the damp made his teeth drop out, he was choked by catarrh at night and suffered vertigo by day. It was probably a relief when plague broke out in the prison in 1576, especially as it killed his jailer.[55] With tens of thousands dying in the city, Donzellini was let out in 1577 in order to tend the sick. His service, and the plague tract which he wrote in his cell without books at his disposal, won him support in government circles, and it was probably diplomatic pressure on Rome which brought his formal release later in the year.[56]

After these experiences Donzellini might well have settled for a quiet, or at least a cautious life. The penalty for a relapsed heretic was death, and he had before him the example of his friend the humanist poet Publio Spinola. Donzellini had secured him employment in Venice only to see him executed there for heresy in 1567.[57] Yet no sooner was Donzellini at liberty than he resumed his correspondence with Joachim Camerarius in Nuremberg, although he did take the precaution of signing his letters with his Greek pseudonym 'ο παρθενιος, and added a postscript in Greek, 'When you write have a thought for my life and do not put your name'.[58] Within a year Donzellini was again brought before the Inquisition. In March 1578 Nassimbene Nascimbene was allowed by the tribunal, on grounds of ill health, to move from his prison to confinement in the house of his friend Donzellini in the parish of Santa Maria Formosa. In the following July Nascimbene fled, and in consequence Donzellini was again subjected to a period of house arrest, which was to last for more than a year.[59] He was later to attribute his sentence to the providence of God, since he spent the time contentedly in his well-stocked library.[60] His mind was turning once again to the necessity for flight, and he looked to his friend the Imperial physician Crato von Craftheim to secure him a post at court. Crato had promised to do so not long before, but Donzellini had hesitated, pleading his old age, and by 1579 the opportunity was lost.[61]

Donzellini remained in Venice, still courting danger through his correspondence and contacts. In March 1583, for instance, he wrote to Theodor Zwinger in Basle, urging him to send a consignment of prohibited books, works which Donzellini had lost in his earlier misfortune. He required Johannes Rivius, *De admirabili consilio Dei in celando mysteris redemptionis humanae*, Paulus Ricius, *De coelesti agricultura*, Huldreich Zwingli, *De providentia Dei*, and Jodocus Willich, *De methodo informanda in omni artium genere*. The books were to be sent with the utmost caution, one by one, by means of students travelling to Italy. If this was not possible, then they could be sent safely if concealed in bales of cloth or other merchandise, but not amongst consignments of other books.[62] Two years later Donzellini requested the same titles by Zwingli and Willich from Joachim Camerarius in Nuremberg.[63]

Finally in 1587 a book sent to Donzellini from Frankfurt by Fridericus Sylbergius fell into the hands of the Inquisition. The author was Johannes Rivius, whose name was on the Index, and this time the fate of Donzellini was sealed. He managed to take flight from Venice to Padua and wrote urgently to Camerarius that he was making for Nuremberg, where he hoped to practise medicine or find a teaching post. He added, with great *sang froid*, that he would have set off already but for the inclement weather.[64] The delay was probably fatal, for he was arrested and taken back to Venice, where, as a relapsed heretic, he was soon afterwards put to death by drowning.[65]

In placing the fate of Donzellini in context, it has to be borne in mind that it was exceptional. Only fourteen Inquisition trials in sixteenth century Venice terminated with a death sentence, although a few more executions (including that of Teofilo Panarelli) were carried out in Rome when cases were remitted there.[66] The fate of Donzellini owed a great deal to his persistence as an offender and to the recklessness of his conduct. In another trial a witness recalled a conversation overheard in the Valgrisi bookshop, in which Donzellini boasted of how he held on to prohibited books despite the Inquisition.[67]

Why did Donzellini persist in taking risks? The answer may lie in part in his theological outlook, which stressed the providence of God. This world, he wrote to Camerarius, was but a game or a fable; a better and heavenly life was to come. In the meantime God who had saved him on other occasions from the mouth of hell was able to keep him safe.[68] He frequently urged his correspondents to bear with equanimity the death of a loved one, since it was the will of God. Camerarius, who had lost his wife, was even told that he would soon find another, since there were plenty of available women.[69]

In addition, the correspondence of Donzellini shows how his intense commitment to humanistic medicine drew him into dangerous waters. He was captivated by his role as an intermediary between the medical humanists of Germany and Switzerland, primarily Crato, Camerarius and Zwinger, and the intellectual life of northern Italy. He was also fascinated by books, publishing and the book trade to the point of bibliomania. In urging Zwinger to send him prohibited books he wrote that he knew these works were condemned, but he could not be without them and his request to Zwinger was insistent (*vehementer etiam atque etiam rogo ut tuo commodo illos mihi compares*).[70] His letters were full of news of the latest medical books passing through the Venetian press, of the possibility of publishing Greek and Latin manuscripts from the Vatican Library, and of the latest progress towards the recovery of theriac, the wonder drug of antiquity. He sent across the Alps not merely letters but parcels of books, jars of theriac, seeds, and even hippo tooth for the cure of haemorrhoids. He was constantly using his contacts, profiting from his friendship with Crato to secure an Imperial privilege for the edition of the letters and *consilia* of Vettor Trincavella,[71] or trying to find German buyers for the library and Greek manuscripts of Sebastiano Erizzo.[72] He loved to move pieces around the board, putting Mercuriale and Zwinger into transalpine cooperation for editorial work on Hippocrates,[73] helping the works of Francesco Patrizi into print,[74] and urging Zwinger into cooperation with Pietro Perna in what was to be one of the most significant partnerships in medical publishing of the century.[75] For Vergerio, exiled in Tübingen, Donzellini was a man 'who knows what is going on in Italy'; he was useful.[76] Crato resolved in 1577 not to write to him any more, since he was too much at risk, but it was a resolution which Crato could not bring himself to keep.[77]

It may also be argued that the humanism and philosophy of Donzellini were important influences on his religious views. It is noteworthy that in his trial he named the Augsburg Confession, drawn up by his fellow humanist Melanchthon, as the statement of faith to which he had adhered. In the preface to his edition of the orations of Themistius he traced the course of wisdom from the beginnings of the world to his own day, a survey which included the Egypt of Hermes Trismegistus. He stressed the continuity of doctrine over time, and the reconciliation of differences. The Renaissance played a fundamental part in his scheme of things. Humanism, he wrote, spreading from Italy to north of the Alps, had brought the revival not only of arts and science but of theology, leading to a purer knowledge of the word of God. The continuity of doctrine in his view was expressed through men of different confessions, such as Vives in Spain, Budé in France, More and Pole in England, Erasmus, Melanchthon, Gesner and Camerarius in Germany.[78] It was, arguably, an outlook which allowed him to hold Protestant beliefs while observing Catholic religious practices in Italy. This synthetic approach was also expressed in the preface which Donzellini wrote for his edition of the commentary of Leonardo Giachini on Rhazes,[79] and he developed it still further in his last work with its strongly autobiographical theme of how to bear misfortune and to suppress anger.[80] Here he brought together philosophy, theology and medicine, blurring the roles of doctor, moral philosopher and priest. He emphasised, for instance, that passions such as anger, hatred, jealousy, love, fear and grief might depend on bodily states. The physician was therefore not only the doctor of the body, but of the soul.[81] Medical humanism and its methods also seemed to offer a justification for reading prohibited books. At his trial in 1560 Donzellini argued that he read Averroes in the light of Aquinas, and Avicenna in the light of Galen; why might he not read heretical works of religion in the light of Catholic orthodoxy?[82]

How typical was Donzellini? This chapter has argued that large numbers of Italian physicians were drawn towards Protestant beliefs. Others came under suspicion for other reasons, for instance when Girolamo Cardano went so far as to cast the horoscope of Jesus Christ.[83] Yet it is also true that Donzellini blamed his denunciation to the Inquisition on doctors in Venice, and he was thrown out of the College of Physicians of Verona in 1575 because of the disgrace of his condemnation.[84] What many doctors appear to have shared with Donzellini was his view that the educated physician was free to make independent intellectual judgments.

Prohibited works of science and medicine continued to be read in Counter-Reformation Italy, as may be seen from probate inventories listing book collections. They were read, too, by men such as Gian Vincenzo Pinelli and Girolamo Mercuriale in Padua whose Catholic sympathies are not in doubt.[85] Donzellini was perhaps typical of the intermediaries who supplied them, and he certainly served Mercuriale in this way. Similarly correspondence between doctors and natural philosophers across the religious divide was not extinguished, although it was necessarily clandestine. Letters from Italian doctors survive in German and Swiss archives, even if the other side of the correspondence is lacking in Italian archives. It is notable that in the lifetime of Donzellini there seem to have been no prosecutions where reading or possession of prohibited works of science and medicine was the sole offence. There were limits to the activity of the Holy Office, and this was low priority. The Index, however, did have an impact. It was impossible for an Italian to engage in print in discussion of a work which was on the Index. The content of what was published might also be affected. Leaving aside censored editions authorized by the Holy Office, there was self-censorship. Donzellini, for instance, begged Zwinger not to mention him in his books, and urged him in revising his *Theatrum vitae humanae* to say nothing which might prevent so important a work from being available in Italy.[86]

The lifetime of Donzellini saw Protestantism virtually extinguished within Italy. It also witnessed the collapse of humanism in theology and the appearance on the Index of the works of Erasmus. The death of Donzellini in 1587 was followed by the decline of humanism in medicine and intensifying attacks on Aristotelianism as the universal basis of knowledge. This was a new era, in which the standpoint of the Church, prefigured in its condemnation of Paracelsus, would lead it into more serious conflict with Bruno, Patrizi and Galileo.[87]

Notes

1. Archivio di Stato, Venice, *Sant' Uffizio, processi*, busta 10.

2. Antonio Rotondò, 'La censura ecclesiastica e la cultura', in *Storia d'Italia*, ed. C. Vivanti and R. Romano, vol. 5 (Turin, 1973), 1399-1492, especially 1399.

3. Paul Grendler, *The Roman Inquisition and the Venetian Press 1540-1605* (Princeton, 1977); Brian Pullan, *The Jews of Europe and the Inquisition of Venice 1550-1670* (Oxford, 1983); Ruth Martin, *Witchcraft and the Inquisition in Venice 1500-1650* (Oxford, 1989).

4. *Sant' Uffizio, processi*, busta 13.

5. On Aldrovandi, *Dizionario biografico degli Italiani*, vol. 2, 118-24; on Falloppia, Giuseppe Favaro, *Gabrielle Falloppia Modense* (Modena, 1928).

6. *Sant' Uffizio, processi*, buste 10 (Gratarolo), 11 (Tomitano), 13 and 17 (Gadaldin), 23 and 32 (Panarelli and Abbioso, implicated together), 39 (Donzellini), 40 (Nifo), 46 (Malvezzi). On Buccella, *Dizionario Biografico degli Italiani*, vol. 14, 750-3.

7. *Sant' Uffizio, processi*, buste 23 (Giuseppe Moscardo, in the trial of his brother Paolo) and 37 (Peranda).

8. *Sant' Uffizio, processi*, buste 23 and 27 (trials of Antonio Volpe and Francesco Anovazzo).

9. *Sant' Uffizio, processi*, busta 13.

10. *Sant' Uffizio, processi*, busta 30. Cf. Carlo Ginzburg, 'Due note sul profetismo cinquecentesco', *Rivista Storica Italiana*, vol. 78 (1966), 184-227.

11. F. Chabod, 'Per la storia religiosa dello stato di Milano', *Annuario del R. Istituto Storico Italiano per l'Età Moderna e Contemporanea*, vols 2-3 (1936-37), 147 note 3.

12. On Gratarolo's militant Calvinism while in Basle, Antonio Rotondò, *Studi e Ricerche di Storia Eretticale Italiana del Cinquecento* (Turin, 1974), 283-6. On Buccella, Aldo Stella, Intorno al medico padovano Nicolò Buccella, anabattista del 500', *Atti e Memorie dell' Accademia Patavina di Scienze, Lettere ed Arti*, vol. 74 (1961-2), 333-361.. On Malvezzi, *Sant' Uffizio, processi*, busta 46.

13. J.J. Bylebyl, 'The School of Padua: humanistic medicine in the sixteenth century', in Charles Webster (ed.), *Health, Medicine and Mortality in the Sixteenth Century* (Cambridge, 1979), 335-70.

14. Biagio Brugi, 'Gli studenti tedeschi e la S. Inquisizione a Padova nella seconda metà del secolo XVI', *Atti del R. Istituto Veneto di Scienze, Lettere ed Arti*, series 8, vol. 5 (1894), 1015-33. Numerous instances are recorded in the minutes of the German students at Padua, *Atti della Nazione Germanica Artista nello Studio di Padova*, vols 1-2 [1553-1615] ed. A. Favaro (Venice, 1911-12).

15. *Sant' Uffizio, processi*, busta 32, Panarelli, 19 Nov. 1571.

16. *Sant' Uffizio, processi*, busta 40; *Atti della Nazione Germanica Artista*, vol. 1, 103.

17. *Sant' Uffizio, processi*, busta 17.

18. Grendler, *The Roman Inquisition*, 94–100 and appendix 1.

19. Grendler, *The Roman Inquisition*, especially Chapters 4 and 5.

20. Richard Palmer, 'The Church, leprosy and plague in medieval and early modern Europe', in *The Church and Healing*, ed. W.J. Sheils (Oxford, 1982), 79–99.

21. *Sant' Uffizio, processi*, busta 35.

22. Gian' Antonio Secco, *De Optimo Medico* (Venice, 1551).

23. Biblioteca Nazionale Marciana, Venice, MS. Ital. VII 2342 (=9695), f.17v., 14 Nov. 1579. Notes from the minutes of the College of Physicians recording a refusal by the College to accept the demands of the Inquisition concerning confession.

24. *Sant' Uffizio, processi*, busta 32.

25. The extensive documentation is scattered through the trials of various members of the group, including *Sant' Uffizio, processi*, busta 23 (trials of Paolo Moscardo and 'una setta di eretici'), 32 (Teofilo Panarelli), 20 and 37 (the Gemma family, sons of the pharmacist at the *Do Colombine*).

26. Mariagrazia Bellorini, 'Un medico italiano alla corte di Elisabetta: Giulio Borgarucci', *English Miscellany* (1968), 251–71; Aldo Stella, *Dall' Anabattismo al Socinianismo nel Cinquecento Veneto* (Padua, 1967), 121 onwards.

27. *Sant' Uffizio, processi*, busta 32.

28. Carlo Ginzburg, *Il Nicodemismo. Simulazione e Dissimulazione Religiosa nell' Europa del 500* (Turin, 1970). The priority of Brunfels is questioned, however, in Perez Zagorin, *Ways of Lying. Dissimulation, Persecution and Conformity in Early Modern Europe* (Cambridge, Massachusetts, 1990).

29. *Sant' Uffizio, processi*, busta 32.

30. The trial records relating to Donzellini (*Sant' Uffizio, processi*, busta 39, amounting to 212 folios) are the source for what follows, except where stated otherwise. Cf. Marie-Louise Portmann, 'Der Venezianer Arzt Girolamo Donzellini (etwa 1527–1587) und seine Beziehungen zu Basler Gelehrten', *Gesnerus*, vol. 30 (1973), 1–6.

31. Istituto per la Storia dell'Università di Padova, *Acta graduum academicorum ab anno 1538 ad annum 1550* (Padua, 1971), number 2790, 28 April 1541. On Donzellini's chair, J. Facciolati, *Fasti Gymnasii Patavini* (Padua, 1757), 367.

32. The translation of *De Ptisana* was published in Venice in the Giunta editions of the Latin Galen, from 1550 onwards. The *Consultationes* and *Opuscula Varia* of Da Monte were published in Basle in 1557 and 1558.

33. Cf. Andrea Del Col, 'Lucio Paolo Rosello e la vita religiosa veneziana verso la metà del secolo XVI', *Rivista di Storia della Chiesa in Italia*, anno 32 (1978), 422–59.

34. Leandro Perini, 'Note e documenti su Pietro Perna libraio e tipografo a Basilea', *Nuova Rivista Storica*, vol. 50 (1966), 145–200.

35. Grendler, *The Roman Inquisition*, 108–10.

36. On the Maggi case, cf. F.C. Church, *I riformatori italiani*, transl. D. Cantimori, 2 vols (Milan, 1967), vol. 1, 330–3.

37. *Sant' Uffizio, processi*, busta 39, ff. 1–14. Cf. Aldo Stella, *Anabattismo e antitrinitarismo in Italia nel XVI secolo* (Padua, 1969), 138, quoting a letter from Vergerio to Bullinger, 6 Sept. 1554, 'Est apud me nunc Hieronimus Donzelinus . . . .'.

38. *Themistii Euphradae Philosophi Peripatetici Orationes Octo* (Basle, 1559).

39. *Sant' Uffizio, processi*, busta 39, ff. 18–76. The abjuration is at ff. 61–2.

40. Archivio di Stato, Verona, *Archivio del Comune*, vol. 610, minutes of the College of Physicians 1469-1569, f. 199r (the admission of Donzellini, dated 30 July 1561, while he was still, in principle, serving his sentence), and f. 225r, Donzellini's election as Prior, 30 June 1566.

41. P.F. Spinola, *Elegorum . . . Libri Quattuor* (Venice, 1563), 44. Cf. Pio Paschini, 'Un' umanista disgraziato nel cinquecento: Publio Francesco Spinola', *Nuovo Archivio Veneto*, new series vol. 37, year 20, 65-186. Spinola was executed as a heretic in Venice in 1567.

42. *Sant' Uffizio, processi*, busta 39, f. 180r, testimony from Valier, 20 Nov. 1573.

43. Twenty-five letters from Donzellini to Zwinger, dating from the 1560s to the 1580s, survive in the Universitätsbibliothek at Basle, Fr. Gr. mss. I and II. Sixty-seven letters from Donzellini to Camerarius are included in the *Briefsammlung Trew* in the Universitätsbibliothek at Erlangen.

44. Donzellini's ownership of Paracelsian works is noted in Zefiriele Tommaso Bovio, *Melampigo Overo Confusione de Medici Sofisti* (Verona, 1585). His anti-Paracelsian tract was written against Bovio under the pseudonym Claudio Gelli, *Risposta dell' Eccellente Dottor Claudio Gelli al Flagello contra Medici Rationali* (Venice, 1584). Donzellini's authorship of this work can be concluded from his letter to Crato, 10 March 1585, printed in Laurentius Scholzius, *Epistolarum Philosophorum Medicinalium ac Chymicarum . . . volumen* (Hanau, 1610), epistola 98.

45. Leonardo Giachini, *In Nonum Librum Rasis ad Almansorem . . . Commentaria. Opera . . . Hieronymi Donzellini . . . Emendata* (Basle, 1564).

46. Girolamo Donzellini, *De Natura, Causis et Legitima Curatione Febris Pestilentis . . . Epistola* (Venice, 1570); Eudoxus Philalethes, *Libri de Natura, Causis et Legitima Curatione Febris Pestilentis Hieronymi Donzellini . . . Apologia per Eudoxum Philalethes edita* (Venice, 1571); Eudoxus Philalethes, *Adversus Calumnias et Sophistmata cuiusdam Personati qui se Evandrophilacten Nominavit Apologia* (Verona, 1573).

47. *Evandrophilactis adversus Acesiam Cacodoxum, qui se falso Eudoxum Philalethem Facit, Antapologia* (Brescia, 1572).

48. Eudoxus Philalethes, *Adversus Calumnias*.

49. Universitätsbibliothek Basle, Fr. Gr. II 4, number 239, Parthenius [ie. Donzellini] to Zwinger, 18 Aug. 1573.

50. Universitätsbibliothek Erlangen, *Briefsammlung Trew*, Parthenius [Donzellini] to Camerarius, n.d., endorsed with date of receipt, 16 Dec. 1577.

51. *Sant' Uffizio, processi*, busta 39, f. 94v.

52. *Sant' Uffizio, processi*, f. 173r. The work by Camerarius was the *Commentarii utriusque linguae . . .* (Basle, 1551).

53. *Sant' Uffizio, processi*, busta 39, ff. 99-102, 23 Nov. 1574.

54. *Sant' Uffizio, processi*, busta 39, ff. 115-16, 12 April 1575.

55. *Sant' Uffizio, processi*, busta 39, ff. 202-3, a long petition by Donzellini and his new and more congenial cell-mate, the humanist Nascimbene Nascimbene, giving a vivid account of the plague in the prison. It was presented on 21 Feb. 1577.

56. *Sant' Uffizio, processi*, busta 39, f. 211r. On 9 August 1577 Donzellini wrote to Camerarius that he was in his own house with his family, practising medicine and gaining in public esteem (Universitätsbibliothek Erlangen, *Briefsammlung Trew*). Cf. Girolamo Donzellini, *Discorso Nobilissimo e Dottissimo Preservativo et Curativo Della Peste* (Venice, 1577).

57. See above, note 41.

58. Universitätsbibliothek Erlangen, *Briefsammlung Trew*, Donzellini to Camerarius (n.d.), endorsed on receipt, 5 March 1577.

59. *Sant' Uffizio, processi*, busta 30, Nascimbene Nascimbene. Included is an instruction from Cardinal Savelli in Rome to the nuncio in Venice, ordering Donzellini to be confined at home and no longer to practise medicine, dated 13 Sept. 1578. Donzellini announced his release and renewed freedom to practise in a letter which reached Camerarius in Nuremberg on 15 Nov. 1579 (Universitätsbibliothek Erlangen, *Briefsammlung Trew*).

60. Universitätsbibliothek Erlangen, *Briefsammlung Trew*, Donzellini to Camerarius, 12 Aug. 1579.

61. *Briefsammlung Trew*, Donzellini to Camerarius, 12 Aug. 1579. The letters from Crato to Camerarius in the Trew Collection provide a useful commentary on this affair, and to the cooling of the Donzellini-Crato relationship in the succeeding years.

62. Universitätsbibliothek Basle, Fr. Gr. II 4, number 241, Donzellini to Zwinger, 2 March 1583.

63. Universitätsbibliothek Erlangen, *Briefsammlung Trew*, Donzellini to Camerarius, 4 Oct. 1585.

64. *Briefsammlung Trew*, Donzellini to Camerarius (n.d.), endorsed on receipt, 13 March 1587.

65. Letters from Padua from Jacobus and Bonifacius Zwinger dated 11 April 1587 (Universitätsbibliothek Basle, Fr. Gr. I. 11 number 418; Fr. Gr. II. 23, number 520).

66. Grendler, *The Roman Inquisition*, 57. Grendler compares these figures with the total of 1560 trials surviving for the same period.

67. Grendler, *The Roman Inquisition*, 192-3.

68. Universitätsbibliothek Erlangen, *Briefsammlung Trew*, Donzellini to Camerarius Jan. 1580 and n.d. (endorsed on receipt 15 Nov. 1579).

69. *Briefsammlung Trew*, Donzellini to Camerarius, 22 Aug. 1577. His comment on the death of Crato's wife was similar: 'What of it? She was mortal, now she is freed from infinite troubles'. (Ibid, 20 July 1585).

70. See above, note 62.

71. Universitätsbibliothek Erlangen, *Briefsammlung Trew*. The interesting prehistory of this edition, published in 1585, may be traced in letters from Crato and Donzellini to Camerarius, 1580-5.

72. *Briefsammlung Trew*, letters from Donzellini to Camerarius, Jan. 1586-Jan 1587.

73. This aspect of the correspondence is dealt with by Portmann, 'Der Venezianer Arzt Girolamo Donzellini'.

74. Universitätsbibliothek Erlangen, *Briefsammlung Trew*, Donzellini to Camerarius, 2 May 1586. Patrizi is frequently mentioned in the Donzellini letters to Camerarius and Zwinger.

75. *Briefsammlung Trew*, Donzellini to Camerarius 24 Nov. 1571. Cf. Rotondò, *Studi e Richerche*, chapter 7.

76. See above, note 37.

77. Universitätsbibliothek Erlangen, *Briefsammlung Trew*, Crato to Camerarius, April 1577.

78. *Themistii Euphradae Philosophi Peripatetici Orationes Octo . . . a Hieronymo Donzellino . . . in Latinam Linguam e Graeca nunc primum Versae et . . . Illustratae* (Basle: Perna, 1559).

79. See above, note 45.

80. Girolamo Donzellini, *Remedium Ferendarum Iniuriarum, sive de Compescenda Ira* (Venice: F. Ziletti, 1586).

81. Girolamo Donzellini, *Remedium Ferendarum Iniuriarum*, ff. 2r. 32r, 40–41. Donzellini also referred to his own case, and the consolation which he drew from the thought that his earthly life was drawing to its end (f. 20r).

82. *Sant' Uffizio, processi*, busta 39, ff. 47–8.

83. Universitätsbibliothek Basle, Fr. Gr. I 13, number 104, Donzellini to Zwinger, 10 Aug. 1577.

84. *Sant' Uffizio, processi*, busta 39, f. 94v, 16 Nov 1574. Donzellini blamed his denunciation in 1553 on his enemies, the physicians Martial Rota and Christoforo dal Legname. On Donzellini's expulsion from the College at Verona, Archivio di Stato, Verona, *Archivio del Comune*, vol. 611, Atti del Collegio dei Medici, f. 44v, 30 June 1575.

85. Grendler, *The Roman Inquisition*, 288–9.

86. Universitätsbibliothek Basle, Fr. Gr. II 4, number 241, Donzellini to Zwinger, 2 March 1583.

87. On the general influence of the Inquisition on Italian culture, see Antonio Rotondò, 'La censura ecclesiastica e la cultura . . .', and Grendler, *The Roman Inquisition*, Chapter 10.

7

The Church, the Devil and the healing activities of living saints in the Kingdom of Naples after the Council of Trent

David Gentilcore

During their rural mission in the diocese of Potenza in 1687, the Jesuit missioners commented on the widespread use of 'superstitions'. According to the definition of the time this meant any of a wide range of popular rituals to heal, cause injury, predict the future or bind someone in love, the efficacy of which – the Roman Catholic Church believed – was due to an expressed or tacit pact with the Devil. In this case, the missioners reported that the principal practitioner was a nun whom the local populace believed to be a living saint:

> Above all, the people were freed from a great error, that of reputing and esteeming to be a saint a woman of a town not far away, to whom they had recourse for all their necessities, and from whom they obtained remedies, all consisting in superstitious things. All these things were gathered together, and having made a great bundle out of them, they were consigned to the flames in front of the people, and God favoured this in such a prodigious way that the people, terrified, did not stop weeping and promised God never again to have recourse to the mentioned witch. And we shall try to notify her Superior of the superstitions, so she receives the punishment she deserves.[1]

Why was this nun such a threat to the Church, personified here by the Jesuit missioners evangelizing in the 'deep south'? Why did it campaign so virulently against the use of 'superstitions'? In this chapter I shall examine the opposition of the Tridentine Church authorities to local attempts to tap the power of the sacred, particularly in response to disease, at a time when these authorities were seeking to define and regulate the access to such power, by laity and clergy alike. I shall begin with a brief discussion of the various healers and remedial forms which made use of sacred power in one way or another, exemplifying the medical pluralism of the period. These include figures like the cunning man or woman, exorcists and 'living saints'. The latter are a special case, in that they embodied the sacred in themselves, while the cunning folk and exorcists simply employed the tools and techniques at their disposal in their healing rituals. Because of the power of these living saints – recognized locally as wonder-working and holy, but not canonized by the Church – and the ever-present threat that the devil might be using them and deceiving them for his own ends, the Church felt that it could never let up its vigilance. In addition to the Church's response I shall also discuss the interpretation of the medical profession and how it perceived the diabolical menace, especially with regard to disease causation. But it is the control exercised by the post-Tridentine Church over sacred healing that will form the underlying theme. The increasingly numerous forays of the Church into the period's medical pluralism – attempting to regulate it, while at the same time encouraging its growth and prolif- eration – constitutes one of the paradoxes which characterize the Baroque.

One example of the medical pluralism of early modern Italy was the frequent recourse to cunning folk for the treatment of a whole variety of ailments. This included diseases ascribed to natural as well as supernatural causation. Cunning folk could be specialized to a degree which we might find surprising: one healer might be considered expert in treating fevers, another headaches, still another pains in the joints. Techniques and rituals were quite varied, the prayers (*orazioni*) and invocations (*scongiuri*) accompanied by simple herbal remedies, or even forming the sole means of treatment. An important part of the healing ritual thus consisted in the use of the sign of the Cross on the afflicted part, or of holy water or oil taken from the church. In this sense popular healing overlapped with the healing rituals of both orthodox Cath- olicism (from blessings to exorcisms) and Galenic medicine. The key element in all this was ritual, so that a particular treatment or ritual formula might not be used for just one disease, and one disease might be treated by more than one such formula. It was through ritual that the healing power of the sacred could be tapped.

The practitioners of these healing rituals were most often women. Healing and health were a natural part of the female domain in southern Italian society, a part of the woman's concern for the well-being of the family. Furthermore, poor, often widowed, women were frequently driven to the margins of society, and so came to depend on such services for their livelihood and development of a social role. Their power came from the ability to distinguish naturally occurring maladies from those caused by the supernatural. It was only once the causation had been determined that an effective cure could be found. But the power to heal also meant the power to harm. The wise woman (*magara* or *fattucchiara*) who undid a spell found to be causing an ailment, was often the one who had cast the spell in the first place.

The Church stressed that only its trained exorcists could ascertain whether an ailment was caused by sorcery and, if this was the diagnosis, only they had the power to treat it. Of course, the patients themselves and their families were generally prepared to use whatever remedy was thought to be efficacious, in a pragmatic search for a cure. But theologians saw the Devil everywhere, even in the healing rituals of the *magare*. Such was the Devil's insidious astuteness that under their apparently pious prayers and 'signings', lay the threat of eternal damnation. This was because such remedies were believed to gain their efficacy – their very efficacy was not in question – through an 'explicit or tacit' pact with the Devil. Because it realized that popular healing was so often employed in good faith or ignorance, the Counter-Reformation Church focussed its campaign against it around the enforcement of orthodox teaching on matters such as sorcery, demoniacal possession and divine intercession. The activity of parish priests, confessors, preachers, episcopal and inquisitorial tribunals was crucial in this campaign, though its impact was a question of centuries rather than decades.

The emphasis placed on the power of exorcists to 'liberate' the possessed from diabolically caused diseases resulted in the mushrooming of extra-canonical exorcists to meet the increased demand. The latter were simply laymen or clerics who practised exorcisms without episcopal training or approval.[2] Sometimes the fame of an extra-canonical exorcist was such that he developed a reputation and a clientele, in much the same way as the 'living saints' we shall examine below. Diocesan synods frequently decreed that no one should perform exorcisms without episcopal licence. If caught, they would be tried by the episcopal courts or the Inquisition. But the typical exorcism was both extremely complicated and vague (not unlike the learned magic of the period), and in terms of the ritual performed it was often difficult to distinguish official from unofficial exorcists. It would also seem that there existed a 'low', domestic form of exorcism, used against diabolically caused maladies, and a 'high' public form, used for demoniacal possession.[3] This situation was exacerbated by the fact that until the Roman Ritual of 1614 there was no standard exorcism format or rite. Even after that date unapproved manuscript exorcisms continued to circulate widely.

Another fundamental aspect of medical pluralism in southern Italy (as in the rest of the Catholic world) was the recourse to the healing powers of saints, through their intercession or the touch of their relics. Intercession could be the result of prayer, pilgrimage or a vow made to the saint. The unceasing demand for sources of healing also explains the thriving trade in relics, which the Church sought to regulate. Church synods forbade people from circulating or making use of new or previously unknown relics, in an attempt to stem the commerce in false relics. They also sought to prevent relics from being taken out of churches and loaned to devoted patients. Even exorcists, who frequently used the saintly relics as part of the ritual means of forcing the devil out of the possessed person's body, had to obtain permission for their use.

Devotion to saints thrived, and new canonizations kept up the supply, despite the more rigorous and standardized procedure of saint-making adopted by the Church in the years following the Council of Trent. The middle decades of the sixteenth century had seen something of a 'crisis of canonizations' within the Church, due in no small part to the Protestant Reformation.[4] Confidence was restored with the establishment of the Congregation of Sacred Rites and Ceremonies in 1588, responsible for canonizations. The revival could be said to have culminated on 12 March 1622 with the canonization of four 'servants of God' in one triumphant ceremony: Theresa of Avila, Philip Neri, Ignatius of Loyola and Francis Xavier. The official making of saints was thus controlled from Rome. However, the initial impetus came from the local level, wherever a cult sprang up around a holy man or woman. For the faithful, the living saint meant a source of sacred power, the function of which was to provide healing. But the Church was looking primarily for saints of the edifying variety. As a result, of these many local cults, some would be recognized and approved by the central authorities, others would be suppressed, and still others would be put in abeyance, neither rejected nor approved, awaiting further developments. Thus, depending on ecclesial reaction, the 'living saints' would end up as either canonized saints, failed saints or saints-in-waiting. The Church regarded devotion to living saints as something of a battleground: where the eager faithful saw visions, ecstasies and healing wonders, the Church saw the possibility of diabolical trickery to lead men and women to damnation. While word of new miracles circulated rapidly amongst the faithful, the Church declared that nothing should be made public as miraculous until it had first been investigated and approved by the local bishop, for fear that fakery or the Devil lay behind it. The result was that a large number of 'living saints' were to be examined by that other entity of the Catholic Reformation designed to define and enforce access to the sacred, the Congregation of the Holy Office, founded in 1542.

Whereas popular religion did not stress the differences between divine and diabolical, grouping them together under the supernatural, the Church, of course, did. This included the ecclesiastical concept of disease and calamity. On the one hand, they could be caused by the wrath of God as punishment for unrepentant sinners. On the other hand, and more menacing still, were the activities of the Devil. He could bring about any sort of malady and misfortune, either of his own accord, or through the influence of spells cast by those in his service. And let us not forget, that even the most humble and devout cunning woman, healing the sick of her village, was considered by the Church to be in league with the Devil. To explore how the Devil was believed to operate in early modern

137

Catholic society, let us turn at last to our two living saints, Maria Manca and Suor Giglia di Fino.

Manca was born in 1571 in the town of Squinzano, near Lecce. Married at the age of nineteen to a local patrician, she was widowed four years later, and made a vow to God to remain chaste and never remarry. However, a local tradesman – a repairer of windmills – fell blindly in love with her. When Maria told him of her vow to God, the tradesman, Lupo Crisostomo, realized he would have to employ other means to win her love. He thus turned to a local cunning man (*fattucchiero*) for a love philtre, which consisted of some powder sprinkled on a mushroom, Maria's favourite food. Brought to her that evening for supper, she ate the mushrooms and soon felt the burning passions of love (her hagiographer refers to its 'burning in her guts'[5]). She immediately went out to find Crisostomo, arriving at his house late that night. When he answered the door she told him that her mill needed repairing, to which he replied that it was her brain that needed repairing. The whole town was soon gossiping about the affair and Maria's relatives decided that she would have to marry him in order to save her honour. The love philtre allows the hagiographer to account for Maria's breaking of her vow and subsequent remarriage, unusual events in a candidate for canonization. But more importantly, it explains the terrible torments that were soon to afflict Maria, after the death of her first child. Demons had been introduced into her body through Crisostomo's spell and started to cause havoc. They began by beating her and causing her terrible visions at night, including a 'black Ethiopian' and 'most shameless embraces and a hundred and a thousand dirty and foul acts'.[6] Visions like these were regarded as real manifestations of the demonic presence.

The physical manifestations began after the death of her second child, immediately after birth. Comparing her to Job, Maria's hagiographer describes her torments:

By reason of the fever having left almost by accident her most worn-out body, which resembled a corpse, having almost nothing more to consume, she soon saw herself covered with wounds, abscesses, gangrene and with the most dreadful pains, which tormented her with all their power all the time, without ever letting up. She offered her most gentle limbs to the knife, flame and every other similar and most painful remedy with a most exemplary and incomparable constancy, but the surgeon worked in vain, because he was incapable of finding a remedy and cure for the grievous diseases of Hell. The wounds grew more cruel in such a way that her most delicate flesh rotted, so as to generate nauseous worms, and these ulcers emanated such a pestiferous stench that whoever came to visit her, fled at once from her presence and held her in abomination, like a plague victim.[7]

Seeing her suffering, Crisostomo asked forgiveness and took her to the Greek rite church in Lecce, whose priests were believed to be expert exorcists. They concluded that she was possessed but could not liberate her of the demons. The same negative result was obtained by Catholic priests who performed exorcisms repeatedly over the next nine months. Crisostomo even went back to the cunning man who had cast the original spell, but he said he was unable to undo it. From this point on, Crisostomo was miserable and melancholic, developed pleurisy and died.

After the physicians and exorcists, Maria offered her ailments up to God, allowing the hagiographer to exercize his descriptive skills once again:

> Her disease having become harsher and, she herself having become a dungheap of putrefaction, a centre of filth and a sink of rot, overwhelmed by unbearable pains, eaten alive by worms, held in abomination, abandoned and shunned by everyone, in imitation of Agatha, she held up her wounds to the Celestial Doctor and, scorning human industry, placed all her hope in him.[8]

Meanwhile, her habit of going to a tumbledown chapel outside the town and praying to an image of the Virgin and Child there eventually paid off. One day a young woman appeared to her and gave her a carnation, telling her to take it to a certain church in the nearby town of Galatone. The rumour of her divine favour spread and the clergy arrived at once to perform an exorcism, taking advantage of what seemed to be a propitious moment. A demon announced he would depart her body the following day on the way to Galatone. Maria was thus finally liberated, vomiting 'a round bone the size of one of the larger pennies, perforated in the middle with a piece of string and a few hairs at the tip'.[9]

It is interesting that on several occasions during the narration of these events Maria's hagiographer, Mauro Paticchio, intervenes with lengthy asides on the means employed by demons to bring about illness. Here, Paticchio puts to use his theological training with the Dominicans in Lecce, citing Scripture, Church councils, demonologists and theologians in support of his statements. The reason that the physicians' cures were ineffective was due to the diabolical, as opposed to natural, origin of Maria's ailments. Spells like the one employed by Crisostomo (*maleficio venefico* or *amatorio*) frequently led to possession and disease, for which Paticchio cites the authority of demonologists like Del Rio, Sprenger and Torreblanca.[10] He also criticizes the 'mad presumption' of 'the Englishman Doctor Mead', who suggested in his *Medica Sacra* that the possessed men and women of the Bible were in fact suffering from incurable natural disease or insanity.[11] The treatise in question by Richard Mead was published in 1749, a time of great change in medical thinking. Paticchio's hagiography of Maria was published twenty years later, and it is clear that he is seeking to affirm the traditional viewpoint of the Church on the subject of possession and disease causation against those of an increasingly secular science. Yet as Paticchio must have been only too aware, during the lifetime of Maria Manca (1571–1668) – the period that concerns us here – the worlds of learned medicine and the Church had been in harmony concerning the belief in diabolical disease causation.

The traditional ecclesiastical view of the manner in which the Devil brought about disease is summarized in Francesco Maria Guazzo's 1608 work, the *Compendium Maleficarum*, the Compendium of Witches.[12] After citing Galen and Avicenna, he quotes the work of the Spanish physician Franciscus Valesius to describe how the Devil brings about disease.[13] Melancholy sickness is brought about by disturbing the bile and dispersing a black humour throughout the brain and the internal cells of the body; he then increases the black bile by introducing other irritations and preventing the purging of the humour.

> He brings epilepsy, paralysis and such maladies by a stoppage of the heavier physical fluids, obstructing and blocking the ventricule of the brain and the nerve-roots. He causes blindness or deafness, bringing a noxious secretion in the eyes or ears. Often again he suggests ideas to the imagination which induce love or hatred or other mental disturbances. For the purpose of causing bodily infirmities he distils a spiritous substance from the blood itself, purifies it of all base matter, and uses it as the aptest, most efficacious and swiftest weapon against human life: I say that from the most potent poisons he extracts a quintessence with which he infects the very spirit of life.[14]

Citing the physician Andreas Cesalpino, Guazzo notes that the 'human skill' of physicians is all but helpless against diseases caused in this way. This is because the devil's poison 'is too subtle and tenacious, too swift and sure in killing, and reaches to the very marrow of the bones'.[15]

Many of the authorities cited by Guazzo in support of his arguments were used by another writer on medicine and magic, Pietro Piperno. Piperno, physician and *protomedico* for the papal enclave of Benevento, published his *De Magicis Affectibus* ('On magical afflictions') in 1634, along with a treatise on the walnut tree of Benevento, the supposed site of witches' sabbaths.[16] The work which concerns us here, the first one, is divided into six sections: magical maladies, superstitious remedies, medical treatment, nonexistent magical maladies, religious therapy and case studies. According to Piperno a malady can be considered 'magical' (i.e. diabolical) if the symptoms are 'beyond the common order of nature without manifest cause, as they do not correspond to the essence of the disease, for which wise men and medics themselves expert in practice are at a loss in getting to know the affliction'.[17] He goes on to list the seven signs which indicate the magical or diabolical nature of a disease: (1) normally effective remedies show no signs of efficacy; (2) symptoms are extreme and out of proportion, 'since the Devil flees from mediocrity'; (3) sacred and consecrated things are insulted; (4) while ranting and then resting the diseased speak in the third person; (5) they speak various languages, not corresponding to their 'regions, practices or occupations'; (6) they prophesy and forecast the future without feeling; and (7) through simple and pious prayer they are healed briefly of lypothymia, syncope, heart palpitation, tremor, epilepsy, and so on.[18]

He suggests that melancholic people are most susceptible to magical maladies, due to their less efficient external senses and more fervent imaginations. This results in a certain 'spiritual somnolence', of which the devil takes advantage. The list of maladies which can be brought about in this way is endless. They include not only those diseases which might be seen as more predictably diabolical, such as neurosis, psychosis, delirium, epilepsy, insomnia, sciatica and extreme feelings of love or hate; but what to us are more everyday ailments, like headache, stomach-ache and sneezing.[19]

The solutions he proposed to these 'magical maladies' are in line with Counter-Reformation orthodoxy. The healing rituals of a cunning woman would prove fruitless. And as for seeking out the man or woman who cast the spell in order to have it undone – the most common practice, he notes – this would only expose the patient to new and more insidious magic. Here he is supporting the opposition of the Church to popular healing rituals, referred to above.

The Church had its own remedies, working in tandem with learned medicine. The Devil could be defeated by taking the inverse route to the one used to bring about the disease. The two-step treatment consisted of first recognizing the maleficient nature of the disease and then proceeding to find and destroy the charm, or exorcise the demon which was causing it. The *curatio medica* of bleedings, cauterizations, fumigations, change of air and diet, baths, poultices and purgations was used in concert with the *curatio divina* of blessings and exorcisms. Because the supernatural had been used to bring about physical disease, exorcisms had to be given a helping hand by medical remedies. The most symbolically effective was no doubt the *purgatio*. Following the tradition of Hippocrates, vomiting was considered a purifying and liberating force against disease. This 'evacuatory purge made a clean sweep of the humoral quagmire, the seat of fermentation for witchcraft',[20] expelling any charms that might be lurking in the body (as in Maria Manca's small bone with a string through it). Indeed, such was the importance of this purgative therapy in the minds of the medical practitioners that it continued to be used on cases of suspected insanity until the end of the eighteenth century, by which time the whole concept of possession and exorcism had been called into question by the same profession.[21]

But to return to the century following Trent. It is striking that the exorcistic treatment was the reverse of the 'superstitious' rituals used to bring about the disease. Divine mirrored diabolical. Such a conception was typical of the period. The demonological, in fact, lacked a language of its own; it was merely the antithesis of the divine.[22] Thus the descriptions of the ecstasies of the mystics and the experiences of the witches have much in common: the rapturous flights to paradise resemble the witches' flights to the sabbath; the languor following ecstatic visions of Jesus is comparable to the exhaustion of witches after being visited by the Devil; the mystical marriage to Christ is analogous to the pact with the Devil. One living saint was even known as 'the witch of God', transported by angels instead of demons, to worship God rather than the devil.[23] So close were the two categories, that the woman held to be a 'living saint' and the woman suspected of being a witch could be victims of the same thing. Women were believed to be especially prone to the devil's deceits, whether in the form of diabolical pacts or simulated sanctity. Their inferior powers of reason, childish curiosity and insatiable lust meant that they were more easily seduced by the devil than men. Paradoxically, the credulity and simplicity that gave them an advantage over men in attaining mystical union with God, also made them more apt to be victims of the devil's snares.[24]

The Church tried to stress and enforce the differences between divine and diabolical visions, as it did the opposition between God and Satan. But in popular culture the devil was but a trickster, easily duped by those sly enough to do so. The pact with the devil was not completely different from a vow made to a saint, and they both could be used to seek protection from malady and misfortune. The divine and the diabolical together formed the sacred and were not yet the opposing forces of good and evil, moral and immoral. Following the Council of Trent the Church did its best to diabolize popular notions of the Devil. A soul not on constant guard against the Devil's presence could easily be deceived and eternally damned by him. This was as much the threat of Protestant heresy as anything else, and the living saint was particularly dangerous in this regard, because she would lead other people astray along with her.

Paticchio's account of the life of Maria Manca is careful to stress her orthodoxy, as well as her practice of the saintly virtues to a heroic degree. In addition to her obvious piety, her charity, humility, patience, obedience and modesty had resulted in her receiving the gifts of healing and prophecy. The Church taught that these gifts were the result of divine favour, its outcome. In other words, the saintliness led to the power to heal. For most of the laity and much of the clergy, however, it was the other way round: the ability to heal was of itself an indication of sanctity, its cause. The living saint was thus torn two ways. Paticchio goes to great lengths to show that, despite Manca's reputation as a saint, she denied it and remained humble throughout. But the temptation to exploit her powers for an increased role in local society must have been great. The people of her town, as well as from other towns further away all came to see her, 'very important and notable personages, to obtain graces, favours and advice'. When she walked past, people would shout 'There's the saint, there's the saint!'[25] In true orthodox fashion, Maria attributed her healing favours to the Virgin working through her touch (the touch of her 'embalsamed hand' which had held the divine carnation).[26] She treats the difficult pregnancy of the Marchioness of Campi by placing her hand on the woman's uterus and addressing the Virgin with the words, '*Madonna mia*, I touch her, you heal her'.[27] Whereas pregnant women were regarded as being particularly vulnerable to witches, the living saints are frequently seen in this role of aiding difficult pregnancies. And of course, Paticchio takes advantage of the account to demonstrate the well-bred nature of her clientele: not just 'dull-witted men and empty-headed women' (*uomini balordi e feminuccie*) who are easily swayed by claims of sanctity. The belief in her holiness was universal, as demonstrated by the general hunt for relics, such as pieces of her clothes, not only whilst she was alive but after her death. Thus – in a *topos* common to saints' Lives – if 'she had not been protected and surrounded by guards assigned for the purpose, since Maria was held by all in great regard and opinion of sanctity, they would have torn her clothes from her body, and divided them in many pieces out of devotion'.[28]

In Maria Manca we have the careful construction of sanctity, following accepted Tridentine models of what qualities and activities constituted holiness. The hagiography itself was compiled by Paticchio from the writings of her spiritual director and other 'reliable' contemporaries.[29] The order to write everything down regarding one's spiritual life was a common practice in convents, for example, allowing for a measure of control over the nuns or even to legitimate future calls for canonization. It permitted the hagiographers to record those events which would add to the candidate's reputation, and eliminate those which would detract from it, especially suggestions of beliefs or practices which might be considered heretical. Print became the ideal means of promoting a cult because it fixed the image of the candidate for canonization according to accepted ecclesial models. It also served to spread the fame of living saints beyond the local area, complementing the traditional modes of diffusion (preaching, travel and within single Orders).[30]

Yet the women themselves, rather than being heterodoxes, were usually seeking a more prominent role in society, employing a religiosity which responded to the affirmation of their own individuality and search for forms of charismatic power within small groups. This put them in a potentially dangerous position. Such is the conclusion of a recent study about the Sicilian nun and living saint Suor Maria Crocifissa (1645–99). She, at least, had a whole 'apparatus' surrounding her – consisting of convent, well-placed family and spiritual directors – which put a complex system of supervision and control into operation, guiding her into safer territory.[31] Less fortunate was the attempt of another seventeenth-century nun, Suor Benedetta Carlini (1590–1661). Her ecstasies, prophecies and healing certainly brought her recognition; but without powerful patrons to protect her, she was examined on several occasions by the Church authorities, suspected of simulated sanctity. Any chances she had of persuading her judges of the authentic nature of her achievements were put to an end by testimony describing homosexual acts with other nuns.

The visions and healing activities of Benedetta and women like her were increasingly suspect because they remained outside the sacramental structure of the Church. Furthermore, in the words of Judith Brown, who has brought us Benedetta's story, the Church 'sought to weaken all competing conduits for grace and to limit the propagation of heresy by well-meaning but ignorant visionaries whose flawed interpretations of their experiences could inadvertently lead them and their followers into doctrinal errors'.[32] Yet even Benedetta had the relative security of the convent walls and the recognized status that being a nun gave. More fragile still was the condition of the tertiary or Third Order nun, from whose ranks most of the living saints were drawn. Our second Apulian living saint, Suor Giglia di Fino of Altamura, was just such a tertiary. Whilst Maria Manca was careful enough to remain humble about the nature of her achievements – which anyway remained within acceptable bounds – and so receive no opposition from the local Church authorities,[33] Giglia's career was to end in disgrace before a representative of the Holy Office.

The tertiary nun was a woman who had taken a simple or private vow of chastity, wore a habit (often Franciscan), observed some sort of religious rule, and lived either in the community of other tertiaries or on her own. A typical tertiary was a single or married pious women who lived at home (for this reason they are sometimes referred to as 'house nuns', *ormonache di casa*), wearing a habit she had made for herself. Why would women join a Third Order as opposed to entering a nunnery? Primarily, given the low social status of most tertiaries, it was because they simply could not afford the dowry payment required to enter a convent. In addition, many may have felt that cloistered life was too restrictive and the life of a tertiary was the ideal compromise.[34] The decision to become a tertiary nun allowed one to partake of both the secular and sacred life. It was an important part of a woman's 'life strategy', particularly if she had no other well-defined role in the community or institutional protection. As for those women who sought to follow established models of sanctity through their role as tertiary, it suggests an awareness of self and individuality, whilst at the same time a greater capacity to adhere and conform to these pre-set models.[35] But seeking to imitate the models of canonized women like Catherine of Sienna and Theresa of Avila was a dangerous business, with the Church on the lookout for sources of heresy or scandal. In the stricter climate of the Counter-Reformation institutional protection was required for the visionary and healer, a protection which the Third Orders did not provide. Sainthood outside of cloistered convents was rendered all but impossible.

While the living saints at the courts of the Italian cities in the first half of the sixteenth century have come down to us through hagiographies, the stories of those mystics, visionaries and miracle-workers esteemed as living saints after Trent are generally told by the surviving records of the Inquisition.[36] Even those living saints who were later canonized, like St Theresa of Avila, had first to pass the test of the Holy Office. Most, of course, never made the grade. All channels to the sacred – and the sources of healing it provided – were now being increasingly regulated and controlled by the Church in order to combat heresy and incorrect belief, as we have seen with regard to cunning folk, relics and exorcisms. But the living saints posed a special threat. First of all, they were women, and the influence they had over their followers meant a disruption of the accepted patterns of relations between the sexes. This, at a time when the Church was seeking to enclose all nunneries and limit the public activities of nuns. Second, living saints subverted the established ecclesial hierarchy by posing as direct channels to divine inspiration and revelation.[37]

The trend of increasing ecclesial control over paths to sanctity was common to all the Inquisitions, Roman, Spanish and Portuguese. Despite being part of the Spanish Dominions, Naples had successfully opposed the introduction of the Spanish Inquisition. Instead, Rome sent representatives of its own Inquisition to sit on the episcopal tribunals. For this reason developments within the kingdom of Naples also influenced the course of local inquisitorial activities. It is no coincidence, then, that the investigation of Suor Giglia follows the controversial case involving Suor Orsola Benincasa (1547–1618), a Neapolitan tertiary nun. Born into a family of noble origin, from a young age Orsola demonstrated great piety accompanied by frequent ecstasies and revelations. She set up a hermitage in 1576, where her fasts, ecstasies, acts of healing and elementary preaching brought her great fame amongst Neapolitans of all classes. By this point, she had already been examined by the archbishop, and the agents of the Inquisition continued to keep an eye on her. In 1582, without the archbishop's permission, she arranged an audience with the Pope, Gregory XIII, to tell him of the dire warnings she had received from God. She went into ecstasy three times during the audience and was unable to deliver her message. The Pope, thinking her experiences might be the work of evil spirits, set up a committee of nine judges to examine her, headed by Philip Neri (and also including one of the chief Inquisitors, Cardinal Santoro, and the General of the Jesuits, Claudio Acquaviva). Rigorous interrogations, exorcisms and purgations continued for the following nine months. This included being completely stripped and shaved to see 'if she had on her, in any place, anything prohibited and pertaining to witchcraft that might be causing the ecstasy'.[38] Rumours even circulated in Naples that she had been burnt at the stake. The committee concluded that her spirit was 'good' and her soul pure and simple.[39] She was allowed to return to Naples but forbidden to preach or prophesy. Her new role was to be private rather than public. In the years that followed pressure was put upon her community to come under some sort of Church control, and the enclosed convent she founded in 1617 was placed under Theatine supervision. She was proclaimed venerable (the first stage to canonization) in 1793.

Even while alive Suor Orsola had become something of an archetype for the tertiary nun in the Kingdom of Naples, though most women were only able to imitate her model on a much smaller scale.[40] Orsola, however, was somewhat exceptional in having had her achievements recognized as divinely inspired. Most of the women who imitated her model and that of other living saints were not so lucky.

Suor Giglia di Fino's story is typical.[41] Giglia (born 1601) was a local tertiary nun, reputed to be a saint because of her visions, ecstasies, prophecies and healing power. Her fame brought her case to the attention of a local delegate of the Holy Office, the Dominican friar Vincenzo di Ferrandina. Aware that such feats could have any of three origins – divine, diabolical or simulation – he began an investigation in 1628. Testimony comes largely from those men who had formed a group around her, calling themselves her 'spiritual children'. In the same way that some living saints had become counsellors and advisors to the princes and courts of Europe, although on a smaller scale, Giglia was asked for advice by her spiritual children based on the revelations she was said to receive from God. They 'associated with her because the said Suor Giglia was reputed to be a saint, and they became attached to the spiritual life, penitential exercises and advice of Suor Giglia as spiritual mother, who had told them that God had revealed to her that she would adopt them as her spiritual children'.[42] One of her 'spiritual children' was Rev. Roberto Campanile, cantor at the church of S. Nicola. He asked for prayers and advice on God's intention regarding his decision to retire to the Dominican monastery in Naples and will his possessions to his brother now, rather than when he died. Her response was to sprinkle holy water in the direction of the door through which she said two devils were fast approaching, and tell him that he was a terrible sinner and ought to perform acts of penitence. She left him with a meditation which she said had been written by her guardian angel.[43]

It was her guardian angel who was ultimately responsible for some of her healing. He had brought her a piece of the Cross, housed in an ornate reliquary, and she used it to heal the sick by having them drink the water in which the relic had been placed momentarily. One man who was at death's door had drunk the water, vomited 'matter of different colours' and was healed. Giglia's physician noted succinctly that 'by making a sign of the Cross [along] along with a Salve Regina' with the oil from the lamp which burned before her crucifix 'she healed every infirmity'.[44] A boy was healed in the following more roundabout way:

> having approached Hell, she touched him and, saying an Our Father and Hail Mary to St Dominic so that he would pray Our Lady of the Rosary for the health of the boy, she held her hand on his stomach, after which the boy vomited certain matter of different colours, asked his mother for food and got better.

On another occasion she sent an ailing priest the relic: his condition improved for eight days, then worsened again and he died. Giglia explained that he had died because he did not want to believe that he had been 'liberated' by virtue of her prayers.[45] Liberation from disease is analogous to liberation from evil spirits. But even more interesting is the suspicion in which Giglia is beginning to be held (at least by some). If her guardian angel was in fact the Devil in disguise then the relic would be fake as well, and the healing attained through diabolical rather than divine favour.

Her guardian angel was also at the centre of her numerous ecstasies. Whilst she was in rapture, enjoying the beatific vision, her body stayed on the ground, her guardian angel directing her, speaking for her and performing other normal actions, like embroidery work.[46] One of Giglia's spiritual children was convinced of the divinity of the spirit speaking through her because it spoke articulate praises of the Virgin, the dignity of the priest, the Blessed Sacrament and Christ's Passion.[47] Her levitations also aroused considerable public interest and curiosity. During them many people would come and watch from behind a closed door. The atmosphere was one of tension and suspense as onlookers took turns peering underneath the bottom of the door to catch a glimpse of the 'saint' in levitation five or six palms off the floor with a crucifix in one hand. On one occasion a cape fell to the ground on the inside of the door, blocking the view, and causing great fear when people tried to move it and it resisted, all of which was followed by a loud thump on the door. A woman named Isabella who lived nearby recounted that

> she too wanted to watch from under the door, [but] while Suor Giglia was raised up in the air she [Giglia] put her hand inside her sleeve and threw a book impetuously at her where she was watching, and the said Isabella, terrified, never wanted to go again.[48]

Giglia accounted for this by saying that her guardian angel did not want her watched when she was closed in her room.[49] In order to prevent her levitations from becoming too much of a public spectacle – especially when doubts about their divine origin were beginning to arise – her confessor had a bar put across the bottom of the door.

In many ways Giglia's experiences imitated those of the female mystics who had gone before her. Indeed, she claimed that St Theresa (canonized in 1622, as we have seen) appeared in all her visions alongside Christ. During one of her ecstasies Giglia had undergone the mystical marriage with Christ in the company of saints and angels (similar to that of St Catherine), although the ring was visible only to her. Other 'wondrous deeds' (*opere maravigliose*) included being taken up into Paradise during the feasts of Christmas and Easter, and celebrating Palm Sunday with the blessed, during which she was given blessed palms for her and her spiritual children. On the feast of Corpus Christi, when she was unable to go to mass to take communion, Jesus gave her communion with his own hands.[50] On another occasion an angel of paradise brought her a jar of 'celestial liquor'. It was the special food of paradise and she drank it 'for the nourishment of her soul', but its intense warmth and sweetness caused her to be sick. Finally, like St Philip Neri, she claimed that the gift of grace had caused her heart to dilate and break her ribs apart (going even further than Neri, whose ribs had only been raised up). Campanile – who was especially devoted to Neri – was told by the guardian angel to feel Giglia's ribs. He did this, and was amazed to be able to put four fingertips into the space.[51]

It was probably this self-confidence and boasting which were Giglia's undoing. Her attempts at constructing her public role as saint began to miscarry. It was one thing to justify her status by referring to her saintly childhood, early manifestations of holiness and daily acts of self-mortification (the most standard of saintly models);[52] quite another to claim that she was more favoured than St Philip Neri. Suspicion about the divine nature of her achivements was aroused when several of her prophecies went wrong. On one occasion she told Dr Cornacchia to cheer up since his pregnant wife was going to give birth to a baby girl; but, instead, she became ill and died within a few days.[53] She was suspected of spending the alms she had supposedly collected for the poor. She was accused of giving such harsh penances to followers that they were brought close to death. Furthermore, a priest from Naples had told Campanile about the blood of a holy man there which had been put inside an ampoule, in which it had occasionally boiled, and with which numerous miracles had been performed (the model is that of the famous Neapolitan reliquary containing the blood of St Januarius). Campanile resolved to try this with Giglia's blood. So, with the help of her physician Cornacchia, a pretext was found to have her bled, and the blood was put into an ampoule. However, the ampoule was then taken by another of Giglia's spiritual children, D. Serio Moro, her favourite. (A word about Moro. Several witnesses say that Giglia was seen in his house one night, naked to the waist, causing much scandal. Serio is also the only one who still frequented Giglia at the time of the trial, despite the charges against her.) Be that as it may, Serio dropped the ampoule, spilling the contents, and Campanile blamed this on the Devil. When asked why by the Inquisitor, Campanile replied that he and Cornacchia had planned to take it, along with Giglia, to the shrine of Monte St Angelo, to give the alleged guardian angel the chance to prove himself before the priests there. The rector of the Jesuit College in Bari had also shown interest in the ampoule. But the trip would have resulted in the clear discovery of the deception.[54]

Giglia's case was weakened further still when her guardian angel told her spiritual children that she had gone to church and had been exorcized by her confessor and another priest, both of whom were now firmly convinced of the guardian angel's divine nature. Campanile decided to ask Giglia's confessor to ascertain the truthfulness of the account, and he responded by saying that the story was a complete lie and advised Campanile not to have anything more to do with her, for the good of his own soul. In fact, Giglia had not even told her confessor and spiritual director about her guardian angel for fear of arousing his suspicion. As Campanile told the Inquisitor, he now came to the conclusion

> that the intention of the Devil was none other than to have the said Suor Giglia credited as a saint in order to prepare some great evil. And I believe that the Lord allowed me to know this because I prayed to him many times that he not let me fall into some evil and I recommended myself to St Philip, who is my particular devotion.[55]

At this point another of her spiritual children, Rev. Giovanni Chiuro, was even courageous enough to confront Giglia's guardian angel with this. On the eve of All Saints' (just a coincidence?) Chiuro was reasoning with her on how she was being deceived by the Devil and how this had occurred to many other holy and devout people, when she mentioned

Paradise and seemed to be leaving herself (*astraersi*) to make way for her spirit. He insisted: 'Stop! stop! Stay with me and listen to what I say.' But in vain, so he addressed the spirit now in her:

> Evil beast, infernal demon! By lying you have kept hold of this poor creature and the rest of us for a long time, pretending to be a good angel. But now the deceit and the lies you told have been discovered . . . Infernal beast, what are you doing inside the body of this creature?

In confusion, the spirit seemed to bow his head and look towards the ground and then said in a low voice, 'God sent me here'. 'How could you have spoken about the greatness of Mary and call her Our Lady?' To which the spirit responded that since he was an angel she was Our Lady for him as well. Then the spirit began to impersonate Giglia, taking her rosary and small reliquary from the head of her bed and kissing it. Chiuro asked where the relic came from, and Giglia – having now returned inside herself – said it was a splinter of the True Cross.[56]

The Inquisitor would seem to have been convinced of the deceit. But the fault was recognized as the Devil's and not Giglia's. She was regarded as a *povera illusa*, the Devil having taken advantage of her simple piety to further his own ends. When confronted with the deceits and told to pray for God's guidance, she replied, in tearful resignation:

> What I have done, I have done and do for this Christ [pointing to the crucifix], who has done and suffered so much for me, and this I understand, if this Christ then in remuneration of my works wants to give me a demon who becomes master of my soul, as master let him do what he wants.[57]

Even Giglia's spiritual director – about and to whom she had lied, and whose instructions she had not respected – believed that she was 'a good Christian, but because of the extravagant things which he saw in her life suspected that she was deceived (*illusa*) by the Devil'.[58] The Inquisitor was also concerned with Giglia's current reputation in the town, for it was important that no one be led astray by the delusion. The three clerics Campanile, Chiuro and Loizzo replied that she was commonly regarded as pious but possessed and deceived by the Devil. Only Cornacchia, her physician, left the court with some doubt, by suggesting that Giglia's healing and prophecy were still in demand:

> For a long time the said Suor Giglia was commonly held to be a saint, but then, when it was discovered that she did not confer with her spiritual director about her things, and then with us, so that we treated her as a liar, and her usual confessor did not want nor wants

to confess her, the people are divided into those who consider her good, and those [who consider her] possessed.[59]

Once women like Giglia began to lose their respectability because of an impending inquisitorial investigation, they were quickly abandoned by many of their followers and soon found themselves all but isolated. After they had recognized the error of their ways, they were generally sent to a convent where they would spend the rest of their days. This not only demonstrated that they had returned to the fold of the Church, but also kept them under strict supervision and prevented them from having contact with any followers that might be left. This is not to say that people in the community ceased to believe in their healing powers. On the contrary. When Benedetta Carlini finally died after thirty-five years of solitary confinement, crowds of people gathered to collect relics from her unburied corpse.[60]

It is not simply a question of the Church reform of local culture. First of all, the power and influence of these living saints could rise to such heights precisely because all levels of society participated. The difference being that the more high-placed her clientele, the more protection the living saint would have, and the more likely that she would have the guidance of those in tune with the accepted limits of holiness. This is what saved Maria Manca. She worked within the confines of what were considered acceptable expressions of piety. Her holiness was of the edifying rather than wonder-working variety, and her piety channelled into the construction of a new church. Suor Giglia, on the other hand, was not told of the limits and the risks of what she was doing. Her model of sanctity was becoming increasingly outmoded as far as the Church was concerned, even if it still satisfied local demands for sources of sacred power for healing, revelation and other wonders. The deeds of living saints would be defined as divinely or diabolically inspired, according to the outcome of the inquisitorial investigation. The women would then be labelled and their actions interpreted accordingly. A 'good' living saint was the antithesis of the witch; a 'bad' living saint, the witch's counterpart. Despite the risks inherent in being a living saint, or in seeking her cures or forming part of her cult, the cultural type survived throughout the early modern period.[61] This is testimony to both the role of saints in medical pluralism and the unceasing quest for manifestations of the sacred. The Church's ongoing struggle to regulate such phenomena – without discouraging their development – demonstrates the ecclesial interpretation of sacred healing after the Council of Trent. The boundary between orthodoxy and unorthodoxy, divine and diabolical, holy and sinful, was a very fine one indeed, and the Church reserved for itself the capability of making the distinction. Those in error, whether wise

151

women, lay exorcists or living saints, risked not only their souls but, like an evil contagion, the souls of the entire community.

Notes

This work was carried out while I was a Wellcome Trust research fellow.

1. 'Breve Notitia delle Missioni fatte nelle Diocesi, e Città di Campagna, Satriano, e Potenza da' Padri della Compagnia di Giesù', Archivium Romanum Societatis Iesu, Provincia Neapolitana, 76 I, f. 174v. (All translations are my own.)

2. One example is the Rev. Giovan Battista Chiesa of Santena in Piedmont studied by Giovanni Levi in *Inheriting Power: the Story of an Exorcist*, transl. L. Cochrane (Chicago, 1988). For the career of a lay exorcist, which also ended before the Church courts, cf. Jean-Michel Sallmann, *Chercheurs de Trésors et Jeteuses de Sorts. La Quête du Surnaturel à Naples au XIVe Siècle* (Paris, 1986), 176–8.

3. Giovanni Romeo, *Inquisitori, Esorcisti e Streghe nell'Italia della Controriforma* (Florence, 1990), 151.

4. Peter Burke, 'How to be a Counter-Reformation saint', in *The Historical Anthropology of Early Modern Italy. Essays on Perception and Communication* (Cambridge, 1987), 49.

5. Mauro Paticchio, *Brieve Riestretto della Vita di Maria Manca della Terra di Squinzano, Fondatrice della Chiesa della Santissima Annunziata di detta Terra. Opera del Sacerdote Mauro Paticchio della Medesima* (Naples: Mazzola-Vocola, 1769), reprinted (Galatina, 1971), 36.

6. Paticchio, *Brieve Riestretto*, 42.

7. Paticchio, *Brieve Riestretto*, 42.

8. Paticchio, *Brieve Riestretto*, 74. St Agatha was a Sicilian virgin and martyr whose breasts were cut off and then miraculously healed after a vision of St Peter. Maria Manca was also a devotee of St Theresa of Avila.

9. Paticchio, *Brieve Riestretto*, 92.

10. Paticchio, *Brieve Riestretto*, 33. The Belgian Jesuit Martín Del Río was author of *Disquisitionum Magicarum Libri Sex* (Louvain, 1600); the German Dominicans Jakob Sprenger and Heinrich Institoris (or von Krämer) compiled the witchfinder's guide, the *Malleus Maleficarum* (1486); and the Spaniard Francisco de Torreblanca y Villalpando wrote the *Epitomes Delictorum, in quibus Aperta, vel Occulta Invocatio Daemonis Intervenit* (Seville, 1618).

11. Paticchio, *Brieve Riestretto*, 41. Richard Mead, MD (1673–1754) was physician to George II for a time, and such was his fame in Italy that the king of Naples wrote to him asking for his works and inviting him to the palace. In his *Medica Sacra, a Commentary on the Diseases Mentioned in Scripture* (1749), he discusses leprosy, palsy and possession, identifying Job's ailment as elephantiasis, Saul's as melancholia and so on. Cf. *Dictionary of National Biography*, XIII, 181–6.

12. Francesco Maria Guazzo (or Guaccio), *Compendium Maleficarum in Tres Libris Distinctum ex Pluribus Autoribus* (Milan, 1608); English translation by E.A. Ashwin with notes by M. Summers (London, 1929).

13. Franciscus Valesius, *De Occultis Naturae Miraculis*, book II, ch. 1.

14. Guazzo, *Compendium*, book II, ch. 8, p. 106.

15. Andreas Caesalpino, *Daemonum Investigatio Peripatetica* (Florence, 1580), ch. 16.

16. Pietro Piperno, *De Magicis Affectibus horum Dignotione, Praenotione, Curatione, Medica, Strategemmatica, Divina, Plurisque [sic] Curationibus Electis & de Nuce Beneventana Maga, Auctore Petro Piperno Beneventano Protomed*

(Naples, 1634). Cf. Michele Miele, 'Malattie magiche di origine diabolica e loro terapia secondo il medico beneventano Pietro Piperno († 1642)', *Campania Sacra*, IV (1973), 166–223.

17. Piperno, *De Magicus Affectibus*, 57.

18. Piperno, *De Magicus Affectibus*, 59.

19. Piperno, *De Magicus Affectibus*, 169–207.

20. Piero Camporesi, *The Incorruptible Flesh. Bodily Mutation and Mortification in Religion and Folklore*, transl. T. Croft-Murray (Cambridge, 1988), 161–2.

21. Michael MacDonald, 'Religion, social change and psychological healing in England, 1600–1800', in W.J. Sheils (ed.), *The Church and Healing* (Oxford, 1982), 123.

22. Michel de Certeau, 'Discourse disturbed: the sorcerer's speech', in *The Writing of History*, transl. T. Conley (New York, 1988), 265.

23. She was the Dominican tertiary Caterina da Racconigi. See Gabriella Zarri, 'Le sante vive. Per una tipologia della santità femminile nel primo cinquecento', *Annali dell'Istituto Storico Italo-Germanico in Trento*, VI (1980), 428.

24. Judith Brown, *Immodest Acts. The Life of a Lesbian Nun in Renaissance Italy* (Oxford, 1986), 52.

25. Paticchio, *Brieve Riestretto*, 54.

26. Paticchio, *Brieve Riestretto*, 125.

27. Paticchio, *Brieve Riestretto*, 145.

28. Paticchio, *Brieve Riestretto*, 164.

29. Paticchio, *Brieve Riestretto*, 11.

30. Zarri, 'Sante vive', 379.

31. Sara Cabibbo and Marilena Modica, *La Santa dei Tomasi. Storia di Suor Maria Crocifissa (1645–1699)* (Turin, 1989), 146–7.

32. Brown, *Immodest Acts*, 51.

33. If the memory of Maria Manca is still alive today in Squinzano it is because she is offered as a model of devotion, and the veneration itself is channelled to the image of Our Lady of the Carnation in the church she built in the town. A more modern-day example of this is the healer and seer Marietta D'Agostino of Orta Nova (Foggia). As observed by the ethnologist Annabella Rossi in 1968, she performed healing activities in a shrine she had set up in her two-room house, attributing her powers to Our Lady of Altomare, to whom the shrine was dedicated. Hundreds of people came everyday for cures and predictions and their contributions enabled her to build a small church in the vicinity. It was consecrated by the bishop, despite earlier trouble with the clergy over her alleged visions of and conversations with the Virgin. Annabella Rossi, *Le Feste dei Poveri* (Palermo, 1986 edn), 61–5.

34. Zarri, 'Sante vive', 409.

35. Cf. Gábor Klaniczay, 'Legends as life strategies for aspirant saints in the late Middle Ages', reprinted in his *The Uses of Supernatural Power: The Transformation of Popular Religion in Medieval and Early Modern Europe*, transl. S. Singerman (Cambridge, 1990), 96.

36. Such was the case in places like Mantua, Ferrara, Milan and Florence in the first half of the sixteenth century, as discussed by Zarri, 'Santa vive', 418–20. After the Council of Trent the activities of such 'court saints' became much more circumscribed and they were subjected to inquisitorial scrutiny. For example, the case of a prioress from Lisbon, Sr Maria de la Visitación, whose visionary powers and stigmata resulted in her becoming one of the most influential women in Europe during the 1580s – consulted by secular rulers and Church officials –

before she was discovered to be a fraud. Cf. E. Allison Peers, *Studies of the Spanish Mystics* (London, 1951 edn), vol. 1, 30–1.

37. This was to be the principal case against the many Spanish *beatas* tried by the Spanish Inquisition, some of whom were linked to the earlier Alumbrado heresy. See the study by Mary Elizabeth Perry, 'Beatas and the Inquisition in early modern Seville', in S. Haliczer (ed.), *Inquisition and Society in Early Modern Europe* (London, 1987), 147–68.

38. Francesco Maria Maggio, *Vita della Venerabil Madre Orsola Benincasa Napoletana Originale di Siena, dell'Ordine del B. Gaetano, Fondatrice delle Vergini della Congregazione e dell'Eremo della Immacolata Concettione* (Rome, 1655), 253.

39. At this point in his hagiography Maggio critized Gregory XIII for not recognizing the need for reform and acts of penance which Orsola had repeatedly called for, the result being the succession of calamities that had followed her death and showed no signs of abating. Maggio, *Vita*, 305–8. This criticism no doubt had a lot to do with his book being placed on the Index. See S. Menchi, 'Orsola Benincasa', *Dizionario Biografico degli Italiani*, VIII (Rome, 1966), 527–30. One calamity which Maggio did not include in his list occurred the year after the book's publication. It was said that Orsola had warned of a great catastrophe for the city of Naples, and when plague struck in 1656, the convent she had founded was the site of many public processions and acts of mortification to placate the wrath of God. Salvatore de Renzi, *Napoli nell'Anno 1656* (Naples, 1867), 39–44.

40. Cf. the discussion by Jean-Michel Sallmann, 'La sainteté mystique féminine à Naples au tournant des 16ᵉ et 17ᵉ siècles', in S. Boesch Gajano and L. Sebastiani (eds), *Culto dei Santi, Istituzioni e Classi Sociali in Età Preindustriale* (Rome, 1984), 683–702.

41. 'Informatio supra Giglia Fino' (1628), Archivio Diocesano, Gravina, Fondo vescovile, Atti del S. Ufficio: materie varie, IV.D9.cl. My thanks to Marisa D'Agostino and Fedele Raguso for their friendly and efficient assistance. The case is discussed briefly, along with other Inquisition trials kept at the Gravina archive, by D'Agostino, 'Religione o magia nella società di Gravina ed Altamura tra XVII e XVIII secolo', *Vedi Gravina. Itinerario III* (Bari, 1987), 89–104. Similar examples of Italian tertiary nuns examined for 'simulated sanctity' by the Inquisition have been studied by Luisa Ciammitti, 'Una santa di meno: storia di Angela Mellini, cucitrice di Bologna (b.1667)', *Quaderni Storici*, XIV (1979), 37–71; and Giovanni Romeo, 'Una "simulatrice di santita" a Napoli nel '500: Alfonsina Rispoli', *Campania sacra*, VIII-IX (1977–8), 159–218.

42. Deposition of Giovanni Gironamo Cornacchia, 'Informatio supra Giglia Fino', f. 15v.

43. Deposition of Rev Roberto Campanile, 'Informatio supra Giglia Fino', ff. 2r–3r.

44. Deposition of Giovanni Gironamo Cornacchia, 'Informatio supra Giglia Fino', f. 19v. The crucifix was itself imbued with sacred power, for it had 'talked and conferred with her' (f. 15r.).

45. Deposition of Rev Giovanni Chiuro, 'Informatio supra Giglia Fino', ff. 24v–25r.

46. Depositon of Rev Roberto Campanile, 'Informatio supra Giglia Fino', f. 4v.

47. Deposition of Rev Giovanni Chiuro, 'Informatio supra Giglia Fino', f. 22r.

48. Deposition of Rev Giovanni Chiuro, 'Informatio supra Giglia Fino', ff. 20v–21r.

49. Deposition of Rev Agostino Loizzo, 'Informatio supra Giglia Fino', f. 35.

50. The Inquisitor made a point of asking how Jesus gave her communion, and the answer was like a priest, giving her the host. Deposition of Rev Roberto Campanile, 'Informatio supra Giglia Fino', ff. 6v–7r.

51. Deposition of Rev Roberto Campanile, 'Informatio supra Giglia Fino', ff. 7v–8r.

52. Deposition of Loizzo, 'Informatio supra Giglia Fino', f. 36v.

53. Deposition of Rev Roberto Campanile, 'Informatio supra Giglia Fino', f. 12v.

54. Deposition of Rev Roberto Campanile, 'Informatio supra Giglia Fino', ff. 8v–9v.

55. Deposition of Rev Roberto Campanile 'Informatio supra Giglia Fino', f. 5v.

56. Deposition of Rev Giovanni Chiuro, 'Informatio supra Giglia Fino', ff. 23r–24r.

57. Deposition of Loizzo, 'Informatio supra Giglia Fino', ff. 38v–39r. In his sympathetic reconstruction of a similar trial for pretence of sanctity against Maria Janis da Vertova (Venice, 1662), Fulvio Tomizza notes that all the evidence meant to ridicule Maria and prove her fakery was 'shown to be inconsistent or irrelevant before the tenacity with which the woman of Vertova, from the age-old poverty of her surroundings, had sought the direct ladder to Paradise, certain as she was, in an era of religious emulation rather than authentic mystic fervour, that sanctity was the equivalent of a feudal privilege extended to the simple people and attainable therefore through the renunciation of material needs and of the very human foundations.' Fulvio Tomizza, *La Finzione di Maria* (Milan, 1981), 208 (English translation by Anne Jacobson Schutte forthcoming).

58. Deposition of Giovanni Gironamo Cornacchia, 'Informatio supra Giglia Fino', f. 14r.

59. Deposition of Giovanni Gironamo Cornacchia, 'Informatio supra Giglia Fino', f. 19r.

60. Brown, *Immodest Acts*, 137.

61. William Christian, *Apparitions in Late Medieval and Renaissance Spain* (Princeton, 1981), 185.

8

The Inquisition and minority medical practitioners in Counter-Reformation Spain

Judaizing and Morisco practitioners, 1560–1610

Luis García-Ballester

The medical history that we read and write today is still based mostly on the *writings* of an *élite* of medical men.

(E.H. Ackerknecht 1967)

Introduction: the problem of the minorities in sixteenth-century Spain

During the fourteen and fifteenth centuries, the Christian-controlled areas of Spain contained two substantial minority groups: the Jews, and those Moslems who had not departed for the lands still controlled by their co-religionists. The members of both minorities underwent persecution during these centuries at the hands of members of the Christian majority, and this became particularly intense from the late fourteenth century (1391) onwards. Many Jews therefore converted to Christianity. These 'New Christians' of Jewish origin were known by the name of 'Conversos'.[1] By contrast, mass conversion did not take place among the Moslem minority until they were forced to adopt Christianity at the beginning of the seventeenth century. After their conversion, the converted Moors were given the name 'Moriscos'.[2]

On a number of occasions I have considered the history of medicine among the Morisco minority in Spain in the sixteenth century and the first decade of the seventeenth century. I have studied the process of disintegration of their medical system, as well as the characteristics of their kind of medicine and of their medical practice.[3] Here I shall undertake a comparative study of the differing attitudes that the Inquisition held towards physicians of these two minorities: towards those who belonged to the Morisco minority, and towards those who were suspected of being descended from the old Jewish population. The different social circumstances of the two groups led to differing modes of action towards them on the part of the Inquisition. I shall concentrate on the period between 1560 and 1610, as these dates coincide with the peak period of the

156

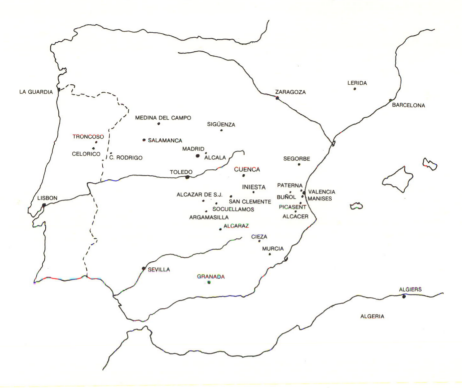

Illustration 8 Map of Spain, Portugal and North Africa, showing towns and cities referred to in chapter 8.

Counter-Reformation in Spain, and since the members of the Morisco minority were expelled from the lands of the Spanish monarchy at the end of this period.

The 'Judaizers' or 'Marranos'

Many of the converted Jews were sincere Christians. Many others believed that it would be possible to lead a double life with respect to their religious beliefs. This gave rise to a new social category, described by the legal and theological term of 'Judaizer' and the popular expression 'Marrano'.[4] As from the fifteenth century, converted Jews were suspected of 'Judaizing' or reverting to their original faith. This suspicion was based on purely ritual indications related to the Jewish religion (cleansing of the hands, washing of meat, rejection of pork, death rituals, among others), and also on forms of religious behaviour which were suspect from the point of view of what was subsequently defined as Catholic orthodoxy (for example, anticlericalism, particularly towards the

157

religious orders; reticence towards the cult of saints, and to the status of the Virgin Mary, and certain forms of messianic expectation).[5]

The Conversos were the victims of riots and massacres in the fifteenth century. But this was not only due to religious reasons. The political complexity and economic difficulties of the Hispanic Kingdoms also played an important part. In 1478, the new monarchy inaugurated by the marriage of the so-called 'Catholic Monarchs' (Isabella, Queen of Castile, and Ferdinand, King of Aragon) introduced the Inquisition.[6] The same monarchs signed the decree expelling the Jews from Spain in 1492. In this way, the Jewish problem disappeared from Spain, although the Conversos continued to be suspected as possible Judaizers.[7] One of the purposes of the Inquisition was precisely to control the religious life of the Conversos.[8] In 1492 many of the Spanish Jews left for Portugal, where they were eventually forced to convert by a wide variety of methods. There was a long frontier between the two countries, and from 1580 to 1640 Portugal was incorporated under the Spanish crown.[9] This brought about a flow of Portuguese Conversos towards Spain, and the two Jewish communities were linked by many family ties as well as by inter-marriage. Thus, as we shall see, it is somewhat artificial to separate Portuguese Judaizers (or suspect Conversos) from Spanish ones in the Counter-Reformation period.[10]

For Jewish physicians, conversion was something more than a personal or collective religious issue. For it also had repercussions in the field of medical practice. In effect, conversion to Catholicism carried with it the prospect of economic improvement for the members of Converso families, and this opened the doors of the universities for them; this was particularly attractive to them because of their traditional high regard for learning. This was a new situation which their ancestors, with their Jewish faith, had not been able to enjoy, for access to the faculties of medicine had been only open to Christians. As we shall see, all the trials of Converso physicians, held in the various Spanish inquisitorial courts (1560–1610), rested upon accusations of Judaizing. In none of them – at least in none of the cases from this half century – were accusations made against them of deviant medical practices, such as the invocation of devils, witchcraft, the use of charms and spells, and other such practices rejected by academic medicine. Almost all the Converso physicians who appeared in the Inquisition's courts had undertaken university studies (see Table 2).

Throughout the sixteenth century, but more especially in the first and last third, the so-called 'condition of purity of blood' was imposed on the 'New Christians' within the lands of Spain, and especially against the Conversos, probably because of the greater social prestige of the posts that they occupied. This measure, which aimed at preventing anyone who might be 'stained' with Jewish blood from holding any post in society (whether civil or ecclesiastic), was contrary to the principle of social unity applying to all those who had received baptism and it was therefore not accepted by Spanish Catholicism; hence it was an element of great social unrest.[11] The 'purity of blood' measures spread to the universities. An example of this movement can be seen in the constitutions of the University College of San Ildefonso (1519), which belonged to the prestigious new University of Alcalá:

> It is ordained that no one shall be admitted nor elected as a member of the college . . . without it first being ascertained that he is neither a son of, nor a descendant of, a Jew, or Moor, or 'Converso' . . . and if on any occasion, whether by error, or by fraud or by negligence, any such person should be elected, he shall be expelled from the College . . . The information should be drawn up concerning his parents and four grandparents.[12]

In spite of these measures to prevent the descendants of 'New Christians' from entering the faculties of medicine, the descendants of the Conversos found ways to get round these prohibitions.[13] The Converso physician, like the Converso population in general, intermingled with the 'Old Christian' population after 1492. They were not an identifiable social grouping. Yet the Conversos were hampered by the climate of suspicion towards them, which varied during the sixteenth century, but which became particularly strong during the Counter-Reformation, leading to an obsession on the part of the Inquisition with particular settlements and instititions, both civil and ecclesiastic, where accusations of Judaizing had accumulated against certain families or individuals.[14]

The Moriscos

By the beginning of the sixteenth century the Spanish monarchy had expelled those of its subjects that belonged to the Jewish faith, but it continued to have in its territories a substantial population which had an Islamic cultural background and practised the Moslem religion. This population was by no means uniformly distributed over the whole country. It hardly existed in the northern parts of the peninsula, nor in Catalonia, with the exception of the southernmost districts forming part of the Ebro valley, while the Moslems formed but a small minority in the extensive territories of Castile and western Andalucia (the Guadalquivir valley). By contrast, they represented a third of the total population in Aragon, Valencia and Murcia, and an even higher proportion in the areas of eastern Andalucia, which coincided with what had been the old Arab Kingdom of Granada. In Portugal there were also Moslems whose background was similar to that of their co-religionists in the other kingdoms of the Iberian Peninsula. Christian society would no longer tolerate the presence in its midst of non-Christians, and thus proceeded with the mass enforced baptism of Moslems. By the 1520s the vast majority of Moslems were officially Christians. These 'new Christians' were, as mentioned above, known as Moriscos. Between 1569 and 1571, the whole Morisco population of the former Kingdom of Granada was expelled, most of them settling in Castile. This expulsion was the punishment imposed on them for the revolt that they had staged against the so-called 'Old Christians' who had been oppressing them. Thus the dream of the first Archbishop of Granada, Hernando de Talavera, to count among his faithful an Arabic-speaking Christian population, was shattered once and for all.[15]

However, the water of baptism would not wash away the fact that they belonged to the Islamic culture, nor their old faith, which the majority of them continued to practise in secret, and which was transmitted – as in the case of many Jewish Conversos – by means of oral tradition. One manifestation of this was the continued survival and the use of the Arabic language (*algarabía*), especially among those living in Valencia, Murcia and Granada, as well as a series of rituals connected with everyday life (such as meals, clothes, and wedding and death rituals) that identified them as a group; an external sign of their continued adherence to Moslem tradition was the continued practice of circumcision, a custom which had a deep cultural significance rather than just a strictly religious one. Furthermore, when the Moriscos constituted a minority of the population of a settlement, then they clustered in particular districts. The 'Old Christians' and the Moriscos were in constant conflict throughout the sixteenth century. As the century progressed, and in particular after the decrees of 1566–7, the 'Old Christians' instituted measures to eradicate the defining differential characteristics of the Morisco population, with the clear aim of marginalizing them in both social and economic terms. One of these characteristics was the form of medicine they practised.[16] Ultimately, between 1609 and 1612, King Philip III decreed the expulsion of all the Moriscos from his realms.[17]

Unlike the Converso, who might be poor but never a serf, the Morisco had a social status typical of that of the serf in feudal society. With few exceptions their new Christian faith did not allow young Moriscos to enter universities in order to study medicine, whereas this was feasible in the case of members of reasonably wealthy Jewish Converso families (such as the sons of physicians, artisans or merchants). Moslem healers – and in general the whole system of medical attention available for the Morisco population – were affected by the general disintegration of their cultural way of life.[18]

The drama affecting the 'New Christians' (both Conversos and Moriscos), the growing tension that they experienced from the last third of the sixteenth century onwards, was the most serious social problem of

Spanish society. The expulsion of the Moriscos, hardly a hundred years after the expulsion of the other great minority – the Jews who refused to accept baptism (1492) – was the greatest social upheaval that Spain underwent during the period of the Counter-Reformation. The vast society ruled by the Spanish Crown (Portugal, Castile, Aragon, other European lands and the extensive overseas territories) may have gained in uniformity, but it lost in freedom and openness. In this process, the Spanish monarchy not only made use of all the political means available to it within secular society to control the life of its subjects, but also reinforced its position by using the authority of the Catholic Church. The ecclesiastical institution which pre-eminently supported this process was the Inquisition.[19]

The Inquisition, minorities and medicine

The role of the Inquisition was decisive in the twofold process of, on the one hand, destroying the Islamic culture of the Morisco minority, and on the other of attempting to assimilate the converted members of both the Moriscos and the Conversos within the orthodox form of Catholic Christianity which was imposed in Spain by the Counter-Reformation. The way this was achieved was by delving into all the acts of the everyday life of the Moriscos and Conversos, even at the most intimate level. The Inquisition made use of all available means, especially anonymous accusations. One of the most negative consequences of this was the introduction of fear and mistrust into human relationships and between social groups.[20] This led to situations like that of the wife of Enrique Leiton (*fl.* 1588), a graduate in medicine, who confessed that her husband was ignorant of her Jewish practices, such was her fear that her husband might be put on trial. Despite his wife's efforts, he was arrested and subjected to torture.[21] On other occasions, it was a wife who accused her own husband, as in the case of Luis Castro (*fl.* 1606), doctor in medicine, who was sentenced in his absence because he had managed to flee to France, abandoning his wife and the rest of his family to their fate.[22] Fear did not always destroy solidarity among those living through such dramatic circumstances. One of the accusations made against the physicians Mateo Nuñez (*fl.* 1595) and Felipe de Nájera (1560–*c.*1610) was that of 'having received into their homes fugitives from Portugal fleeing from the Holy Office'.[23] Mere possession of the medical works of Isaac Israeli came to be a motive for suspicion for the Inquisition 'because the author was Jewish'.[24] For this reason, it is not at all surprising that the Inquisition should have been perceived by Moriscos as the very symbol of repression, especially from the 1570s onwards, and that the Converso accused of being a Judaizer should consider it to be worse than 'the devil himself'.[25]

161

Table 1 Offences recorded by the Court of the Inquisition of Toledo (1575–1610)

Offences	Number of cases
Judaizers	174
Moriscos	190
For not considering fornication as a crime	264
Blasphemy	46
Witchcraft	18
Heresy	62
Soliciting in confession	52
Total	806

Source: H. Kamen, *The Spanish Inquisition*, London, 1965.

The Inquisition's state of near obsession with the Jewish and the Moslem minorities of medieval and Renaissance Spain becomes immediately apparent simply by reading and comparing the tables of those cases recorded by the court of the Inquisition of Toledo between 1575 and 1610, the period of the full social implementation of the Counter-Reformation in Spain (see Table 1).

As can be seen, trials of Judaizers and Moriscos amount to 364 (45 per cent); those of the Moriscos alone made up almost a quarter of the total.

While these figures are highly revealing, those referring to the numbers of healers (physicians, surgeons and barbers) are not so striking. Hardly a dozen Morisco healers can be traced in all the Inquisition courts (not only those of Toledo). Between 1560 and 1610, the number of Converso physicians, or members of their families, tried by the Inquisition (according to the material surviving from all the courts) is 36, nine of whom were of Portuguese origin (see Table 2).

It is true that the death sentence was in general hardly ever applied to Moriscos by the Inquisition courts. The ratio between death sentences/ sentences in the courts of Zaragoza (Aragon), Cuenca (Castile), Granada and Murcia in the late sixteenth century, was in the region of 1 to 40.[26] For the Conversos, while no such ratio is available, it can be safely said that the Inquisition was much stricter and that Conversos were often condemned to death.[27] In the case of Judaizing physicians put on trial in the period 1560–1610, the ratio was 1 to 5. Generally speaking, the Inquisition preferred to impose fines, stimulated as it was by the increasing need for money to cover the expenses incurred by its own bureaucracy. For this reason, special contributions were agreed upon with Morisco communities, and in the case of Conversos sentences included the confiscation of their worldly goods and possessions. For example, of the 36 Converso physicians or members of the families of Converso physicians, 26 had their property confiscated, two were heavily fined, seven were acquitted and seven were condemned to death. The

Inquisition's greed for money was so infamous that one of the physicians put on trial, the bachelor of medicine Felipe Nájera (1609), at one stage of the interrogation, after undergoing torture,[28] said to the inquisitors: 'if you are doing this because of my estate, take it'.[29] In the case of physicians or healers, professional disqualification for life was added to the sentences (this is made explicit in the sentence imposed upon the Morisco healer Gaspar Capdal).[30]

As a result of all these measures those who were tried were reduced to poverty, together with their families. In the case of the Moriscos, the more numerous and better organized social group, this measure was deliberately taken into account as a means of preventing any improvement in their social status. The Archbishop of Valencia, Juan de Ribera (1532–1611), a typical eccclesiastical representative of the Spanish Church during the Counter-Reformation, was very clear on this matter: 'There is also a great advantage in this measure [punishing them with fines and imposing special taxes], which is that it makes them poor.'[31] The Dominican Friar Bleda, also from Valencia, maintained in the same vein: 'These dogs should not be given the bread of their children, but they must be expelled from colleges and assigned to the galleys, and never to the liberal arts [the step prior to the study of medicine].'[32]

The Inquisition kept up a relentless campaign of harassment against the Morisco minority. The aim was to try to bring about the disappearance of the Morisco cultural identity as such by means of judicial persecution. The magical forms of Morisco healers' medical practice attracted the hostile attention of the Inquisition. The confrontation between the Inquisition and Morisco healers was a confrontation between academic medicine and popular forms of medical practice steeped in magic and empiricism. The very system of medical attention that had been gradually created among the Moriscos (with their own healers), the physician–patient relationship when a Morisco was one of the parties involved, and the body of medical doctrine used by Morisco healers, which was considered to be effective by Morisco (and non-Morisco) patients, these were all carefully monitored and undermined by the Inquisition.[33] The inquisitorial trials in the courts of Toledo, Cuenca and Valencia, against Moriscos who practised medicine, increased in the last third of the sixteenth century and in the first few years of the seventeenth century: that is to say, in the final phase of the disintegration of the medical subculture in the Morisco community and in a Spain dominated by the Counter-Reformation. The Spanish monarchy linked its methods of political control to the Counter-Reformation movement, which was concerned with the preservation of Catholic dogma. Thus a mixture of political, religious and legal ideas was achieved, a mixture that clouded the life of the whole of Spain in this period.[34] What was collected by means of the Inquisition's interrogations demonstrates

Table 2 Medical training of the Judaizing practitioners prosecuted by the Inquisition (1560–1610)

University training	No. of cases	Training unrecorded	No. of cases
Doctors	4	Physicians	6
Licenciates	16	Barber surgeons	2
Bachelors	7		
Student of medicine	1		
Total	28	Total	8

Source: AHN, Inquisitorial records; J. Contreras, Database (personal information).

undeniably the increasingly desperate situation of the Moriscos, the fear and the mistrust permeating the whole of Spanish society, and the wish of the Moriscos to live unmolested and hence in freedom. Christian society in Counter-Reformation Spain was unable to integrate into itself the Morisco attitudes towards illness and medicine, and endow them with social dignity. Faced with these problems, it opted for the easiest solution, which was at the same time the most traumatic: to make the Moriscos disappear.[35]

The fact that Converso physicians were fully integrated within the medical system of the 'establishment' and that they practised the form of medicine that was usual among the Christian majority (I leave aside here the popular forms of medicine, as yet unstudied by historians) meant that the situation that affected Morisco healers did not arise among the Conversos. Converso physicians were tried by the Inquisition for being Judaizers, but not for medical practices deviating from what was considered 'normal' in the neo-scholastic Galenism that flourished in Spanish faculties of medicine in this period.[36] It must be remembered that as from 1559 Spanish universities and their members, both staff and students, were forbidden by Royal decree to maintain intellectual contacts with any other university centre in the rest of Europe. One year earlier (1558) strict control over intellectual publications (from theology to natural philosophy and medicine) had been introduced also by Royal decree; this in fact was the establishment of a proper censor's office, which had negative repercussions on Spanish intellectual life. This kind of measure was another consequence of the Counter-Reformation movement in the Spanish realms.[37]

The Conversos did not possess their own form of medicine, nor did they organize a system of medical care and attention specifically for their own community. The thirty-six Converso healers suspected of Judaizing who were put on trial by the Inquisition between 1560 and 1610, belonged to the medical establishment. Their medical training was as shown in Table 2.

Inquisitorial trials as a source for the study of Morisco and Converso healers

Any Morisco or Converso was liable to be prosecuted by the Holy Office simply because of his status; for this reason, he distrusted all those around him. Whereas civil courts only intervened in the ordinary circumstances to be found in contemporary civilized European society (including Spain), the Inquisition poked into the most remote corners of society without respecting the norms of other courts. Although the degree of strictness it employed was by no means the same in all regions, it was omnipresent. Because of its power and methods, it kept the Moriscos and the Conversos in a state of permanent worry and fear. The Inquisition even prosecuted Moriscos and Judaizers in the Americas and India (Goa), when Goa was incorporated into the territories of Portugal and finally into those of the Spanish Crown between 1580 and 1640.[38]

Paradoxically, the strictness and efficiency demonstrated by the Inquisition enable us to further our knowledge of the medical sociology of the Moriscos, Conversos and Judaizers, providing us with material on their healing activities which would otherwise be very difficult, if not impossible, for us to reconstruct. The same is the case with Converso and Judaizing physicians.[39] The zeal of the Inquisition has enabled us to discover the existence of a not inconsiderable number of general practitioners (the majority of whom were university-trained physicians) who were Conversos, many of them Judaizers, who served as town physicians throughout the length and breadth of Spain. They were the protagonists of a dramatic situation which led many of them into exile, in search of a place where 'they might be well received' and where they could live 'with freedom to be Jews', as a Judaizer confessed,[40] or in order to 'be able to renounce our Holy Catholic faith and apostatize and live in greater freedom in the sect of Mohammed', in the words of a Morisco healer.[41] According to the evidence of Conversos themselves (either directly from those on trial or indirectly from those who had fled), these places were: Italy, and especially Rome (because of the tolerance shown by the Popes themselves in their own territories), France (Bordeaux, Paris, Rouen), the Low Countries (Amberes), Germany (Hamburg), North Africa (Algeria), Turkey (Constantinople) and overseas territories (the New World and Goa).[42]

The current state of research does not allow us to quantify the number of Converso or Morisco physicians who had to go into exile, or to measure the effects that this movement must have had on the sixteenth and seventeenth century Spanish medical system. Even though we are aware that there were more, we have only traced one case of exile among the Morisco healers sought by the Inquisition: that of Jerónimo Jover, which will be considered below. More numerous were the Judaizers who opted for exile. We can instance, among others, the famous physician and naturalist Garcia d'Orta,[43] the pattern of whose life was to be repeated by many Conversos. The son of Spanish Jews who had been deported and who were converted while in Portugal, he undertook medical studies in the Castilian universities of Salamanca and Alcalá (between 1515 and 1522-3). In 1534, he left for Goa, where he died in 1568, without having been troubled, even though the Inquisition had been established there in 1560. His sisters were prosecuted by the Inquisition in Portugal; one of them (Catalina) was tried for a second time in 1568 and burnt at the stake the next year. The trial gave rise to suspicions about Garcia d'Orta, who was tried *post mortem*. On 4 December 1580, his remains were exhumed and burned. His work as a naturalist (*Coloquios dos Simples e Drogas da India*, Goa 1563) was permeated by the memory of his parents' expulsion from Spain (1492) and by his fear of the Inquisition because of his status as a Converso.[44] Another famous contemporary of Garcia d'Orta was Amato Lusitano or Joao Rodriguez de Castello Branco, who, after studying medicine in Salamanca, left for Italy and the Low Countries in 1534, where there was a sizeable colony of exiled Conversos, especially in Amberes.[45] We might also mention Rodrigo de Castro (born in 1548), who went into exile in the Low Countries and later in Hamburg, where he was still living in 1629.[46] To a later generation belonged Zacuto (born 1575), who also studied in Salamanca and who graduated from the minor University at Sigüenza. He was a descendant of the Spanish Jewish astronomer, Abraham Zacuto,[47] who was also exiled to Portugal in 1492. After practising in Lisbon, he went back to Castile in 1625, but subsequently his fear drove him into exile in Amsterdam. It was there that he wrote his history of the most important physicians, *De Medicorum Principum Historia* (Amsterdam, 1629), which is of great interest for this subject, since it informs us, by means of his medical correspondents, of the widespread network that the Conversos formed in the various lands of Europe (including Castile) and overseas, ranging from the Low Countries, Germany and France as far as Turkey and Goa. Their evidence allows us to gain an idea of the importance this continual gradual drain of exiled physicians meant, an outflow that was increased in the period of the Counter-Reformation.[48]

Heresy and minority medical practitioners

The theological and doctrinal justifications for the prohibition of the practice of medicine by Morisco or Converso practitioners were based on a puristic Catholic attitude which had its roots in the years when the early Christian communities had to ask themselves the question: who cures? is it Christ, or the pagan physician who is treating them?[49] Likewise, was it permissible for an 'Old Christian' to be treated by a 'New Christian' who was suspected of being a secret Moslem or Jew?

It is true that the Moriscos and many Conversos were Christians, even if only outwardly. Being constantly suspected by the Church and society of continual deviation, the Inquisition stigmatized them as 'heretics'. This was a very wide term which, according to the famous declaration of the University of Paris in 1398, included all forms of superstitious practice on the part of a Christian, whose results could not reasonably be explained either to be proceeding from God or from nature.[50] This was precisely the way in which the Inquisition attacked Morisco practitioners.

Explicitly or implicitly, it was considered that any cure achieved by a Morisco physician could be nothing other than the work of the devil, and consequently the result of a pact with him. Continuing the line of the theological authorities in Paris, in 1492, Bernardo Basin, a canon of Zaragoza, using a solid (!) scholastic argument, concluded that every pact with the devil, implicit or explicit, should be treated as if it were heresy, whether it was so or not.[51] In the same tradition, in 1552, Bishop Simancas declared that the devil entered all superstitious practices and charm rites, whether man so desired or otherwise.[52] In this way, everything was to be attributed to the 'arts of the devil'. Torreblanca, a Spanish theologian of the late sixteenth century, even suggested in his *Epitome Delictorum sive de Magia*,[53] that in any cure we have to assume the presence of a pact if recited or murmured words are used, even if it involved the merest touch, or the use of a simple piece of clothing with no special properties. There is also a suspicion of a pact if verbal imprecations against the disease are used; these are approved of by the Church but can only be used by those who are in holy orders. And in general, there is suspicion of a pact in any cure of a disease which physicians cannot explain. Consequently, all the activities of healers and charlatans fell under the jurisdiction of the Inquisition. These measures were finally endorsed by Sixtus V's Bull of 1585 (*Caeli et Terrae*).[54] The wide and unrestricted field in which the Inquisition moved meant that any cure carried out by Morisco practitioners which Inquisition experts (that is, physicians at the service of the Holy Office)[55] found difficult to explain was open to the suspicion of having been carried out by means of a pact with the devil. In the trial of the physician Gaspar Casal[56] – a Morisco physician who practised medicine in the town of Buñol, western Valencia, an area with a large number of Morisco inhabitants – the prosecutor concluded:

1. I accuse him especially of having an express pact with the devil, with whom he communicates freely, and from whom he knows the

future and also many other things which human knowledge could not encompass, and in view of this it is very probable that he obeys, venerates and adores the devil. 2. . . . and in accordance with the contents of the preceding chapter, the said 'Morisco' is held to be a physician who carries out extraordinary cures, which could not be achieved by human art, nor by other physicians, and that many people come to him, drawn by his reputation. . . .[57]

To these arguments should be added those derived from professional competition with 'Old Christian' practitioners, in which money and prestige were involved. This is clearly stated by one of the Morisco physicians: 'And since the Morisco received both honour and money [from attending rich patients], he was hated by the [Old Christian] physicians'.[58] This sort of reason gave support to a feeling which we could call 'professional anti-Semitism', both against Converso and Morisco practitioners.[59]

Reasons of a religious/pastoral nature (i.e. those related to the care that religious authorities, as shepherds of their flocks, are supposed to take) gave support to the argument against both Morisco and Judaizing physicians: 'how can a Morisco or a Judaizing physician encourage a patient to confess his sins if he himself does not consider confession a sacrament, or receive Holy Communion either?'[60] If 'Old Christian' physicians were negligent in this respect, how much more probable was it that 'New Christian' physicians would be so? In view of this, Catholic moralists even rejected the consolation that every doctor could offer a patient – even a hopeless case – namely the possibility of a cure. The intransigent moralists of the Spanish Counter-Reformation did not hesitate to condemn one of the most venerable aspects of medical behaviour in the Western medical tradition:

> We must reject the advice of Galen, who taught that a physician should comfort a patient and promise him health, even though it is in fact impossible to save him. This is rejected by St Ambrose, who affirms that the medical precept, in this case, is contrary to the divine condition [i.e. to properly prepare the sick to go to the next life through confessing their sins].[61]

So, 'it is proper for the service of God and for good government that "New Christians" should be prohibited from curing and using the arts of medicine with "Old Christians" '.[62]

The members of the Inquisition courts took special care to establish the degree of Christian training possessed by suspect Converso physicians. They were interrogated about their fulfilment of the obligations to confess and to take communion at least once a year, about their knowledge of the prayers, especially the Lord's Prayer and the Creed, and the Inquisition carefully investigated whether they demonstrated the necessary external signs of pious behaviour (the cult of the saints and devotion to the Virgin Mary). All of these were practices which were encouraged in the Counter-Reformation, following the Council of Trent. Any relaxation on the part of a physician as regards the fulfilment of these practices – having totally or partially forgotten the necessary prayers, indifference towards or rejection of the external signs of devotion – strengthened the suspicions that were harboured about their being Morisco or Judaizing physicians. The evidence in this respect is particularly abundant. There is for instance the case of Felipe de Nájera, bachelor of medicine, who was accused of Judaizing in 1607 before the Inquisition in Toledo, two years after having been accused of homosexuality. He was observed by his cell-mates, who reported him to the Inquisition judges; they noticed that he did not pray in prison[63] – that he even made fun of his fellow prisoners who did[64] and nor did he know how to recite the Creed properly.[65] It was obvious therefore that the precept concerning the need to induce a sick patient to make his confession was not being fulfilled with the diligence that the Fourth Lateran Council (1215) had required.[66] The poorly defined frontier between the physician of the soul and the physician of the body was made use of by the Inquisition, who dusted off this old medieval precept.[67]

Morisco physicians, by contrast, were to be prohibited from treating their own Morisco patients at all. As there was no clearly demarcated professional status amongst Moriscos (which was characteristic of their culture), many of them were 'alfaquíes', meaning individuals practising as teachers, religious and political leaders, and also as healers. For this reason, according to Catholic moralists, 'under the pretext of administering physical remedies or drugs [they] were really spreading the impiety of Mohammedanism'.[68] For these same reasons, Morisco midwives were forbidden to practise in Granada (Synod of Guadix, 1554) and Valencia (1561) since, 'when the children are born, they usually circumcise them. They are only allowed to attend a delivery in the presence of a Christian [i.e. 'Old Christian'] physician or surgeon, who should prevent the rite of circumcision.'[69] Thus the physician was used not to improve medical conditions or to supervise the delivery, but to play a religious and political role. Non-Morisco surgeons who did not carry out this order or those who attempted to resist the pressure of the Church, backed as it was by Royal authority, were frequently prohibited from practising at all.[70] This kind of measure against Morisco practitioners was possible because the Moriscos were a minority who not only lived close together but who also possessed external cultural signs which were easily identifiable,

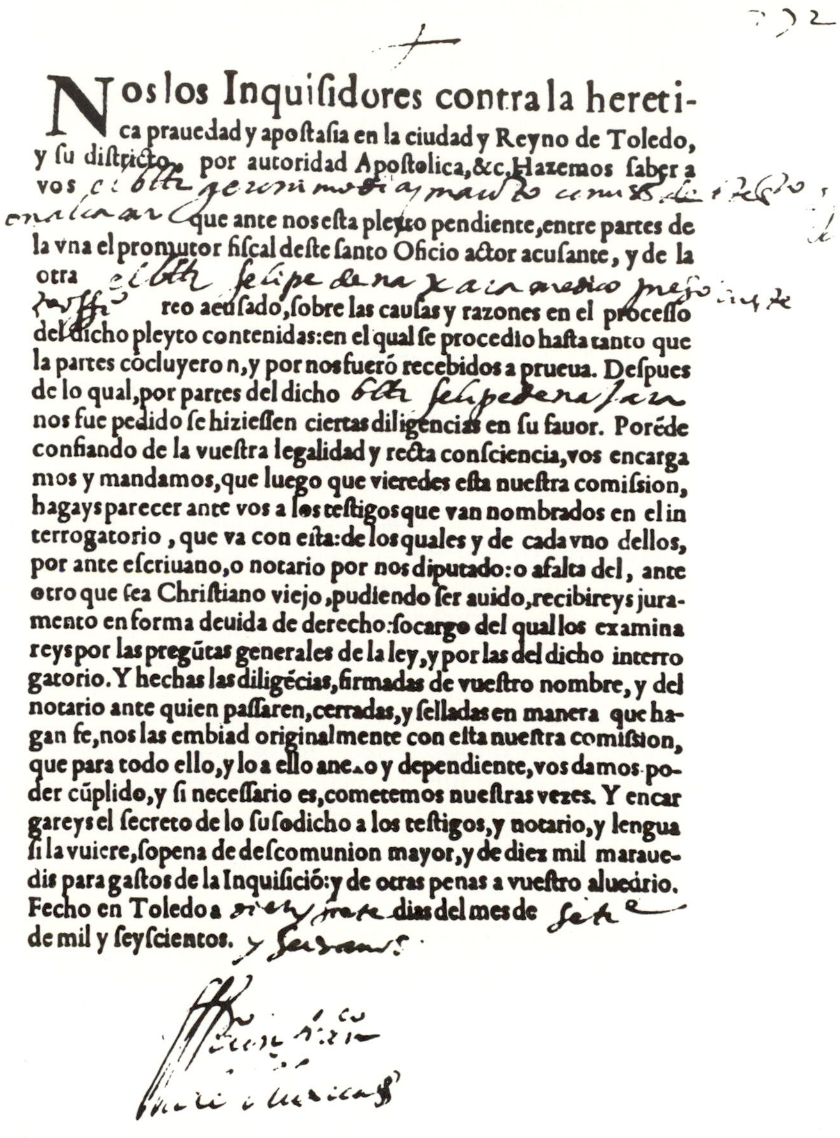
Nos los Inquisidores contra la heretica prauedad y apostasia en la ciudad y Reyno de Toledo, y su districto, por autoridad Apostolica, &c. Hazemos saber a vos que ante nos esta pleyto pendiente, entre partes de la vna el promutor fiscal deste santo Oficio actor acusante, y de la otra reo acusado, sobre las causas y razones en el processo del dicho pleyto contenidas: en el qual se procedio hasta tanto que la partes cócluyero n, y por nos fueró recebidos a prueua. Despues de lo qual, por partes del dicho nos fue pedido se hiziessen ciertas diligencias en su fauor. Poréde confiando de la vuestra legalidad y recta consciencia, vos encargamos y mandamos, que luego que vieredes esta nuestra comision, hagays parecer ante vos a los testigos que van nombrados en el interrogatorio, que va con esta: de los quales y de cada vno dellos, por ante escriuano, o notario por nos diputado: o a falta del, ante otro que sea Christiano viejo, pudiendo ser auido, recibireys juramento en forma deuida de derecho: socargo del qual los examinareys por las pregútas generales de la ley, y por las del dicho interrogatorio. Y hechas las diligécias, firmadas de vuestro nombre, y del notario ante quien passaren, cerradas, y selladas en manera que hagan fe, nos las embiad originalmente con esta nuestra comission, que para todo ello, y lo a ello anexo y dependiente, vos damos poder cúplido, y si necessario es, cometemos nuestras vezes. Y encargareys el secreto de lo susodicho a los testigos, y notario, y lengua si la vuiere, so pena de descomunion mayor, y de diez mil marauedis para gastos de la Inquisició: y de otras penas a vuestro aluedrio. Fecho en Toledo a dias del mes de de mil y seyscientos.

Illustration 9 Warrant signed by the Inquisitor of Toledo, Don Francisco de Múxica, calling witnesses against the Converso physician Felipe de Nájara, bachelor of Medicine, suspected of Judaizing. Archivo Histórico Nacional, Inquisition of Toledo, leg. 168, 1, fol. 232. Reproduced by permission of the Spanish National Archive, Madrid.

whereas Converso individuals and physicians were scattered among the population as a whole and thus stood out less.

Two case-studies: the Morisco healer Jerónimo Jover and the Converso physician Felipe de Nájera

Jerónomo Jover

The case of the Morisco physician Jerónimo Jover (*fl.* 1577–80) quite clearly illustrates a number of points: the difficulties that Morisco healers were faced with in order to graduate from a faculty of medicine; the empirical and magical nature of their cures, which were basically used among members of the Morisco community, but also among 'Old Christians'; and the problem that many of these healers had to consider – whether or not to go into exile in order to escape the Inquisition and death.[71] As far as we know (for all our information comes from the records of the Inquisition), he was born in Segorbe, a town in the north of the Kingdom of Valencia where the Morisco population was dominant; for part of his life he lived in Zaragoza, where he must have started his medical activity and where he got married. His mother had been responsible for instructing him in the practices of the Moslem religion; he learnt Arabic and read Castilian perfectly, and probably Latin as well. He subsequently left Zaragoza for Valencia, where he remarried. His second wife was a rich 'Old Christian', the widow of a notary. He practised medicine with noteworthy success, his practice extending to towns and villages around Valencia, which were densely inhabited by Moriscos. In Valencia, however, he experienced professional difficulties as a result of the problems he encountered in obtaining a licence to practise medicine.

From the later Middle Ages, university-trained physicians – all of whom were Christians – aimed at uniting their monopoly of knowledge (for medicine could only be studied in faculties of medicine) with a monopoly of medical practice (only those who had graduated from a university were allowed to practise medicine). In this aim they could count on the support of the civil, municipal and ecclesiastical authorities. This double monopoly took shape in the course of the sixteenth century, and in Spain it was linked with the increasing bureaucratization carried out by Philip II (1527–98).

In the last third of the sixteenth century, one could gain access to the practice of medicine through such non-university institutions as the guilds of surgeons and barbers. Their medical practice was controlled and regulated by a state organization (the 'Protomedicato' council) and by the municipal bodies themselves, which could rely on the support of the tribunals which authorized (or not) practice of a profession after the necessary examinations.[72] Both the 'Protomedicato' council and the municipal tribunals were dominated by university-trained physicians and surgeons and became very sensitive to the practice of ensuring 'blood purity'.[73] In the case of Valencia, for example, the municipal tribunal was a jury of doctors appointed by the city council. Anyone who wanted to practise legally had to appear before the jury, who examined them on theoretical as well as practical aspects of medicine. The jury's decisions varied from outright rejection to admission. Licences were granted for a shorter or longer period of practice under the supervision of an experienced doctor, and in some instances licences were granted which did not allow their holders to treat certain diseases which required complicated therapy.[74] In the period under consideration, these tribunals and the university itself were not left unscathed by the social tension existing between 'Old' and 'New Christians'. For reasons which have already been explained, the Morisco healer lacked university education. In spite of this, his services were required, both by the Morisco population and by 'Old Christians' who were suffering illnesses. This gave rise to confrontations between university-trained physicians and Morisco healers. If we consider the documentary sources, the clearest and most explicit confrontations took place after the 1570s and the 1590s, and the motives were clear: '. . . and since [the Morisco] carried off the prestige and the money, the physicians bore him so much hate'.[75] Some of these Morisco physicians who had acquired an improved financial position wished to get round the conflict by obtaining a university qualification, which would protect their medical activity. Let us consider the difficulties involved.

The case of the Morisco healer Jerónimo Jover illustrates the monopoly of knowledge/monopoly of practice binomial very clearly, the first term being expressed by possession of a university qualification, and the second by medical activity which was derived from such a qualification. One of the witnesses of the inquisitorial trial to which Jover was subjected said:

> that the said doctor [Jover] endeavoured to go to Lérida [Catalonia] to graduate, for the physicians would not let him cure since he held no university qualification, because in fact the aforesaid doctor possessed no qualification at all.[76]

An 'Old Christian' from Paterna (a small town near the city of Valencia), an ex-patient of Jover's, pointed out the difficulties that these unqualified Morisco healers continually came across, and also mentioned that they were gradually driven into a corner by the pressure from professionals with a university qualification:

> [The witness] said that in the month of June in the previous year, 1577, doctor Jover, a 'Morisco' physician, went to visit his patients in Paterna and admitted that the physicians of Valencia were doing everything possible to make sure that he did not heal the sick, and that, as a consequence, he had considered departing for the Faculty of Medicine at Lérida to obtain a degree. For that purpose, he was

carrying quite a substantial sum of money and [he hoped] that, if all went well, he would obtain it within three or four months.[77]

Why, when there was a Faculty of Medicine in Valencia, did he plan to go off to that of Lérida, in Catalonia? From other trials of the Inquisition against other Morisco physicians, we know that the Faculty of Medicine in Valencia was particularly hostile towards Moriscos and that its best-known professor, Luis Collado, a former student of Vesalius, indulged in public debate, and even came to blows, with a Morisco physician who mocked him in front of his patients on more than one occasion. Moreover, university qualifications could be obtained with greater ease in Lérida because of the corruption of its governing board. Certain universities are known to have been responsive to bribes and to the pressure of 'ties of relationship' on the part of 'New Christians' (especially converted Jews) when awarding university degrees,[78] and this seems to have influenced Jover. Another of the witnesses, the Frenchman, Père Cassot, a farmworker in Valencia, declared that Jover had asked him for 100 coins 'saying that he wanted them in order to go to Lérida to graduate'. Another witness stated

> that he heard him [say] that as the physicians of the [municipal] tribunal of Valencia would not give him a licence to practise medicine, he wanted to go to Lérida to be examined. He also heard him [say] that he had received a letter from Lérida in which he was informed that he should go before St John's Day [the end of the academic year], because on that date the examiners were changed, and those that there were at that moment were friends of the person who was writing the letter of recommendation. And that made the said doctor Jover make haste in his departure for Lérida.[79]

The letter of recommendation had been written by don Jerónimo Fajardo, an influential figure in the world of finance in Valencia and Catalonia.

Jover's difficult situation of being a Morisco and not having a university education led him to take the decision to depart for Lérida, taking advantage of the friendship existing between don Jerónimo Fajardo and the examiners. Nevertheless, the difficulties must still have been considerable by the time when, despite his evident professional success, he drew up a plan for going into exile in a country where he could practise the Moslem religion openly and where he would be allowed to practise medicine without the need to obtain a degree. Another witness stated:

> that the said Jover had a very wealthy brother in Constantinople and that he had explained to him that if the physicians here [Valencia] did not give him a municipal licence to practise, he was considering

leaving; he wanted to go to Lérida to graduate, and that if he did not succeed, he would not return, but he would go to where his brother was . . .; his wife said that since the physicians ['Old Christians'] would not let him practise medicine, he should try to do so in those new lands, and that she would rent their houses and she would join him there.[80]

In the end he fled to North Africa, where he practised medicine. The route that he took in order to reach Algeria was, as in the case of many other Moriscos, via the ports of the south of France, principally Marseilles. Once in Africa, impatient and homesick, and anxious for news of his loved ones, he wrote a letter, in Arabic, to his family in Valencia, which was intercepted by the Inquisition. It was translated by a Morisco who was being held prisoner in the Inquisition's gaol. Among other things Jover wrote:

> . . . I shall tell you what heppened to me after I left Barcelona, whence I went to Marseilles by sea, whence I departed and went to Bône in the land of the Moors [near Tunisia]. The journey took twenty-one days, and I made it together with three other companions. My intention is to go to Algeria. But in Bône I found the mayor sick and I cured him of his illness. In payment he gave me a horse, a suit of clothes and ten gold coins. But I want to go to Algeria. Do not worry about me; the only thing that I lack is your presence.[81]

The Inquisition submitted the circulation or mere possession of books or papers in Arabic to strict control. In the second half of the sixteenth century, it was enough to be caught with a brief note written in Arabic – even if it was a matter of a legal contract or a medical prescription – to be put on trial by the Inquisition as suspected of practising the religion of the 'degraded sect of Mahomet'. Naturally, this has not aided the survival of this type of literature. However, we should not lose sight of the fact that, in spite of the existence of a true clandestine network of 'alfaquíes', who taught people to read and write Arabic and who thus acted as focal points for maintaining Arab learning, the vast majority of Moriscos were illiterate. Nevertheless there is evidence for the continued existence and circulation of medical literature in Arabic among the Moriscos.[82] In the trial of Jover, whom we know to have read, written and spoken Arabic, it was said of him that 'when he left Valencia [with the intention of enroling at the Medical Faculty at Lérida], he took with him some books in Arabic. He left another Arabic book at home, which the witness gave to the Holy Inquisition'.[83]

Unfortunately, the subjects of the books are not mentioned, nor are they attached to the trial documents, by way of proof, as happened in other cases, nor is there any mention of their contents. Were they medical volumes? This is quite likely, since he left for the Medical Faculty of Lérida and may well have already been contemplating going into exile. From the evidence of a Christian apothecary who was an old friend of his, we are able to ascertain that he read Castilian and probably also Latin, which was by no means usual. In fact, from this same testimony we know of some of the books to be found in his library: 'The said doctor [Jover] auctioned all the Christian books he had, including a book by St Thomas Aquinas and a book by Friar Luis of Granada and a book called *Memorable Things of Spain*'.[84]

We do not know how Jover acquired his medical training. From what we know of other Morisco healers, it could have been a question of family apprenticeship and learning, in which medical training was transmitted from father (or mother) to son by oral tradition. However, this does not seem to have been the case here, considering Jover's wide knowledge of other languages. He may have been trained in a tradition of medical education that still existed in the sixteenth century following what we might call an 'open' model, under which anyone who had medical knowledge to impart might pass it on, outside any institutional framework. In such an open system, teaching activity reflects the interests of an individual teacher, not the requirements of a set curriculum, and the success of education, a student's qualification for practice, can be tested only by his success at curing his patients; it is ultimately the patient who will judge who is a physician and who is not. Where books for medical instruction are relatively scarce, as in Morisco communities, the open system, built round the master–disciple arrangement, further encourages the oral transmission of knowledge and consequently a tradition of empirical and family medical practice.[85] The Morisco doctor Gaspar Capdal, a contemporary of doctor Jerónimo Jover, who also practised in the Kingdom of Valencia, followed this model of professional training step by step. He did not know Arabic and he learnt medicine from an 'Old Christian' doctor and was able to read medical books in Spanish; he received his training on patients and his expertise in the preparation of drugs from a Morisco doctor, Master Damian, a 'New Christian', and the apothecary Ynca of Valencia.[86] Both Jerónimo Jover and Gaspar Capdal were totally integrated within a society consisting of 'Old' and 'New Christians' in which everyday living together was evidently more normal and less intense than appears from the narrow perspective provided by the Inquisitorial trials. Their training and family lives allow us to obtain some small idea of the complex co-existence of different cultures in sixteenth century Spanish society.

From the evidence of other witnesses we know that Jerónimo Jover practised medicine and used to carry out blood-letting; this he did at the correct and proper points of the body in accordance with orthodox

Galenism.[87] His clients were numerous and consisted mainly of Moriscos, as another witness indicates: 'many Moriscos with their urine used to enter and leave Doctor Jover's houses, and they came from the towns of Paterna and Manises',[88] towns near Valencia which had a largely Morisco population. However, he was also visited by 'Old Christians', both from the towns and villages and from the city of Valencia itself, as another witness reminds us: 'those with whom he had most dealings were the Moriscos of Picasent, Alcacer, Paterna, Manises and Moriscos from all the Kingdom [of Valencia] would come, and many "Old Christians", as is public knowledge and well-known in this city [Valencia]'.[89] Individuals from all manner of trades visited his house (tailors, shepherds, merchants, students, farmworkers, servants, weavers, even members of the families of university-trained physicians!) and he maintained a good relationship with the apothecaries who made up his prescriptions. Another witness tells us that he spoke *algarabía* (the dialect of Arabic spoken in Valencia) with Moriscos and spoke in their own language (Catalan or Castilian) with 'Old Christians'.[90] He used standard cures on all of them, but he also made use of invocations and spells, as one of his patients testified.[91] Jover's prestige must have been great, for it spread to far-flung parts of the Kingdom of Valencia, and he formed partnerships with 'Old Christian' apothecaries, and with them he used to organize visits to these distant areas. All this work produced substantial profits, as one of the apothecaries who had been a partner of his testified.[92] 'Old Christians' and Moriscos thus consulted the Morisco healer. At the popular level, and given the levelling effect that illness imposes across society as a whole, it would appear that the condition of the Morisco – 'the most despicable caste in the world', as one Morisco healer said of his own status before the Inquisition judges[93] – did not point to any special differences. The Inquisition, however, was not of the same opinion.

Felipe de Nájera, bachelor of medicine

The proceedings against the bachelor of medicine Felipe de Nájera are of considerable length and provide information, not only about Judaizers, but also about many other aspects of the medical milieu in late sixteenth and early seventeenth century Spain.[94] The trial procedure of the Inquisition court, which allowed and encouraged anonymous accusations without proof, based only on the infomer's testimony, was used to settle personal vendettas of every type: these could range from those resulting from the poor relationship of a physician with his patients to sheer spite in a sentimental relationship.[95]

The particular economic conditions of medical practice were the cause of confrontations between Converso physicians and their 'Old Christian' clients. From the financial standpoint, the physician–patient relationship in this period might be based on one of three models: (1) the contracting of the physician by a municipal council to attend to the needs of the population or a part of it (normally the so-called poor, a concept which it is difficult to define by present-day criteria); (2) the fee agreed (*iguala*) between the physician and the potential client. This agreement gave rise to a wide range of casuistry – from specific agreements for a particular illness (whether or not of a surgical nature) to total medical cover for a limited period of time (six months, one year); this might also be personal, for a family or for an institution (for example, to satisfy the medical requirements of a religious community[96] or a cathedral chapter); (3) payment for a visit when a client called a physician with whom he had had no previous established financial agreement.[97]

In practice, many of the witnesses who presented themselves voluntarily before the court of the Inquisition to give evidence against the Judaizing physician did so, in fact, to avenge themselves for the problems that derived from the financial system upon which the physician–patient relationship was based.[98] The Converso physician took great pains to warn the inquisitor:

> Your Lordship should be aware that I have many open and declared enemies in this town of Alcazar and also in Argamasilla [two towns in New Castile], not only because my personality is somewhat violent but also because I collected the agreed fees and salaries that I was owed by means of judicial summons. This has meant that I have had serious arguments with many of my patients.[99]

Some of them took advantage of the Inquisition's zeal for acting against Conversos suspected of Judaizing in order to get their revenge for what they considered to be the physician's greed. On other occasions, those who testified were endeavouring to get their revenge for a poorly performed cure or a consequence that the patient attributed to negligence or error on the part of the physician and which the ordinary courts had not considered as such (for instance, becoming blind in one eye as a consequence of an eye disease treated by the physician Felipe de Nájera).[100] Another prosecution witness was unmasked by the Converso physician himself, who was able to demonstrate that the person who was accusing him of being a Jew in actual fact wanted to get his revenge on him because, as a physician, he had refused to certify falsely that a relative of his was insane in order to have him declared unfit and thus to obtain his inheritance.[101] Another gave evidence out of sheer spite 'because the physician did not want to marry a daughter of his and spurned her'.[102]

In the same way, the trial against Felipe de Nájera allows us to catch a glimpse of the social milieu of the medical profession in late sixteenth and early seventeenth century Spain. We might notice the standard evolution of a university-trained physician's career, which starts with his university qualifications as his one and only possession: from the hard beginnings in financial terms of the young graduate, at the age of 25 (in 1588), 'who could not change his shirt for two weeks, nor change his sheets, because he did not have the funds',[103] until the moment, some fourteen years later, when 'his position as a physician, and the large number of clients that he had to attend to, both in his city and the surrounding towns' allowed him to employ maidservants as well as a house of some standing.[104] A brief description of his goods and chattels offer further evidence of his social position – both from an economic and an intellectual point of view – especially the size of his private library.[105] The trial allows us to see a cash-orientated society,[106] and to note the greed of physicians who frequently resorted to the civil courts in order to be paid the so-called *igualas* in the form of their equivalent in consumable goods (normally wheat, which the physician subsequently traded)[107] or precious metals (most commonly, worked silver).[108] This gave rise to tense situations, quarrels and even violent confrontations (on one occasion swords were drawn by the physician and a furious client).[109]

In the previous case, that of the Morisco physician Jover, we saw how anti-Semitism was used in connection with 'professional' problems. In the trial of the physician Felipe de Nájera, such 'professional anti-Semitism' also appears, but on this occasion among healers who acted within the bounds of legality. More precisely, there was friction between him and a barber-surgeon who had felt humiliated by what he believed to be arrogance on the part of the physician in the exercise of his profession.[110] Such were the typical rivalries between members of two categories of doctor with a certain social position, but with rather poorly defined functions: those of the physician with his university background, and those of the barber-surgeon with training of a more artisan nature. The tensions were emphasized not least because the barber-surgeons were the ones who actually provided most of the medical service for the population.

Contemporary Spanish society accepted the Inquisition as just one more element in social interaction, to the point of having it placed at the service of private interests, including those of the physician–patient relationship itself, as far as financial matters were concerned. This relationship brought together a medical professional belonging to the social and university establishment, and clients coming from a wide variety of different social categories: clergy, merchants, farmworkers, artisans, noblemen, lawyers, physicians, notaries, civil servants of the royal administration, even institutions such as monasteries or municipal councils; they all passed through the Inquisition court as a consequence of the trial against the physician Felipe de Nájera.

By a rare stroke of fortune for us, Felipe de Nájera shared an Inquisition cell in Toledo for almost a year with a Morisco healer, 'doctor' Juan de Toledo. This enables us to be certain about the very different medical training that they had each received, as well as to observe the different charges that the Inquisition laid against the Morisco healer and the Converso physician, who was accused of Judaizing.[111]

Felipe de Nájera belonged to a family of Converso merchants and farmers related to 'Old Christians' of some wealth. As in the case of many of the Converso physicians, among his family there were some who had undertaken medical studies. His maternal grandfather, Antonio de Nájera, was also a bachelor of medicine, as was one of his brothers, Pedro Alvarez de Mezquita, a resident of Madrid. His father's family was related to Portuguese Conversos. He himself was born in Portugal.[112] His case illustrates the tight control the Inquisition exercised over Spanish society, not only concerning problems directly connected with what was generically called 'heresy', but also concerning those connected with the moral standards of society. As we shall see, this particular physician had his first confrontation with the Inquisition when he was accused of being a homosexual. This was a serious matter in a society considerably less permissive than the present day.[113]

As he himself explained, he was born in Trancoso (Portugal) in 1563, where he received his primary education. He then moved to a nearby town, Celórico, where he continued studying grammar, in preparation for university entrance. When he reached the age of seventeen, his family sent him to the University of Salamanca to study arts and medicine. Eight years later he obtained his bachelor's degree in medicine and he began to practise as a physician. For eighteen years he travelled around Murcia and New Castile, working as a physician.[114] His route was typical of such university-trained village physicians, who sometimes worked for themselves but on other occasions were contracted by town councils to give medical attention to their inhabitants. Municipal councils held university-trained physicians in high esteem and their offers of employ-ment (which included salary, tax benefits and accommodation) made up the principal job market for young graduates. These contracts might be for widely varying periods of time: they ranged from periods of a few months to a year or more. They were normally renewed annually providing the financial terms were satisfactory.[115]

After leaving the Faculty of Medicine at Salamanca, Nájera spent his whole career in the Kingdom of Castile. He started in the city of Cuenca, where he formed part of the medical staff of the Hospital of Santiago, acquiring professional experience there. From there he moved to Cieza (Murcia) with a contract from the town council for just three months. He then moved on to the town of San Clemente and almost immediately afterwards to that of Argamasilla de Alba, where he held a six-year contract from the council. He returned to his home town, Trancoso, for a few months, probably for family reasons, before leaving for Ciudad

Rodrigo with a contract for a further year. He returned to his home town for several months again, and then went back to San Clemente for one year more. From there he went on to provide medical services in a nearby town, Iniesta, for a two-year period. He was taken on by the municipality of San Clemente once again, and from there he moved on to that of Socuéllamos, for two and a half years. His last six years were divided between Argamasilla and Alcázar de Consuegra (nowadays Alcázar de San Juan), where he was under contract to the respective town councils. He never married.[116] During this final period, prior to his stay in Alcázar de San Juan, and while he was in Socuéllamos and Argamasilla, a housekeeper, Agueda García, a 40-year-old widow, took care of him.[117] It was in these two settlements that he had problems with the Inquisition: first of all, he was accused of practising homosexuality and thereafter of Judaizing. His career as a physician thus took place in the region of La Mancha, so familiar to his contemporary Don Quixote.

Felipe de Nájera's first brush with the Inquisition was in 1605, during his last stay in Argamasilla, and it arose from a conversation that his housekeeper had with a neighbour, in which she expressed her suspicions about her master's possible homosexuality. During interrogation, Agueda García spoke of her suspicions as well as the fact that, in her opinion, her master did not show due respect towards the images of saints or to the image of Christ himself, which demonstrated a lack of religiousness. The hearing was relatively rapid: the witnesses and the accused himself gave their evidence between May and September 1605; the defence managed to refute the evidence and the judge of Alcázar de San Juan acquitted him.[118]

Two years later, in November 1607, the inquisitor of Toledo, Don Francisco de Múxica, appeared in Alcázar de San Juan in order to make inquiries about certain Converso families who were living in that town. The atmosphere in the town was one of great unease. Three Converso physicians of the town were suspected of Judaizing: Doctor Yepes, the bachelor Barroso, and Felipe de Nájera, who was also a bachelor.[119] A lawyer neighbour of Nájera appeared before the Inquisitor voluntarily and accused him of practising rites that were typical of Judaizers and of maintaining friendship with Conversos; at the same time, he recalled the hearing of two years earlier, in which Nájera had been accused of a lack of respect towards holy images. He claimed

> that he heard Alonso Sánchez de la Serna, a priest, say that he had seen the bachelor Nájera, a Portuguese physician, wash meat before putting it into the cooking pot. Similarly, that he had frequent dealings with Conversos and that there had been proceedings against the said physician in which it was established that he treated images [of the saints] badly, which makes him a suspect individual.[120]

This was the usual way of presenting an accusation against someone suspected of Judaizing: besides the washing of meat, immediately afterwards another witness claimed to have seen him, on occasions, rejecting pork, removing the fatty excrescences from a leg of lamb (*landrecilla*), changing his shirt on Saturdays and Sundays, and seeking books written by Jews (these were the medical works of Isaac Israeli).[121] All this was sufficient to have him transferred to the secret prison of the Inquisition in Toledo (March 1608). There he shared a cell for a year with a Morisco healer, Juan de Toledo. The confidential comments that the bachelor made to the Morisco healer were used to add further information about his situation as a Judaizer. On the basis of all this information, the prosecuting counsel formulated the definitive accusation of

> Heretic, apostate from our Holy Catholic faith and Evangelical Law, excommunicant and perjurer, a Judaizer descended from Conversos; that being a baptized Christian, with danger for his soul and to the great scandal of the Christian people, he has said and has believed . . . that he is a Jew.[122]

The interrogation started immediately afterwards: first in Alcázar de San Juan (18 Feburary 1608) and subsequently in Toledo. Nájera was then 46 years old. The first point that the Inquisitor considered was the problem of 'blood purity' as he asked him 'about his caste and about the identity of his parents, grandparents and other transversal and collateral lines, and whether any of them has ever been held prisoner, sentenced, acquitted or condemned by the courts of the Holy Office of the Inquisition'.[123] The physician's reply reveals something of the complex network of family relationships among Portuguese and Spanish Conversos. His father was a Castilian merchant, from Medina del Campo, a new convert from Judaism, who had fled to Portugal during the civil war (1520-1) which set the Castilian municipalities against King Charles. He had five brothers and sisters, one of whom, also a bachelor, Pedro Alvarez de Mezquita, was a physician and practised medicine in Madrid.[124] He too must have experienced difficulties with the Inquisition because from a later declaration by Felipe de Nájera (who used his mother's surname) we discover that he fled to France together with his father.[125] Another of his brothers, Enrique de Nájera, left for Angola, where one of his father's brothers, Diego de Mezquita, traded in slaves, 'buying and selling negroes'.[126] Another brother was a cloth merchant and his two sisters were both married to merchants, one of whom was settled in La Guardia (Galicia).[127]

Despite such a background, he did not recognize his position as a Converso, stating that he was an 'Old Christian' and that none of the members of his family had been prosecuted by the Inquisition.[128] The long interrogation of the Converso physician, which lasted almost two years, offers a good example of inquisitorial proceedings, involving the confidential remarks made by the Judaizing physician to the Morisco healer and the latter's accusations before the judges, the intelligence and dialectical cunning of the judges, the unfeeling use of torture as a standard technique,[129] plus the fear that the court and the torture itself induced, as well as the use of lies, intelligence and even irony as defensive weapons in a desperate defence in which the very real threat of being burnt alive constantly appears.

At the beginning of his interrogation, Felipe de Nájera was a man proud of his qualifications as a university physician and his current social standing:

> I am an educated man and a graduate of an approved university, from the faculty of medicine, and by the mercy of God, I have a good name and a good salary in the town of Alcázar and its neighbourhood.[130]

He conducted his own defence against the accusations that were based on his dietary habits, suspected of being Jewish rituals, by resorting to his knowledge of medicine:

> I gave up eating bacon some time ago when I was suffering from an attack of gout or another internal illness for which bacon and other salted meats are harmful, according to Galen's opinion, which is expounded in his work *De alimentorum facultatibus*.[131]

A fellow physician, Gaspar López, called by the Inquisition, confirmed the diagnosis.[132]

Eventually, after two prolonged sessions of torture, which were noted down in detail with dispassionate detachment by the Inquisition scribe, we find ourselves present at the collapse of a man 'full of fear and bewildered . . . with his arms and body destroyed',[133] who concludes by confessing under torture that he has been a Jew:

> I have been a Jew from time to time. If your Lordship wishes me to say more, I shall sign it; but if I state anything else, it is so that I do not have to undergo torture. Do not kill me your Lordship, I cannot withstand any more torture. If I have already admitted that I am a Jew, what else does your Lordship require?[134]

The accusation centred totally upon his situation as a crypto-Jew. What concerned the Inquisition above all else throughout the interrogation was to discover the names of Judaizers, to find out the network of relationships and assistance among the Conversos;[135] to investigate the contacts between the Conversos of Spain and Portugal and those in other countries, those who had fled to France, to Rome, to Germany, and with whom they were in correspondence;[136] to attempt to reconstruct the

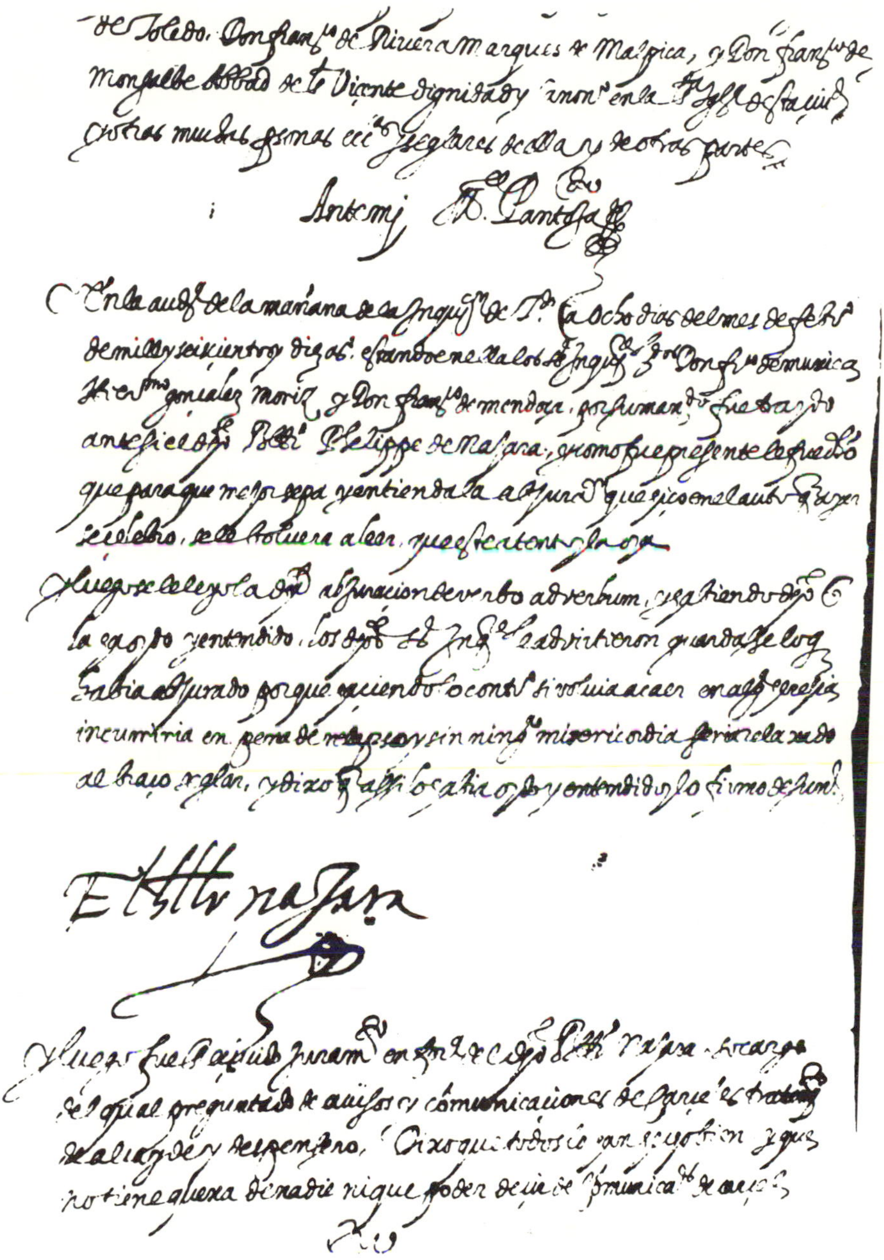

Illustration 10 Signature of the Converso physician, Felipe de Nájara, bachelor of Medicine, confirming that he was aware of the sentence on the morrow of auto-da-fe (8 February 1610). Archivo Histórico Nacional, Inquisition of Toledo, leg. 168, 1, fol. 365r. Reproduced by permission of the Spanish National Archive, Madrid.

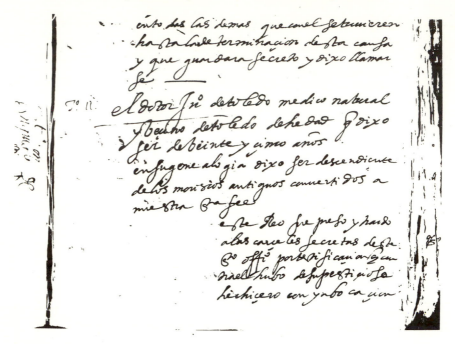

Illustration 11 Fragment of the Inquisition trial of the Morisco healer, Juan de Toledo, where he confesses that he is a descendant of Moriscos and that he is accused of superstitious behaviour and witchcraft with the invocation of demons. Archivo Histórico Nacional, Inquisition of Toledo, leg. 168, 1, fol. 172r. Reproduced by permission of the Spanish National Archive, Madrid.

crypto-Jews' clandestine system of religious education;[137] and, last but not least, to find out in as much detail as possible the financial situation of Felipe de Nájera the physician.[138]

Felipe de Nájera's skill in conducting his own defence, the dishonesty of many of the witnesses, and his insistence on stating after the sessions of torture 'that what I have confessed under torture has been said because I am much afraid',[139] was enough to cause disagreement among the five judges of the court of the Inquisition of Toledo: two of them condemned him to be burnt alive, but the other three opted for 'public exhibition in a habit in an auto-da-fe, life imprisonment, confiscation of his possessions, and five years at the oars in His Majesty's galleys, without pay' (1 October 1609).[140] Another way to be a condemned man.

The most compromising information for Nájera turned out to be that which he himself had told the Morisco healer with whom he shared a cell and secrets for a year. The difference in status and treatment by the Inquisition of the two cellmates, one a Judaizer, the other a Morisco, typifies the way the two minorities were persecuted. The Judaizer, Nájera, was a university-educated physician who found himself in trouble on what appeared to be purely ethnic/religious grounds. At no point in his trial was he accused of malpractice, superstition or other irregularities. His medicine appears to have been that practised by a traditional, university-educated Galenist. The Morisco healer, Juan de Toledo, aged 25, was called a 'physician' by the inquisitors and he himself stated that that was his title. When, of his own volition, he appeared to accuse the Converso physician of being a Jew, he began his statement by saying: 'I lived in Toledo and was a descendant of the old Moriscos who were converted to our Holy Faith'.[141] He had no objection to acknowledging that

> he was taken prisoner and brought to the secret prison of this Holy Court, having been accused of superstitious behaviour, of witchcraft with the invocation of demons and of making use of judicial astrology in his practice of medicine.[142]

These were exactly the same accusations as were hurled against all Morisco healers tried by the Inquisition up to the expulsion of the Moriscos from the Spanish realms between 1609 and 1612. They demonstrate that, as opposed to the Judaizers, the Morisco healers found themselves in trouble with the Inquisition particularly because of the way they practised medicine, and not only because of their supposed religious and cultural leanings.

Notes

I am indebted to Jaime Contreras and Ricardo G. Cárcel, who have allowed me to use their database of inquisitorial records. Thanks are also extended to Alvar Martínez-Vidal and Jon Arrizabalaga, who read the draft and made valuable comments, to Philip Banks who improved the English text, and to the editors for their help and kindness. Funding for the research was provided by CICYT grant number PB/89–0066.

1. See Y. Baer, *A History of the Jews in Christian Spain*, 2 vols. (Philadelphia, 1961).

2. L. Cardaillac, *Morisques et Chrétiens. Un Affrontement Polémique (1492–1640)*, (Paris, 1977); A. Domínguez Ortíz and B. Vincent, *Historia de los Moriscos. Vida y Tragedia de una Minoría*, (Madrid, 1978). The reality, at least at the intellectual level, was more complex; see L. García-Ballester, L. Ferre and E, Feliu, 'Jewish appreciation of fourteenth-century Scholastic medicine', *Osiris* 6 (1990), 85–117, and L. García-Ballester, 'A marginal learned medical world: Jewish, Muslim, and Christian medical practitioners faced with Arabic medical sources in late medieval Spain', in L. García-Ballester, R.K. French, J. Arrizabalaga, A. Cunningham (eds), *Practical Medicine from Salerno to the Black Death* (Cambridge, 1993); E. Gutwirth, 'Actitudes judías hacia los cristianos en la España del siglo XV: Ideario de los traductores del latín', *Actas del II Congreso Internacional 'Encuentro de las Tres Culturas', 3–6 Octubre 1983* (Toledo, 1985), 189–96.

3. See my work *Los Moriscos y la Medicina* (Barcelona, 1984); 'Academicism versus empiricism in practical medicine in sixteenth-century Spain with regard to Morisco practitioners', in A. Wear, R.K. French and I.M. Lonie (eds), *The Medical Renaissance of the Sixteenth Century* (Cambridge, 1985), 246-70, 338-42.

4. C. Roth, *A History of the Marranos* (Philadelphia, 1947). The dictionary defines 'Judaizer' as a person who conforms to the spirit, character, principles or practices of Judaism. See also H. Beinart, *Conversos on Trial. The Inquisition in Ciudad Real* (Jerusalem, 1981). This work, although focussing on fifteenth-century New Castile, is a very good survey of the relationship between the 'Conversos' and the Inquisition.

5. J. Caro Baroja, *Los Judíos en la España Moderna y Contemporánea*, 3 vols., 2nd edn (Madrid, 1978), II, 289-510; Beinart, *Conversos on Trial*, 237ff. Interesting evidence on these topics is to be found in Archivo Histórico Nacional, Inquisition of Toledo, leg. 168, 1, ff. 291v-292v, 334v-336v.

6. A good brief survey is in H. Kamen, *The Spanish Inquisition* (London, 1965). See also, H.C. Lea, *A History of the Inquisition of Spain*, 4 vols. (Philadelphia, 1906; repr. New York, 1966). Two recent accounts are, A. Alcalá (ed.), *The Spanish Inquisition and the Inquisitorial Mind* (New Jersey, 1987); and G. Henningsen and J. Tedeschi (eds), *The Inquisition in Early Modern Europe. Studies on Sources and Methods* (Dekalb, Illinois, 1986).

7. 'In the forced or voluntary conversion of the Jews of Spain, State and Church did not find a solution to the internal difficulties that beset the country in the 14th and 15th centuries. Nor did the establishment of the Inquisition and the Expulsion of the Jews of Spain provide the answer. For centuries Spain was to continue to grapple with the problem of the absorption within it of an entire population group,' Beinart, *Conversos on Trial*, 235-6.

8. Caro Baroja, *Los Judíos en la España Moderna*, I, 149; Beinart, *Conversos on Trial*, 25. See also Alcalá, *Spanish Inquisition*.

9. Good surveys are H. Kamen, *Spain 1469-1714. A Society in Conflict* (London, 1983); and J. Casey, 'Spain: a failed transition', in P. Clark (ed.), *The European Crisis of 1590* (London, 1985), 209-31.

10. Caro Baroja, *Los Judíos en la España Moderna*, I, 207-226.

11. A. Domínguez Ortiz, *La Clase Social de los Conversos en Castilla en la Edad Moderna* (Madrid, 1955), 36-73; Caro Baroja, *Los Judíos en la España Moderna*, II, 285ff.

12. *Constitutiones Insignis Collegii Sancti Ildefonsi . . .* (Alcalá, 1716), 10.

13. J.T. Lanning, *The Royal Protomedicato. The Regulation of the Medical Profession in the Spanish Empire*, ed. J.J. TePaske (Durham, N.C., 1985), 175-200.

14. A.A. Sicroff, *Les Controverses des Statuts de 'pureté de sang' en Espagne du XVe au XVIIe siècle* (Paris, 1960); Domínguez Ortiz, *La Clase Social de los Conversos*; and Caro Baroja, *Los Judíos en la España Moderna*.

15. On the Archbishop of Granada, see T. Herrero, *Vida y Obras de Fray Hernando de Talavera* (Granada, 1966).

16. See references quoted in note 2.

17. See Cardaillac, *Morisques et Chrétiens*; and Domínguez Ortíz and Vincent, *Historia de los Moriscos*.

18. García-Ballester, 'Academicism versus empiricism', 246.

19. The Royal decrees were published by P. Boronat, *Los Moriscos Españoles y su Expulsión*, 2 vols. (Valencia, 1901), II, 190-285. See the books mentioned by Cardaillac, Domínguez Ortíz and Vincent (note 2).

20. See the works of R. García Carcel, *Orígenes de la Inquisición Española. El*

Tribunal de Valencia, 1478-1530 (Barcelona, 1976); and *Herejía y Sexo en el Siglo XVI. La Inquisición en Valencia, 1530-1609* (Barcelona, 1979). The updating edited by A. Alcalá on the Inquisition, quoted in note 6, is useful.

21. Archivo Histórico Nacional, leg. 1988, case record 23, ff. 22r-3v.

22. Archivo Histórico Nacional, leg. 2106, 4, f. 10r-v.

23. Archivo Histórico Nacional, leg. 1988, 49, f. 16r; leg. 168, 1, ff. 283v-4r.

24. Archivo Histórico Nacional, Inquisition of Toledo, leg. 168, 1, ff. 124r-v.

25. Archivo Histórico Nacional, Inquisition of Toledo, leg. 2106, 9, ff. 41r.

26. García Carcel, *Herejía y Sexo*, 187ff.

27. Caro Baroja, *Los Judíos en la España Moderna*, II, 209ff.

28. On the use of torture, see F. Tomás y Valiente, *La Tortura en España* (Barcelona, 1973); on the rules of procedure of the Inquisition, see Beinart, *Conversos on Trial*, 105-94.

29. Archivo Histórico Nacional, Inquisition of Toledo, leg. 2106, 9, f. 46r.

30. Archivo Histórico Nacional, Inquisition of Valencia, leg. 549.

31. 'Ay también en este medio una gran conveniencia que es hacerlos pobres', Archivo del Colegio del Patriarca, Valencia, I, 7, 8, 275. The letter was written *c.*1590. See Boronat, *Los Moriscos Españoles*, I, 24ff.

32. 'Non igitur est dandus panis filiorum his cannibus, sed abigendi sunt ab illis seminariis et ad sordidas artes, aut ad triremes destinandi, non ad studia literarum,' Bleda, *Defensio Fidei in Causa Neophitorum sive Morischorum Regni Valentiae* (Valencia, 1610), 374.

33. See García-Ballester, 'Academicism versus empiricism', 251ff.

34. See Domínguez Ortíz, Vincent, *Historia de los Moriscos*, 129ff.

35. García-Ballester, *Los Moriscos y la Medicina*, 211-12.

36. On neo-Scholastic medicine in the Spanish faculties of medicine in the period we are considering, especially that of Valladolid, see J. Riera, *Vida y Obra de Luis Mercado* (Salamanca, 1968).

37. See, J.M. López Piñero, *Ciencia y Técnica en la Sociedad Española de los Siglos XVI y XVII* (Barcelona, 1979), 126-8, 140-8; J. Pardo Tomás, *Ciencia y Censura. La Inquisición Española y los Libros Científicos en los Siglos XVI y XVII* (Madrid, 1991).

38. See, Caro Baroja, *Los Judíos en la España Moderna*, II, 175ff.

39. See H. Beinart, 'The records of the Inquisition. A source of Jewish and Conversos history', *Proceedings of the Israel Academy of Sciences and Humanities*, II (Jerusalem, 1968), 211-16.

40. Archivo Histórico Nacional, Inquisition of Toledo, leg. 168, 9, ff. 42r, 44r.

41. Archivo Histórico Nacional, Inquisition of Valencia, leg. 552, 9.

42. All these places are mentioned in the inquisitorial records for 1560-1610. See also, Caro Baroja, *Los Judíos en la España Moderna*, I, 227-88; Beinart, *Conversos on Trial*, 209, and the references therein.

43. See a brief biographic survey in Caro Baroja, *Los Judíos en la España Moderna*, II, 189-93; see also, A.G. Keller, 'Garcia d'Orta', in Charles C. Gillispie (ed.), *Dictionary of Scientific Biography* (New York, 1980), X, 236-8.

44. It was edited by the Count of Ficcalho, 2 vols. (Lisbon, 1891-5). The passages I am referring to correspond to *Coloquios*, I, 24.

45. See, A. Hernández Morejón, *Historia Bibliográfica de la Medicina Española*, 7 vols. (Madrid, 1842-45; repr. New York-London, 1967), I, 100-1; M. Lemos, *Amato Lusitano. A sua Vida e a sua Obra* (Oporto, 1907); Caro Baroja, *Los Judíos en la España Moderna*, II, 193-4.

46. Hernández Morejón, *Historia Bibliográfica de la Medicina Española*, I, 107-8; Caro Baroja, *Los Judíos en la España Moderna*, II, 194.

47. See, L. de Alburquerque, in *Dictionary of Scientific Biography*, XIV, 583–4.

48. Hernández Morejón, *Historia Bibliográfica de la Medicina Española*, I, 104–6; M. Lemos, *Zacuto Lusitano. A sua Vida e a sua Obra* (Oporto, 1909); Caro Baroja, *Los Judíos en la España Moderna*, II, 195–8.

49. See, P. Laín Entralgo, *Enfermedad y Pecado* (Barcelona, 1961); O. Temkin, *Hippocrates in a World of Pagans and Christians* (Baltimore-London, 1991), 249–56.

50. See Lea, *A History of the Inquisition of Spain*, IV, 185.

51. Quoted by Lea, *A History of the Inquisition of Spain*, IV, 185.

52. D. Simancas, *Institutiones Catholicae . . .* (Vallisoleti, 1552), cap. 30, n. 10, 11.

53. F. Torreblanca, *Epitome Delictorum*, 2 vols. (Hispali, 1618), II, 9.

54. 'Statuimus et mandamus ut tam contra astrologos, mathematicos, et alios quoscumque dictae astrologiae artem, praeterquam circa agriculturam, navigationem et rem medicam inposterum exercentes, aut facientes iudicia et nativitates hominum . . ., qui supradictas damnatas, vanas, fallaces et perniciosas divinandi artes sive scientias exercent, profitenturet docent aut discunt, quive huiusmodi illicitas divinationes, sortilegia, superstitiones, beneficia, incantationes . . .', *Bullarum Diplomatum . . .* (Augustae Taurinorum, 1873), vol. 8, 650.

55. The collaboration between physicians (including Converso doctors) and the Inquisition has been studied by D. Gracia, 'Judaism, medicine, and the inquisitorial mind in sixteenth-century Spain', in Alcalá (ed.), *The Spanish Inquisition*, 375–400. He does not use the inquisitorial records, which form the basis of the present essay.

56. His medical training has been described in García-Ballester, 'Academicism versus empiricism', 267–70.

57. Archivo Histórico Nacional, Inquisition of Valencia, leg. 175, 1.

58. Ibid., leg. 840.

59. The concept 'professional anti-semitism' was first used in this way, but applied to Converso physicians, by Caro Baroja, *Los Judíos en la España Moderna*, II, 175ff.

60. 'Quomodo igitur monebit aegrotum peccata sua confiteri medicus, si Sacramentum Confessionis contemnit, et nunquam legitime confessus est, nec sacra communione refectus?', Bleda, *Defensio Fidei*, 366.

61. Bleda, *Defensio Fidei*, 367.

62. Cortes de Castilla's Proceedings, Madrid 13 November 1607, vol. 23, 583–7.

63. Archivo Histórico Nacional, Inquisition of Toledo, leg. 168, 1, f. 173r.

64. Archivo Histórico Nacional, Inquisition of Toledo, leg. 168, f. 187r.

65. Archivo Histórico Nacional, Inquisition of Toledo, leg. 168, f. 206r.

66. 'Quod infirmi prius provideant anima quam corpori. Cum infirmitas corporalis nonnunquam ex peccato proveniat . . .', J.D. Mansi, *Sacrorum Conciliorum Nova Amplissima Collectio* (repr. Graz, 1960–2), vol. 22, 1010–11.

67. See, L. García-Ballester, M.R. McVaugh and A. Rubio, *Medical Licensing and Learning in Fourteenth-century Valencia* (Philadephia, 1989), 42–4.

68. '. . . ac pretextu, et colere medicinae corporalis erunt seminatores Mahometanae impietatis', Bleda, *Defensio Fidei*, 365.

69. Ordenanzas de la Real Audiencia y Chancillería de Granada (Granada, 1610), f. 370.

70. Among the various pardons granted to the Morisco population of Granada, 'the surgeon who has practised circumcision' is specifically excluded. See Archivo de la Alhambra (Granada), leg. 159.

71. Archivo Histórico Nacional, Inquisition of Valencia, leg. 552, 9. A part of the extensive proceedings of his inquisitorial trial has been transcribed and reproduced (in Spanish) in García-Ballester, *Los Moriscos y la Medicina*, 179–89.

72. See, L.S. Granjel, *El Ejercicio Médico y Otros Capítulos de la Medicina Española* (Salamanca, 1974), 11–86; J.M. López Piñero, 'The medical profession in sixteenth century Spain', in A.W. Russell (ed.), *The Town and State Physician in Europe from the Middle Ages to the Enlightenment*, (Wolfenbüttel, 1981), 85–98.

73. *Recopilación de las Leyes, Pragmáticas Reales, Decretos, Acuerdos del Real Protomedicato . . .*, by Don Miguel Eugenio Muños . . . (Valencia, 1751; repr. Valencia, 1991), 71-3; see Lanning, *The Royal Protomedicato*, 175–200.

74. See a description of the procedure in García-Ballester, McVaugh and Rubio, *Medical Licensing and Learning*, 12-18.

75. Archivo Histórico Nacional, Inquisition of Valencia, leg. 840.

76. Archivo Histórico Nacional, Inquisition of Valencia, leg. 552.

77. Archivo Histórico Nacional, Inquisition of Valencia, leg. 552.

78. This was the case at the small University of Sigüenza, which is briefly described by V. de la Fuente, *Historia de las Universidades, Colegios y Demás Establecimientos de Enseñanza en España*, 4 vols. (Madrid 1884–89), II, 328ff.

79. Archivo Histórico Nacional, Inquisition of Valencia, leg. 552, 9.

80. Archivo Histórico Nacional, Inquisition of Valencia, leg. 552. 9.

81. Archivo Histórico Nacional, Inquisition of Valencia, leg. 552, 9.

82. García-Ballester, 'Academicism versus empiricism', 266; A. Labarta, 'Los libros de los moriscos valencianos', *Awrat*, 2 (1980), 72–80; *idem*, 'Textos para el estudio de la terapéutica entre los moriscos valencianos', *Dynamis*, 1 (1981), 275–310.

83. Archivo Histórico Nacional, Inquisition of Valencia, leg. 552, 9.

84. Archivo Histórico Nacional, Inquistions of Valencia, leg. 552, 9.

85. A description of this so-called 'open' model of medical teaching in the training of late medieval Jewish physicians is given in García-Ballester, Ferre and Feliu, 'Jewish appreciation of scholastic medicine', 93-7.

86. A description of the medical training of Gaspar Capdal is given in García-Ballester, 'Academicism versus empiricism', 267-70.

87. Archivo Histórico Nacional, Inquisition of Valencia, leg. 552, 9.

88. Archivo Histórico Nacional, Inquisition of Valencia, leg. 552, 9.

89. Archivo Histórico Nacional, Inquisition of Valencia, leg. 552, 9.

90. Archivo Histórico Nacional, Inquisition of Valencia, leg. 552, 9.

91. Archivo Histórico Nacional, Inquisition of Valencia, leg. 552, 9.

92. Archivo Histórico Nacional, Inquisition of Valencia, leg. 552, 9.

93. The Morisco healer was Román Ramírez, see Archivo Diocesano de Cuenca, Inquisition, leg. 343, 48.

94. Archivo Histórico Nacional, Inquisition of Toledo, leg. 168, 1, ff. 1–370; leg. 2106, 9, ff. 40v–46r. Caro Baroja used the first inquisitorial proceeding, see *Los Judíos en la España Moderna*, II, 211–20.

95. Archivo Histórico Nacional, Inquisition of Toledo, leg. 168, 1, f. 234r-v.

96. For example, Felipe de Nájera was the doctor of the Franciscan monastery at Argamasilla, Archivo Histórico Nacional, Inquisition of Toledo, leg. 168, 1, f. 28v.

97. The doctor–patient relationship has not been studied from the financial standpoint in sixteenth-and seventeenth-century European medicine, at least not in the Spanish realms. See L.S. Granjel, *La Medicina Española Renacentista*,

Salamanca, 1980. The three models we are summarizing were shaped in the late medieval centuries, see V. Nutton, 'Continuity or rediscovery. The city physician in Classical Antiquity and Mediaeval Italy', in Russell (ed.), *The Town and State Physician in Europe*, 9–46, repr. in V. Nutton, *From Democedes to Harvey: Studies in the History of Medicine* (London, 1988), no. vi.; also L. García-Ballester, 'Medical ethics in transition in thirteenth–fourteenth century Latin medicine: new problems with the physician–patient relationship, and the doctor's fee', in J. Geyer-Kordesch, A. Wear and R.K. French (eds), *A History of Medical Ethics* (in preparation).

98. Archivo Histórico Nacional, Inquisition of Toledo, leg. 168, ff. 228r–9v.

99. Archivo Histórico Nacional, Inquisition of Toledo, leg, 168, f. 226r.

100. Archivo Histórico Nacional, Inquisition of Toledo, leg. 168, f. 229v.

101. Archivo Histórico Nacional, Inquisition of Toledo, leg. 168, f. 234r.

102. Archivo Histórico Nacional, Inquisition of Toledo, leg. 168, f. 234v.

103. Archivo Histórico Nacional, Inquisition of Toledo, leg. 168, f. 230r.

104. Archivo Histórico Nacional, Inquisition of Toledo, leg. 168, f. 226r.

105. Archivo Histórico Nacional, Inquisition of Toledo, leg. 168, f. 22r–v. The library contained 121 volumes of different sizes. Unfortunately the scribe did not describe the incipits.

106. See, E.J. Hamilton, *American Treasure and the Price Revolution in Spain, 1501–1650* (New York, 1970), 73–103.

107. Archivo Histórico Nacional, Inquisition of Toledo, leg. 168, f. 228r.

108. Archivo Histórico Nacional, Inquisition of Toledo, leg. 168, ff. 228r–229v.

109. Archivo Histórico Nacional, Inquisition of Toledo, leg. 168, f. 229v.

110. Archivo Histórico Nacional, Inquisition of Toledo, leg. 168, f. 229v.

111. Archivo Histórico Nacional, Inquisition of Toledo, leg. 160, 1, ff. 172r–201v, 282r–302r.

112. Archivo Histórico Nacional, Inquisition of Toledo, leg. 160, 1, f. 205r.

113. Archivo Histórico Nacional, Inquisition of Toledo, leg. 160, 1, ff. 1–25.

114. Archivo Histórico Nacional, Inquisition of Toledo, leg. 160, 1, f. 206v.

115. See references cited in notes 94 and 97.

116. Archivo Histórico Nacional, Inquisition of Toledo, leg. 160, 1, ff. 205r–6r.

117. Archivo Histórico Nacional, Inquisition of Toledo, leg. 160, 1, ff. 50r–51v.

118. Archivo Histórico Nacional, Inquisition of Toledo, leg. 160, 1, ff. 3r–107r.

119. Archivo Histórico Nacional, Inquisition of Toledo, leg. 160, 1, f. 296v.

120. Archivo Histórico Nacional, Inquisition of Toledo, leg. 160, 1, f. 110r.

121. Archivo Histórico Nacional, Inquisition of Toledo, leg. 160, 1, f. 124r–v. See above on the large library Felipe de Nájera had in his house at Argamasilla, with a total of 121 volumes of different sizes; ibid., f. 22r–v. The subjects of the books were not noted down by the scribe. On the Jewish life of the Conversos see Beinart, *Conversos on Trial*, 237–85.

122. Archivo Histórico Nacional, Inquisition of Toledo, leg. 160, 1, f. 210r.

123. Archivo Histórico Nacional, Inquisition of Toledo, leg. 160, 1, f. 206r.

124. Archivo Histórico Nacional, Inquisition of Toledo, leg. 160, 1, f. 206r.

125. Archivo Histórico Nacional, Inquisition of Toledo, leg. 160, 1, f. 337v.

126. Archivo Histórico Nacional, Inquisition of Toledo, leg. 160, 1, f. 205v.

127. Archivo Histórico Nacional, Inquisition of Toledo, leg. 160, 1, f. 205v.

128. Archivo Histórico Nacional, Inquisition of Toledo, leg. 160, 1, f. 206r.

129. See the book by Tomás y Valiente, *La Tortura en España*, cited in note 28.

130. Archivo Histórico Nacional, Inquisition of Toledo, leg. 160, 1, f. 224v.

131. Archivo Histórico Nacional, Inquisition of Toledo, leg. 160, 1, f. 225v. See Galen, *Opera Omnia*, ed. C.G. Kühn (repr. Hildesheim, 1964), VI, 528, 661–3.

132. Archivo Histórico Nacional, leg. 230r, marginal note.
133. Archivo Histórico Nacional, leg. 230r ff. 332, 334v.
134. Archivo Histórico Nacional, leg. 230r f. 334r–v.
135. Archivo Histórico Nacional, leg. 230r f. 286v.
136. Archivo Histórico Nacional, leg. 230r ff. 292v, 294v, 297v, 309r, 337v; Archivo Histórico Nacional, Inquisition of Toledo, leg. 2106, 9, f. 42r.
137. Archivo Histórico Nacional, Inquisition of Toledo, leg. 168, 1, ff. 328–9v.
138. Archivo Histórico Nacional, Inquisition of Toledo, leg. 168, 1, f. 209r–v.
139. Archivo Histórico Nacional, Inquisition of Toledo, leg. 168, 1, f. 345v.
140. Archivo Histórico Nacional, Inquisition of Toledo, leg. 168, 1, f. 348.
141. Archivo Histórico Nacional, Inquisition of Toledo, leg. 168, 1, f. 172r.
142. Archivo Histórico Nacional, Inquisition of Toledo, leg. 168, 1, f. 172r–v.

Index

Abano, Peter of 34
Abbioso, Ludovico 119, 121
Abumashar 34
Acquaviva, Claudio 146
Alberti, Salomon 14, 22, 23, 26
Alcalá, University of 159, 166
Alcázar de San Juan 180, 181
alchemy 87, 95
Aldrovandi, Ulisse 118
Alfaqúies 169, 174
Algeria 165, 174
almanacs 36
Ambrose, Saint 168
Amsterdam 166
anabaptists 119
anatomy, anatomising 2, 3, 6, 11–32,
    82, 83, 84, 85, 86, 88, 92, 93, 94, 95,
    102
angel, guardian 146, 148, 149
Anti-Christ 67
anti-clericalism 157
Apocalypse 70, 74
apothecaries 15, 175
Aquinas, Saint Thomas 37, 128, 175
arcana 68, 95
Arendt, Johann 78, 91
Argenat, Francesco da (Francesco
    Severi) 119
Aristotle, aristotelianism 6, 16, 18, 21,
    23, 34, 35, 37, 38, 39, 43, 71, 124, 129
Articella, The 13
Asa 106
Aslaken, Cort 89
astrology 6, 33–56, 59, 83; faculty of,
    34
astronomy 38, 45, 46, 59, 120
atheism 20, 25, 109
atomism 20

Augsburg Confession 124, 127
Augsburg 123
Augustine, St 4, 101
Averroes 128
Avicenna 13, 24, 71, 81, 82, 128

Bannister, John 95
Barcelona 174
Bartholin, Caspar 7, 78–100
Basin, Bernardo 167
Basle, University of 58, 83, 84, 87, 88,
    89, 90, 122
Bayly, Lewis 111
Baynes, Paul 104
Becon, Thomas 104, 105
Bellantius, Lucius 43, 44
Bellarmine, Cardinal Roberto 118
Bellebuono, Decio 119
Benedetti, Alessandro 17
Benincasa, Suor Orsola, *see* Orsola,
    Suor
Berengario da Carpi 11
Bible 4, 42, 69, 78, 79, 92
blasphemy 162
Bologna 11, 24, 34
Bolton, Robert 107
Borgarucci, Giulio 121
botany 14, 83, 84, 85, 86, 88, 92, 93, 94,
    95, 102
Bradwell, Stephen 104
Brahe, Tycho 86, 87, 89
Braunschweig 70
Brendel, Zacharias 24
Brenz (Brettiades), Johannes 2
Brochmand, Jesper 93
Brown, Judith 144
Brunfels, Otto 120, 121
Bruno, Giordano 129

192

Buccella, Niccolò 118, 119, 121
Bugenhagen, Johannes 82, 83
Bunyan, John 111
Burchard, Peter 13, 14, 16
Burghall, Edward 108

Caius, John 17, 122
Calvin, John 2, 42, 43, 109, 119, 121
Calvinism, Calvinists 7, 119
Calvinist theology 101–17, 121
Calzaveglia, Vincenzo 124
Camerarius, Joachim 44, 123, 124, 125, 126, 127
Campanile, Roberto 146, 148, 149, 150
canonisation 143
Capdal, Gaspar 163, 175
Capiteyn, Peter 85
Cardano, Girolamo 128
Carinthian Trilogy 71, 73
Carion, Johannes 59
Carlini, Benedetta 151
Carlini, Suor Benedetta 144
Casal, Gapar 167
Castro, Luis 161
Castro, Rodrigo de 166
Catherine of Siena, Saint 145
Catholic Church 8, 61, 78, 134–55
Catholic Doctrine 8
Catholics 7, 112
Cesalpino, Andreas 140
Charles V, Emperor 8
Chesne, Joseph du (Quercetanus) 7, 95
Christ 3, 4, 65, 66, 72, 73, 103, 107, 109, 124, 128
Christensen, Anders 86, 89
Christian I, Elector of Ernestine Saxony 15
Christian III, King of Denmark 81, 85
Christian IV, King of Denmark 88, 93
Cicero 124
circumcision 160, 169
Coburg 2
Cogan, Thomas 102
Collado, Luis 173
College of Physicians of London 17
College of Physicians of Venice 120
College of Physicians of Verona 123, 128
Colmar 59
Colombo, Realdo 24
Congregation of Sacred Rites and Ceremonies (1588) 137

Congregation of the Holy Office *see* Inquisition
Constantinople 165, 173
Conversos Physicians *see* Jewish Physicians
Copenhagen, University of 7, 78–100
Copernicus, Nicolas 46
Copp, Johannes 59
Cornarius, Janus 17, 45, 120
Counter-Reformation 7, 8, 118, 128, 156–91
Cracow 37
Crafftheim, Crato von 125, 127
Crisostomo, Lupo 138, 139
Crocifissa, Suor Maria 144
Cuenca, Court of the Inquisition 163
Cunning Folk 134, 135, 137, 138, 139, 141, 151–2

Danaeu, Lambert 43
Del Rio, Martín 139
Denmark 7, 78–100
Devil 41, 42, 64, 66, 67, 72, 104, 111, 134–55, 167, 168
Dioscorides 44
disease causation 140
Donzellini, Cornelio 122
Donzellini, Girolamo 118–33

Eber, Paul 2, 24, 45
Eck, Johannes 125
ecstasy 145, 146, 147, 148
Elizabeth I, Queen of England 121
English medicine 101–17
Epicurean atomism 20, 25
Erasmi, Bonifacius (Bonifazius) 37
Erasmianism 8
Erasmus, Desiderius 58, 123, 129
Erastus, Thomas 89
Erizzo, Sebastiano 127
eschatology 59, 61, 95
Espich, Valentin 23
Euclid 34, 37
exorcism, exorcists 134–55

Fabri, Matteo 123
Fabricius, Hieronymus, of Aquapendente 11, 14
Fajardo, Jerónimo 173
Fallopio, Gabrielle 11, 14, 17, 118
Ferdinand, King of Aragon 158
Ferra, Court of 122
Ferrandina, Vincenzo di 146

Ferrara 12
Ficino, Marsilio 43, 44
Fincke, Thomas 84, 89, 90, 91
Flock, Erasmus 45
Forio, Marc' Antonio 119
fornication 162
Frankfurt 118, 126
Fransden, Hans 85, 86
Frederick the Wise, Elector of
    Ernestine Saxony 12, 13, 35
Frederik II, King of Denmark 85, 86,
    87
Fries, Lorenz 59
Friis, Christian 88
Fuchs, Leonhard 22, 44, 85, 86
Fugger Library 123
Fuiren, Jørgen 90

Gabler, Matthias 81
Gadaldin, Agostino 118, 119, 120, 123
Galen, Galenism 5, 13, 14, 15, 16, 18,
    21, 24, 26, 39, 44, 69, 70, 71, 73, 81,
    86, 88, 120, 121, 128, 164, 168, 176,
    182
Galilei, Galileo 129
Gatta, Giovanni 121
Geneva 2
Gengenback, Pamphilus 59
George, Duke of Augustine Saxony 13
Gerhard, Johann 78
Germanus, Johann 25
Germany 12, 16, 85
Gesner, Conrad 120, 124, 127
Giachini, Leonardo 128
Giglia, Suor (Suor Giglia di Fino)
    138, 144–52
Giudici, Pietro 119
Glover, Mary 104
Goa 166
God 7, 18, 20, 22, 25, 37, 38, 39, 40, 42,
    45, 65, 66, 67, 69, 72, 73, 79, 82, 92,
    126, 139, 147, 150, 168
Goslar 70
Gratarolo, Guglielmo 118
Greek 6
Gregory the Great 4
Gregory XIII, Pope 146
Griefswald University 24
Gronenburg (Groneberg), Simon 25
Grün, Johann 24, 25, 26
Grünpeck, Joseph 59
Grynaeus, Symon 37, 38
Guazzo, Francesco Maria 140

Hakewill, George 102
Hall, Joseph 103, 106, 108
hallucinations 21
Harris, Robert 109
Hartlib, Samuel 92
Hartmann, Johannes 95
Harvey, William 11
Harvel, Edmund, English Ambassador
    to Venice 122
heathens 79
Heidelberg, University of 14, 90
Hellenism 16
Hemmingsen, Niels 86, 87, 90
Herbert, George 117 n86
heresy 118, 124, 162, 166
Hermes Trismegistus 127
Hezekiah 106, 109
Hildesheim 70
Hippocrates 5, 13, 16, 21, 38, 39, 81,
    102, 127, 141
Hoby, Lady Margaret 104, 107
Holy Office see Inquisition, Roman,
    and Inquisition, Spanish
Holy Spirit 4, 20, 73
homosexuality 179, 180
Hooker, Thomas 112
horoscopes 33, 34, 39, 42, 128
Hugenots 7, 114 n16
humanism 5
Hunnius, Aegidius 15

Illuminism 8
Illyricus, Mattaeus Flacius 2
Index of Prohibited Books 120, 126,
    128, 129
Ingolstadt 14, 17
Inquisition, Portuguese 145
Inquisition, Roman (Congregation of
    the Holy Office) 8, 9, 121, 122, 136,
    137, 145, 146; Venetian 118–33
Inquisition, Spanish (Congregation of
    the Holy Office) 145, 156–91; see
    also Toledo, Court of the
    Inquisition; Valencia, Court of the
    Inquisition, and Cuenca, Court of
    the Inquisition
Isabella, Queen of Castile 158
Israeli, Isaac 161, 181
Italy 8

Jacobaeus, Vitus 2
James I, King of England 108
Jena University 24

Jessen, Johann 14, 15, 23
Jesuits 8, 112, 134, 146
Jewish Physicians 9, 156–91
Jews 8, 79, 158, 177, 181, 182
Joachimites 59
Job 138
Jover, Jerónimo 165, 171–6
Judaizers 156–91
Jüterbog 24

Karsthans 70, 71
Kepler, Johannes 46
Knobloch, Tobias 22
Knollys, Lord 110
Kragh, Anders 89
Kynghorn, Alexander 81

Lateran Council, Fourth 169
Lausanne 2
Leiden, University of 90
Leipzig, University of 12, 13, 36, 69,
    87
Leiton, Enrique 161
Lemvig, Anders 89
Leoniceno, Niccolò (Nicolao) 12, 36
Lérida, University of 172, 174, 175
levitation 147–8
licences to practise medicine 172, 173
Lichtenberger, Johannes 59;
    prophecies 61, 70
Lindemann, Caspar 14
Liuzzi, Mondino dei 13
Lochitius, Peter 86
Locke, Anne, Dowager Duchess of
    Suffolk 109
López, Gaspar 182
Loyola, Saint Ignatius 137
Lusitano, Amato 166
Luther, Martin 2, 3, 4, 6, 11, 20, 26, 35,
    57, 78, 81, 118, 121
Luther, Paul 20, 23
Lutheran medics 33–56
Lutheranism 7, 16
Lutherans 4, 44

madness 21
Maggi, Vincenzo 122
magic 46, 68, 69, 73, 140, 163, 167, 171
Malmø 90
Malvessi Pier Paolo 119
Manca, Maria 141, 142, 151
Marranos 156–91
Marseilles 174
Mathesius, Johann, the younger 22, 23

Mayerne, Theodore de 7
Mead, Richard 139, 140
medical profession 64
melancholy 140, 141
Melanchthon, Phillip 2, 5, 11, 12, 14,
    16, 17, 20, 21, 23, 24, 26, 33–56, 78,
    81, 82, 87, 118, 127
Mellerstadt, Martin Pollich von 12, 13,
    35, 36, 37
Mercurialis (Mercuriale), Girolamo
    127, 128
middle ages 22
midwives 169
Milich, Jacob 14, 22, 38, 39, 44
miracles 41
Mirandola, Gianfrancesco Pico della
    43
Mirandola, Giovanni Pico della 36,
    38, 43, 44
Monte, Giovanni Battista 122, 123
Montpellier, University of 34, 69, 83
Moriscos, Morisco Physicians 156–91
Morsing, Christian Torkelsen 81–6,
    90, 94, 95
Moscardo, Giuseppe 119, 121
Moslem Physicians, *see* Morisco
    Physicians
Moslems 8
Mostelius, Thobias 23
Múxica, Don Francisco de 180

Nájera, Antonio de 179
Nájera, Felipe de 161, 163, 169, 176–85
Naples, Kingdom of 134–55
Nascimbene, Nascimbene 119, 125
natural philosophy 23, 37, 39, 40, 41,
    42, 45, 46, 65
Neo-Platonism 44
Neri, Saint Philip 137, 146, 148
Newton, Isaac 46
Nicander 44
Nicodemites, Nicodemism 121, 123
Nifo, Fabio 118, 119
Nuñez, Mateo 161
Nuremberg 58, 59, 61, 62, 123, 125

Ochino, Bernadino 121
Odense 92
Odoni, Angelo 123
Oeclampadius, Johannes 83
Orsola, Suor (Suor Orsola Benincasa)
    145, 146
Orta, Garcia d' 166
Osiander, Andreas 59

Padua, University of 3, 8, 11, 12, 14, 24, 34, 69, 91, 118, 122
Palladius, Peder 87
Panarelli, Teofilo 119, 121, 126
Papacy 67
Paracelsus (Theophrastus von Hohenheim), and Paracelsians 6, 7, 57–77, 83, 86, 88, 108, 124; his 'religion of medicine' 68, 129
Paris 34, 69
Paris, University of 167
Paticchio, Mauro 139, 142
Patrizi, Francesco 127, 129, 132 n74
Paul, St 82
Paulli, Simon 88
Peasants' War 57
Pegolotto, Francesco 121
Peranda, Giovanni Battista 119
Perna, Pietro 122, 123, 127
Peucer, Caspar 14, 22, 23, 26, 38, 45
Peypus, Frederick 61, 62
pharmacies 121
Philip II, King of Spain 8, 171
Philip III, King of Spain 160
philosophy 22, 23, 24, 119
physiology 22, 23
Pigafetta, Antonio 14
Pinelli, Vincenzo 128
Piperno, Pietro 140
Pistoris, Simon 12, 36
Pius V, Pope 120
plague 69, 70, 103, 107, 108, 109, 116 n63, 118, 125
Plato 18
Platter, Felix 85, 89, 90
Pliny, The Elder 44, 45, 71
popular medicine 8, 9
Portugal 158, 159, 161, 166, 179
possession, *see* witch
Potenza 134
Pratensis, Johannes Philip 86, 88
prayer 21
priesthood of all believers 58
prognosis 33, 34
prognostications 59, 61
Protomedicato 171
Providence 7, 35, 42, 43, 44, 45, 46, 83, 101–17, 125, 126
Ptolemy 34, 39, 44
Puritans 46

Rainolds, John 107
Ramist philosophy 86, 88, 90

Ramus, Petrus 24
Reformed 4
Regiomontanus 38
Reinhardt, Martin 81
relics 112, 136, 137, 143, 145, 146, 151
Resen, Bishop Hans Poulsen 94
Revelation 69, 70
Reynmann, Leonhard 59
Rhazes 13, 82, 128
Ribera, Juan de, Archbishop of Valencia 163
Ritual, Roman (1614) 136
Rivius, Johannes 126
Robinson, John 105
Rodrigues, Joao, de Castello Branco 166
Rome 119, 121, 124, 126, 165
Rosenborg Palace 88
Rosenkrantz, Holgar 81, 91, 92, 93
Rüdinger, Esrom 24
Rudolph II, Emperor 88

Sachs, Hans 59
Sacrobosco 34, 37
saints, living 134–55
Salamanca, University of 166, 179
Salerno 69
Salzburg 58, 71
Santoro, Cardinal 146
Sascerides, Gellius 89
Satan *see* Devil
Saxony 15, 25
Schaller, Hieronymus 23
scientific revolution 57
Secco, Gian' Antonio 120
Seven Years' War 85
Severinus, Petrus 79, 86, 87, 88, 89, 95
Ship of Fools 72
sin 21, 41, 42, 101–17
Sixtus V, Pope 167
Smith, Henrik 82
sorcery, *see* witch
Sorø, Academy 89
soul 12, 20, 21, 24, 25, 26, 101–17
Spain 8, 11, 156–91
Spangenberg, Cyriacus 2
Spinola, Publio Francesco 123, 125
spiritual physic 101–17
Sprenger, Jakob 139
Staetz, Dr Benedict 13
Stöffler, Johannes 43, 44
Stoic philosophy 40
Strasburg, University of 58, 89, 90

Sturm, Johannes 89
Suor Giglia di Fino *see* Giglia, Suor
superstitions 134, 185
surgeons, surgery 24, 89, 169, 171, 178
Susio, Giovanni Battista 119, 123
Sylbergius, Fridericus 126
Sylvius, Jacobus 17
syphilis (the 'French disease') 36, 62, 69

Tandler, Tobias 15, 16
Tannstetter, Georg 59
tartar 73
Taylor, Thomas 109
Tertiary (Third Order) Nuns 144, 145
Themistius 123, 127
Theodoricus, Sebastianus 45
theology 12, 34
Theresa of Avila, Saint 137, 145
theriac 124, 127
Thirty Years' War 92
Thomas, Keith 5
Toledo, Court of the Inquisition 162, 163, 169, 180, 181, 184
Toledo, Juan de 179, 181, 185
Tomitano, Bernardino 118
Torreblanca, Francisco de 139, 167
torture 161
Trent, Council of 8, 134–55, 169
Trincavella, Vettor 127
Trinity 73
Tübingen, University of 43, 85, 86
Turner, Jane 104
Turner, William, 116 n68

Ussher, Archbishop James 103

Valencia, Court of the Inquisition 163
Valencia, University of 173
Valesius, Franciscus 140
Valier, Bishop Agostino 123
Vatican Library 127
Velcurio, Johannes 21
Venice 8, 118–33
Vesalius, Andreas 3, 11, 14, 16, 17, 22, 23, 24, 26, 44, 173
Vienna 69
Vinci, Leonardo da 11
Virdung, Hans 59
Viret, Peter 2
Virgin Mary 143, 147, 158, 169
Volmar, Johannes 37, 39

Ward, Samuel 108
Wild, Stephen 14
Wimpina, Konrad 13
witch, witchcraft, sorcery, possession 134–55, 158, 162
Wittenberg University 2, 6, 7, 11–32, 35, 36, 37, 43, 44, 46, 70, 81, 82, 85, 87, 90, 91
Woolton, John 105
Worm, Ole 84, 90, 91, 92, 95

Xavier, Saint Francis 137

Zabarella, Jacopo 24
Zaragoza 162, 167, 171
Zwinger, Bonifacius 132 n65
Zwinger, Jacob, 85, 90, 132 n65
Zwinger, Theodor 85, 88, 89, 90, 124, 125, 127, 128
Zwingli, Ulrich (Huldreich) 2, 126